Henry Theophilus Finck

Lotos Time in Japan

Henry Theophilus Finck

Lotos Time in Japan

ISBN/EAN: 9783337166168

Printed in Europe, USA, Canada, Australia, Japan

Cover: Foto ©Suzi / pixelio.de

More available books at **www.hansebooks.com**

LOTOS-TIME IN JAPAN

BY THE SAME AUTHOR.

LOTOS-TIME IN JAPAN. Illustrated. Cr. 8vo . . $1.75

THE PACIFIC COAST SCENIC TOUR. From Southern California to Alaska. Illustrated. Cr. 8vo 2.50

SPAIN AND MOROCCO. Studies in Local Color. 12mo 1.25

CHOPIN, AND OTHER MUSICAL ESSAYS. 12mo . 1.50

WAGNER AND HIS WORKS. The Story of his Life, with Critical Comments. With Portraits. 2 vols. Cr. 8vo 4.00

GEISHA PLAYING SAMISEN

LOTOS-TIME IN JAPAN

BY

HENRY T. FINCK

ILLUSTRATED

NEW YORK
CHARLES SCRIBNER'S SONS
1895

Norwood Press:
J. S. Cushing & Co. — Berwick & Smith.
Norwood, Mass., U.S.A.

Cordially Dedicated

To

HENRY VILLARD

PREFACE

FLOWER festivals are the great national holidays in Japan, where every month has its floral favorite. Lotos-Time extends through July and August. In some respects midsummer is not the most favorable season for tourists, because of the damp heat and copious rains. But while the autumn air is drier and more bracing, it is only in summer that one can climb Fuji or visit Yezo to advantage; and summer has this further advantage, that the heat compels the natives to remove the fronts of their flimsy houses, so that the tourist can see every detail of family life, in countless interiors. Thus a trained observer might get material enough in a week or two for a volume of description, by taking either "the beaten, because most interesting tracks," or the more remote regions, where foreigners are rarely or never seen. And the longer he remains, the more will he realize the truth of Professor Chamberlain's remark that in Japan the subject-matter for an author is so plentiful that "the chief difficulty is to know what to omit."

If the reader expects to find in this preface an abject apology for adding another volume to the long list of books on Japan, he will be grievously disappointed. Have I not just as much right to try my hand and luck as my "seventy-times-seven-hundred" predecessors? Herodotus wrote about Egypt twenty-four centuries ago, yet books on that country continue to appear every year. Asiatic Japan is certainly not less interesting than African Egypt, yet the first European who described it lived only two centuries ago, and after he had done his work Japan remained hermetically sealed to the rest of the world until about forty years ago, so that it still preserves many mediæval customs, the contrast and clash of which with the imported elements of our Occidental civilization produce a multitude of picturesque phenomena that will continue to fascinate and tempt authors and artists for many years to come. The story of Rip van Winkle is, like so many other things, reversed in Japan, where it is the country that has gone to sleep, and the visitor that is up to date.

That there is room for another volume on this remarkable country I may perhaps be allowed to infer from the fact that, among the hundreds of books in various languages that I have looked over, I have not found one in which is given a convenient bird's-eye view, in a few brief chapters, of the principal points in which Japanese civilization is superior to our own. In attempting to do this, in a modest way, I have fortified my arguments with quotations from the authoritative and admirable volumes of Messrs. Griffis, Chamberlain, Hearn, Black, Alcock, Mitford, Misses Bacon and Bird, and others, to all of whom I am indebted for much instruction and pleasure. Such a bird's-eye view is, it seems to me, particularly timely and desirable, in view of the American tendency to estimate Japanese civilization from a purely material and military point of view. I have tried to show that the Japanese have as much to teach us as we have to teach them, and that what they can offer us is, on the whole, of a higher and nobler order than what we can offer them. Japanese civilization is based on altruism, ours on egotism. Mr. Howells's *Traveller from Altruria* might have almost hailed from Japan, and Mr. Bellamy, while *Looking Backward*, might have benefited by looking across the Pacific for ideals of social refinement and happiness. The comparison of Japan with America is particularly suggestive, as her virtues balance our vices, and *vice versa*.

The bulk of the present volume is, however, innocent of didactic purpose, its sole object being to present a few realistic and unbiassed sketches from life and nature, and to exhibit to the reader and possible tourist specimens of the every-day experiences he would be likely to have in Japan. Personal details of a trivial nature are given only in situations where it was believed that they would increase the vividness of the local coloring. Tourist luck was against me in the matter of Fuji, while it greatly favored me in Yezo.

among the Ainos. For my excellent opportunities to study certain phases of life in Tōkyō, I am especially indebted to the courtesy of Mr. Heromich Shugio, a Japanese gentleman who is as well known in New York society and clubs as in the aristocratic circles of Japan's capital. I also wish to express my gratitude to Mr. Yabi, my native travelling companion, whose encyclopædic knowledge of things Japanese helped me to avoid misleading the reader, and added greatly to the pleasures of my travels.

The use of the word "native" in this book calls for a line of explanation, in view of the fact that it may possibly be read by some of the numerous Japanese who now speak English, and whose feelings I do not wish to hurt. It appears that there is current prejudice against the word "native," because a standard dictionary translates it as *dojin*, which means aborigines in their barbarous condition. Of course I use the word merely in its ordinary sense, as the opposite of "foreign," and to avoid too frequent repetition of the word "Japanese."

H. T. F.

NEW YORK, March 2, 1895.

CONTENTS

PAGE

TO JAPAN, VIA HAWAII . . . .

    Time and Expense — Five Hours at Honolulu — Mount Fuji — Are American Indians Japanese? — Scenes in Yokohama Bay — Perry and his Oyster

YOKOHAMA — FOREIGN AND NATIVE . . . .

    Baby Carriages for Adults — Half-way House to Japan — Barbers and Bar-rooms — The Bund and the Bluff — Clubs — Scarcity of Foreign Women — Staring at Foreigners — Young Beggars — Oriental Bowery Shows — Queer Music — Godowns and Green Tea — An Apology for Yokohama

RAILWAY AND KURUMA 22

    America in Japan — Locomotives and Natives — A Typical Station — Clog Dance — A Eurasian Hotel — A Polite Clerk — A Plea for Lemons — A Quiet City — Bird's-eye View — Hills and Parks — Traits of Kuruma Coolies — What is Degrading Work?

STREET SCENES IN TŌKYŌ 37

    Recent Changes — Daimyos and Samurai — Yashikis and Moats — Policemen — Attacks on Foreigners — Safety in City and Country — Shops and Homes exposed to View — Bazaars — Trades Flocking Together — Comic Signboards — Ungrammatical Costumes — Brunettes in Blue — Modest Exposure — Japanese Children — Bowing — How the Poor Live — Fires and Godowns

	PAGE
FROM MORNING TILL MIDNIGHT	54

Tōkyō at its Toilet — Dogs and Chickens — Fish Market — Dangerous Wells — Nap Time — A Foolish Law — Coolies versus Horses — Street Sprinkling — Planed Ice — Stewed Tea — A Carriage Drive — Where Missionaries Live — Scenes about a Buddhist Temple — Religion and Fun — Archery Girls — A Night Crowd — Flower Show — River Festival — Day and Night Fireworks — The City Band

WINE, WOMEN, AND SONG	75

Beauty of Japanese Women — Brunettes only — Waiting Maids and Singing Girls — Like the Ancient Greeks — An Esthetic Banquet — Music and Banter — Fireboxes — Rice Wine — Soup and Fish — Chopsticks — Dancing and Drums — Gilded Vice — A Slave Market — Trap for Criminals

A THEATRE AND A SCHOOL	91

Only Seven Hours — Behavior of the Audience — Social Status of Actors — Trailing Trousers — The Kneeling Nation — Expression of Emotion — Chinese Falsetto — Scenery and Music — Stage Illusions — Count Okuma's School — Speeches and Prizes — Lunch in the Count's Garden

THE MIKADO AND THE EXHIBITION	103

A Vast Curio Store — Visitors — Semi-Foreign Picture Gallery — A Gastronomic Insult — An Imperial Prisoner — The Mikado's First Outing — Invisible No Longer — Editorial Punishment — A Remarkable Monarch — Personal Appearance — Evening Dress in the Morning — Japanese Journalists — Emperor or Mikado? — A Foreign Dinner

OFF FOR JAPANESE SIBERIA	117

Climate of Japan — Monkeys in the Snow — Skating in Tōkyō — Yezo versus Hondo — Damp Days — Climate and Literature — Professors at Home — Coolie Traits — Guides — A Literary Companion — Unusual Privileges — Mulberry Plantations — An Inn at Sendai — Transforming a Room — Quilts and Pillows — The Bill

ON A COAST STEAMER 128

The Famous Pine Islands — The Island Empire — Melons and Eels — Japanese Steamers — High Fare — Meals in "Foreign" Style — Yankees Out-Yankeed — Passengers and Cargo — A Large Fishing Village

JAPANESE GIBRALTAR 135

Sights in Hakodate — New Buddhist Temple — An Interview — A Japanese Interior — Toy Garden and Fish Pond — Barber and Taylor — How to please Girls — Taken to the Bath — Courtship and Marriage — Odors and Noises — Dining and Climbing — A Sea Bath — Round the Island — "Irish Stewed" — Otaru Peasants — Marvel of Politeness — A Mixed Inn

AMERICAN SAPPORO 151

Natives in the Ocean — Capitol of Yezo — Russian Designs — American Farms and Factories — Expensive Experiments — City and Suburbs — Calling on the Governor-General — A Eurasian House — Beer and Fruit — The Superintendent's Kindness — A Unique Museum — A Dairy — Seeing the Factories — Tea-house Girls — Lamps and Washstands — American and Asiatic Correspondence — A Comic Resemblance

INTO THE VIRGIN FOREST 166

A Greek Idyl — In a Japanese Coal Mine — Convicts — Ride on a Coal Train — A Pond and a Bathing Scene — Caught in the Rain — Horses and Guides — Treating the Ainos — Bear Fights and Poisoned Arrows — American Clearings — Japanese Pioneers — Forest Enchantment — Nightingales and Flowers — Polite Convicts — A Yezo Song — Centre of the Island — More Ainos — Newspapers and Magazines

xiv   CONTENTS

	PAGE
THE AINOS AND THE WHALE	192

Yezo Apples — Time not Money — Stage Ride to Mororan — A Useful Lotos Pond — Japanese Chivalry — Along the Wild Coast — Beach Roses — Fireboxes — A Deserted Aino Town — Excitement on the Beach — Whale Ashore — Blubber and Prayers — Aino Women — Revenge on the Kodaker

FROM MORORAN TO HAKODATE	203

Escorted to the Inn — Crossing the Stormy Bay — Suburbs of Hakodate — Expense of the Yezo Trip — Bath in the Sulphur Springs — The Typhoon

THROUGH MEDIÆVAL JAPAN	208

Bear Cub — Melons — Roofs — From Railway to Kuruma — Early Morning Scenes — Ravages of the Storm — Changeable Rivers and Coolies — Silkworms — Foreigners as a Curiosity — A Remarkable Runner — Types of Female Beauty — Ditches and Deaths — Rainy Japan — How Coolies Eat — Babies and Pickles — Naked and not Ashamed — An Exciting Ferry — A Grand Avenue

A PILGRIM'S PARADISE	224

A Rainy Region — Nikko's Long Street — Our Summer House — Pilgrim Processions — Nature and Religion — Ieyasu — The Temples — Art Works — A Sacred Dance — Ferns, Mosses, and Sun Jewels — Lotos Roots — What Japanese Houses Need

NIKKO LAKES AND WATERFALLS	231

Back View Cascade — Tea or Lies — Kegon-No-Taki — Lake Chūzenji — A Lakeside Inn — Dragon's Head Cascade — Moor of the Red Swamp — Lake Yumoto — Public Baths — The Hot Springs — Foam Cascade — Nearly a Waterfall — Snake Stories — A Cholera Scare — A Night half way up Fuji — Sleeping under an Umbrella

	PAGE
RAILWAY GENRE PICTURES	248

The Legend of Fuji and Biwa — A Popular Railway — How Japanese Women Smoke — A Married Beauty — The Dress Problem — Fat Wrestlers — Lunch Boxes — Cheap Tea Sets

FASCINATIONS OF KYŌTO 255

Watermelons and Cholera — The Japanese Rome — A City of Temples — The Corean Ear Mound — Buddhist Chanting — Rascally Priests — Silk Factories — Southern Female Beauty — The Spanish Type — Photographs of Geishas — A Blind Musician — Koto Concert — Cheap Art Treasures — An Oriental Nocturne

LAKE AND LOTOS POND 267

Otsu — Puns and Poetry — Japan's Largest Lake — Acres of Lotos Flowers — Difficult to Paint — The Lotos in Japan, India, and America

ARE THE JAPANESE TOPSY-TURVY? 273

Two Funny Incidents — Social Antipodisms — A Perverse Language — A Japanese Letter — Lacquer and Wind — When we are Topsy-Turvy — How to stable Horses — Proper Way to address Letters

THE MOTE AND THE BEAM 280

Six Hundred Missionaries — Denominationalism — An Agnostic's Opinion — Creeds and Deeds — Occidental Bunkum — Indians and Slavery — Getting Civilized — Commercial and Sexual Morality

NUDITY AND BATHING . . . 286

Public Baths — Modest Exposure — A Foolish Law — Nudity and Climate — Customs of Various Countries — Shocked at our Habits — No "Great Unwashed" — A Sensuous Luxury — Bathing to get Warm — Scenes in Bath Houses — An Esthetic Question — Neglect of the Nude in Art

	PAGE
THE ESTHETIC NATION	298

Music and Nationality — Future of Japanese Music — Sculpture and Architecture — Great in Small Things — Decorative Art — Impressionism — Irregularity — Love of Nature — Flowers versus Bouquets — Flower Seasons — Poetic Names — Mottoes on Screens — Japanese Poetry — Love Letters on Trees

A SUPERIOR CIVILIZATION 313

Care for Parents — A Paradise of Babies — Children born Civilized — School and Holidays — A Thousand Years of Politeness — A Language without Profanity — Smiling in Grief — Altruism versus Egotism — American Rudeness — No Flaunting of Wealth — American Plutocracy — Inside and Outside — Kindness to Animals — Transition Period — Three Kinds of Patriotism — Shintoism — Criminals and Crowds — Sailors' Amusements — How to enjoy Life

LIST OF ILLUSTRATIONS

Geisha playing Samisen	*Frontispiece*
	FACING PAGE
Kuruma	10
Beggars	16
A Kago	38
Silk Store	46
Carrying Children	50
Pleasure Boat	70
Glimpse of an Interior	78
Tea Plantation	124
Rain Coats	172
Hairy Aino	200
Fuji, from Hakone Lake	244
Koto and Samisen Players	264
Lotos Pond	270
Artificial Landscape Garden	306
A Flower Lesson	308

TO JAPAN VIA HAWAII

TIME AND EXPENSE — FIVE HOURS AT HONOLULU — MOUNT FUJI — ARE AMERICAN INDIANS OF JAPANESE ORIGIN? — SCENES IN YOKOHAMA BAY — PERRY AND HIS OYSTER

To most Americans a trip to Japan seems almost equal to a globe-trotting expedition, yet it involves to-day little more expenditure of time and money than a trip to Europe did to our fathers. Thirty or forty years ago it was still customary to cross the continent from the Mississippi River to California in five months in "prairie schooners." The Panama steamers reduced that to five weeks from New York to San Francisco, and to-day we cross in a Pullman car in five days, half expecting that Mr. Edison will before long reduce that to five hours. The further reduction to five minutes will then be a matter of secondary importance. From San Francisco or Vancouver the best steamers of the Pacific Mail, the Oriental and Occidental, and the Canadian Pacific companies make the trip to Japan in twelve to sixteen days, which is about the time it used to take to cross from New York to European ports until about two decades ago, when the "ocean greyhounds" were first let loose. And although the Japanese round trip involves about 10,000 miles more travel than the European, a New-Yorker can leave home with $1200 in his pocket, spend three months in Japan, and return with enough left for a dinner at Delmonico's, or an opera ticket, or both, if he has been fairly economical.

The Canadian line has more fast steamers than any other, and the distance from Vancouver to Yokohama — 4330 miles — is 230 miles less than from San Francisco, but the sea is apt to be rougher at all seasons, the route being so much further north. To insure smooth sailing, you can choose one of the steamers of the Pacific Mail when (about once in three months) they take a southern course, so as to include a stop at the Hawaiian Islands. This implies an addition of 800 miles to the voyage and three days more in time; but the calm sea and the half-day at Honolulu more than compensate for this. When I engaged my passage on the *City of Peking*, I did not know she was going *via* Hawaii; but the discovery was a pleasant surprise, for I had long wished to get a glimpse of the "Paradise of the Pacific," so long misnamed the Sandwich Islands.[1] The *City of Peking* is a slow steamer, and it took us twenty days to reach Yokohama, whereas the *China*, of the same line, has made the trip *via* Hawaii in fifteen days and eight hours. But we were comfortable, and that was the main point. The *China* has made the direct trip from San Francisco to Yokohama in less than twelve days, and could probably do it in ten if

[1] They were so called after the Earl of Sandwich by Captain Cook. But Cook was not the first explorer who discovered these islands, and he had no right to inflict on them a name which inevitably suggests a ten-cent lunch. The Hawaiians themselves greatly dislike to be called Sandwich Islanders, and it was gratifying to see, during the troubles of 1894, that that name for them was gradually displaced in American newspapers by the original term Hawaiians. As in the case of Mount Tacoma (long misnamed Rainier) and Lake Tahoe (misnamed Bigler), such arbitrary proceedings and aberrations of taste are usually cured by the lapse of time.

necessary. But ocean racing from California ports is not popular, owing to the high price of coal.

It took us a week to reach Honolulu, and when we got there, the captain allowed us only five hours to see its sights. To travel 2100 miles to a group of islands, world-famed for their palm groves, flowers, sugar plantations, dusky Polynesian beauties, luscious melons and mangoes, tonic breezes, balmy climate, and the most sublime ever-active volcano in the world, and stay only five hours seemed, indeed, like the craziest kind of globe-trotting. If we had had only a week, we might have visited the volcano; but under the circumstances it was impossible to see it unless we were willing to wait three months for the next P.M. steamer stopping here, or else take one of the occasional Japanese steamers which are probably ill-equipped for Occidental passengers. We consoled ourselves with the thought that a trained observer can see more in five hours than a careless spectator in five months. We did see enough to fill a chapter of description, but the temptation to do so must be heroically resisted, as our subject is Japan, which claims so much space for itself that it brooks no rival. I must omit, too, the many characteristic international episodes of our voyage, and pass on at once to its last day.

Before going to Japan I had often dreamed that, in the tour of the world, there must be one sight which would fill even the shallowest globe-trotter with a thrill of awe, and make him a worshipper of nature. Imagine the situation. For two or three weeks you have been confined in a floating prison, until you have almost forgotten that there are such things in the world as trees, fields, houses, rivers, mountains; and the gray-blue ocean is merged with the gray-blue sky in one sensation of unfathomable globular monotony. At last, one morning, if the sky is blue, you discover a mysterious phantom — a small, white cone standing in the midst of the ocean. As you approach, the cone rises higher and swells visibly, till, at last, it looms up as a shapely mountain top. It is Fuji, the sacred mountain of Japan, whose snowy crown pierces the celestial blue at a height of almost three miles above the ocean, whence you see it. Yet, at first, the globe's rotundity had made it appear to rise but a foot above the sea. For hours the pilot steers straight for that snowy landmark, which seems to grow larger and larger, like an avalanche rolling toward us. In the hazy atmosphere its base is invisible, so that the snow cone continues to float in a gray ocean of air, even after the peaks and ridges of surrounding mountain ranges have come dimly into view, confirming our approach to land, and giving us a standard wherewith to measure the grandeur of Fuji.

Such was my day-dream — a dream which youthful experiences among the snow cones of Oregon made it easy for my imagination to realize vividly. But alas! it was to remain a pleasure of the imagination. Our blue sky had turned gray as we neared rainy Japan, and Fuji was invisible. I had to console myself with the malicious satisfaction that few visitors to Japan have had better luck. Captain Marshall, of the steamship *Abyssinia*, told Mabel Loomis Todd that "entering Yokohama harbor very frequently, during nearly twenty years, he had but twice seen clearly this great landmark." In this respect a ticket to Japan is a lottery ticket; and the worst of it is that a second ticket would cost another $350 and involve a return trip of

9000 miles more. Nor could you obviate this by sailing, say, on a yacht or fishing boat from Yokohama till Fuji was out of sight, and then returning. You would, indeed, in that case have Fuji revealed to your eyes gradually, but it would not be the same ocular feast without the preceding ocular fast.

Yet even without Fuji and under a leaden sky, the approach to Japan is fascinating. To me the first sight of land on the voyage between Europe and America is always a fresh delight, a thrill which repetition does not weaken. How much keener, therefore, must be the sensation of catching the first glimpse of a country a journey to which tourists have united in declaring to be like a visit to another planet. Look at the map — readers of travel sketches should always have a map at hand; it makes everything so much more definite and impressive — and note, first the large bay, then the smaller one, which it takes the steamer several hours to traverse before Yokohama is reached. At the entrance to the large bay, just half-way between the promontories on the right and left, lies the island of Oshima, formerly a convict settlement, guarded by a volcano whose constant smoke threatens an eruption on the slightest provocation. It forms a fine background to the scenery left of the steamer's course, while the promontory to our right is adorned with curious villages, wonderfully green hillsides, and one of those fine lighthouses of which the government has erected a hundred on this dangerous coast within the last quarter of a century. The guide book assures us that here "luxuriant beds of jonquils and other flowers abound near the seashore, and fill the air with their fragrance at Christmas time."

"You would have to travel far in China to find such scenery as this," a German passenger residing at Shanghai said to me, as we made our way up the bay. I assured him he need not have limited his comparison to China. Nor was it the landscape alone that feasted the starved eyes; the ocean itself had lost its ruffled monotony, and was now a smooth mirror of gay Oriental life. During the four or five hours that it took us to steam up the bay, with slackened speed, we passed several Japanese coasting steamers and innumerable smaller vessels, fishing boats mostly, with large white sails, junks of various sizes, going out to fish in the Kuro Siwo — the warm, black ocean current which traverses the cold Pacific all the way to Alaska and down to California, modifying the climate of our Pacific coast. In centuries past many a Japanese junk has been carried across the Pacific by this 400-mile wide current, whence the not improbable inference that America was originally peopled by the Japanese. The faces of the Pacific coast Indians, from Alaska to Oregon, certainly bear a striking resemblance to the lower-class Japanese physiognomy, and there are not a few customs (notably those of carrying infants on the back and of walking with the toes in) that suggest a common origin. If this theory be accepted, the Japanese would be the "only genuine and original Americans" — which is the first of the innumerable paradoxes we shall find on Japanese soil.

Distant Japan is linked to America by the two further curious circumstances that it is indirectly responsible for the discovery of America, and that it was the American Commodore Perry who re-discovered Japan. It was the tales of Marco Polo about a mysterious gold country, named Jipangu, that fired the zeal of Columbus to start on his voyage of discovery; and it was through the diplomatic shrewdness and perseverance of Perry (fortified by his gunboats) that Japan was opened up to the world in 1853, after it had been hermetically closed for more than two centuries, except at a small island off Nagasaki, where a few Dutchmen were kept as a sort of European menagerie. It may be that, as Professor Chamberlain bluntly puts it, "Perry triumphed by frightening the weak, ignorant, utterly unprepared, and insufficiently armed Japanese out of their senses." But I, for one, shall not blame him; for from the tourist's point of view — the only one I am bound to recognize — he did a great thing when he opened this stubborn old pearl oyster, and gave everybody a chance to see the pearl, though it was rather cruel to the oyster.

Perry's expedition is still recalled by the names of Treaty Point, Mississippi Bay, and Perry Island, which are pointed out to the passengers. As soon as we enter the inner bay, we catch sight, to the left, of Yokohama, which was a mere fishing village in Perry's day, but is now the chief foreign port, with a mixed population of 122,000 inhabitants. The nearer we get to it, the denser becomes the throng of vessels, among which we have to pick our way slowly — vessels of all sizes, from the huge war-ships of various nations, nearly always lying anchored there, to the local sampans, which crowd around us, and which are sculled by dark-skinned natives in various stages of undress. Some wear only a sort of blouse of blue cotton; others, only a pair of trousers. The small boys have no use for any sort of covering; and it is easy to guess that the men, too, would not encumber themselves with any were they not compelled to do so by laws enacted since the advent of foreigners. Some of the boats we passed carried the female members of families too, engaged in cooking, eating, or other domestic occupation, while the wind or oars were carrying them to the fishing grounds. Products of the farm and garden filled up some of the other junks. We just missed coming into closer contact with the natives; for hardly had we cast our anchor, a mile from shore, when some of the boats came alongside. A rope ladder with a hook was fastened by means of a long pole to the deck railing, and the coolies began clambering up like monkeys. Just then our quartermaster came along, seized the hook, and compelled the coolies to choose between a hasty retreat and a plunge into the bay. It looked, for all the world, like an attack by pirates, except that our assailants were unarmed, and probably had the most peaceful wage-earning intentions.

YOKOHAMA — FOREIGN AND NATIVE

BABY CARRIAGES FOR ADULTS — HALF-WAY HOUSE TO JAPAN — BARBERS AND BAR-ROOMS — THE BUND AND THE BLUFF — CLUBS — SCARCITY OF FOREIGN WOMEN — STARING AT FOREIGNERS — YOUNG BEGGARS — ORIENTAL BOWERY SHOWS — QUEER MUSIC — GODOWNS AND GREEN TEA — AN APOLOGY FOR YOKOHAMA

THE two largest "foreign" hotels in Yokohama send their own steam launches to meet the steamers and bring passengers ashore. Getting into one of these, we were soon on Asiatic soil. The custom-house officers did not detain me a minute, as I was luckily provided with one of the thousand invitations extended during the exhibition year to "distinguished visitors" from abroad. There was nothing Asiatic in hotel launches or custom-house officers, but our next experience was specifically Japanese. Had we landed ignorant of native customs, we should have looked about for a conveyance to take us and our baggage to the hotel; we should have been disgusted not to find a single cab or 'bus, and wondered what that long row of two-wheeled baby carriages was there for, with men between the shafts. Did they expect a shipload of infants from America? Our astonishment would have increased on seeing our fellow-passengers — sober adult men and women — get into these baby carriages and trot off with a man-horse between the shafts, as if it were the most self-evident thing in the world.

Fortunately we were posted, not only in regard to these man-power carriages (jinrikishas, as the Chinese word is, or kurumas, as the Japanese more musically call them), but even in regard to the ways and tricks of the two-legged horses who draw them, and I was thus able to astonish at least one native before I had been on shore fifteen minutes. Getting into a kuruma, I said "Grand Hotel" in purest Japanese accents. The intelligent kurumaya understood me perfectly, turned to the left, and started down the Bund, as the beautiful wide street facing the ocean is called, past cosy private residences and fine curio stores, soon reaching the Grand Hotel. Here I handed him ten cents (the legal fare for an hour, and I had used him only five minutes). He held the coin in his hand, looked at it and at me with well-feigned astonishment, and exclaimed, "Ten sen?" in a tone of injured innocence. I paid no attention to him whatever, and moved towards the hotel door. Turning again after a few steps, I found him getting ready to go, with a resigned expression on his face, of "Well, that fellow has evidently been in Japan before."

Yokohama is a sort of "half-way house" to Japan. You might live in its foreign settlement a year without seeing a Japanese house, eating a Japanese meal, or knowing as much of native life and sights as you might learn of Chinese life by an hour's visit to Chinatown in San Francisco. The Grand Hotel typifies this situation. A long two-story stone building, it is in Japan, but not of Japan. It has rooms with foreign furniture and beds, carpeted parlors with a hotel piano, a foreign

KURUMA

office, billiard and bar-room, a barber shop, separate foreign bath rooms, and a spacious dining room, with scores of small tables on which are served dishes cooked in foreign style and eaten with knife, fork, and spoon. The tea is foreign (Chinese or Indian) and is taken in the barbarous foreign way, with milk and sugar. But the waiters — called "boys," as everywhere in the East — are Japanese, and know very little English; wherefore all the dishes are ordered, like the wines in our own restaurants, by their numbers. "European" wines are obtainable in Yokohama hotels and restaurants, Europe being, as the reader is doubtless aware, situated in California. Some of the leading San Francisco wine-houses have agencies in Yokohama. The Japanese take naturally to foreign wines and are especially partial to champagne, which, however, few can afford to drink at their own expense. The amusing incidents related in Perry's account of his expedition show that the Japanese took to the exhilarating sparkling wine as ducks to water.

The hotel bar-room is entirely American in appearance, and here you can get all the American mixed drinks, at American prices. American treating is customary, and is rendered still more of a temptation and nuisance by the use of "chits," or slips of paper on which drinks are recorded with the drinker's signature, the bill to be settled once a month, or whenever convenient.

The hotel barber is less prosperous than the barkeeper. The one who shaved me complained that he was patronized only by the new arrivals, and that most of these soon followed the example of the foreign residents, who engage a Japanese barber to come to their room every morning to shave them, cut their hair whenever necessary, and take care of their hands and feet — all for one dollar a month!

It is not only in shaving and shampooing that the foreign residents in Japan economize by relying on the natives. A kuruma costs seventy cents a day, but if you engage your own man, the expense is only $10 a month, on which the kurumaya can easily support his family on fish and rice; fortunately he needs no hay or oats, for in his sphere every man is his own horse. Should you want a real horse and carriage, you would be charged $5 a day, but by paying $30 a month you can have your own horse and carriage, besides a betto, or runner, who always accompanies the horse. Real horses and carriages are, however, little used except for pleasure-driving and the display of wealth; for business purposes everybody uses the kuruma.

I have just said that one might live a year in Yokohama without seeing much of Japanese life; nor need one remain shut up in a hotel to attain this undesirable result. The streets of the foreign settlement are absolutely un-Japanese, except as regards the displays of tempting curios and works of art in the large windows. Otherwise you will see just what you see in our own towns of from 20,000 to 50,000 inhabitants, — stone sidewalks, solid stone buildings of one or two stories, drug stores, groceries, haberdashers, bookstores with the latest English, French, and German novels, and so on.

The handsomest street in Yokohama is the Bund, on which every visitor takes his first kuruma ride. It ends at the Grand Hotel; and as no houses are built on its ocean side, it presents everywhere a fine view of the harbor, with its international mixture of American, English, German, French, and other men-of-war, Japanese junks, sampans, and yachts. The one row of houses on the Bund sublimely illustrates man's confidence in his luck. Yokohama and the neighboring Tōkyō have about fifty earthquake shocks a year. True, most of them are insignificant, but the experiences of 1894 showed that they will, on occasion, knock over a foreign-style building like a card-house.[1] Nevertheless, the houses on the Bund and on Main Street are all of stone and often two stories high, whereas the more wary Japanese build their dwellings of the lightest possible materials, — wood, bamboo, paper. Typhoons, too, annually visit these shores; and only a few years ago a tidal wave at Kobe lifted up a steamer, and left it high and dry on the beach. Yet the Yokohama Bund is so close to the ocean that the waves often dash

---

[1] During my stay in the third story of the Tōkyō Hotel I experienced two earthquake shocks. They were so slight that I should hardly have noticed them had it not been for the moving to and fro of the mirror on the wall. I do not know whether to envy or to pity the witness of the terrible earthquake at Gifu, whose experiences are described in the *Japan Mail* of Nov. 21, 1891. The following is certainly one of the most graphic little pen pictures of an earthquake ever written: "He had just finished dressing when the first shock came. . . . He crawled and dragged himself out of the house, for to walk was next to impossible. The next moment, so highly strung were his nerves, he burst into laughter at seeing the remarkable way a girl was moving down the garden path, lifting her legs high into the air, as it seemed. Then, looking over his shoulders, he saw a great and ancient temple, which he had been admiring the previous day, leap into the air and fall in dreadful ruin. Looking again to his front, the whole town was in an instant swept away before his eyes, and out of the great cloud of white dust came a screaming, gesticulating, wildly frantic crowd of men, women, and children, rushing hither and thither, they knew not where, for refuge from the great destruction which had come upon them."

into the middle of the street, and create sad havoc with it. One afternoon in September, as I was sitting on the Grand Hotel piazza, I heard feminine screams. Looking up the Bund, I saw a party of ladies on kurumas, being drenched by the ocean spray, although the runners were as close to the houses as they could get. That night the solid hotel shook and trembled like a ship, from the force of the wind; and in the morning I found that many of the stone posts lining the ocean side of the Bund had been washed out and upturned by the angry waves.

We consider the Japanese topsy-turvy in many ways, but in one respect the foreigners at Yokohama beat the natives on their own ground. They have numbered all the houses in the settlement continuously, regardless of street names. Thus, if you wish to go to the English Club, you simply say, " No. 5 " to your kuruma man; if the Germania Club is your goal, " No. 235 " will take you there. Just as London and New York firms will often give their cable address in their advertisements, so it is customary in Yokohama to print the "'Rikshaw" address. One bank, for instance, is " ni ban," another " hachi-jiu ban." The bank, of course, is the first place you will visit, in order to get Japanese money, which, luckily, is identical with our own, a yen being a dollar, a sen a cent, and the coins similar in size and appearance to our own. Formerly every Daimyo, or provincial nobleman, had his own paper money; but those good old times are no more. But foreigners are still pleased on finding that they can buy a dollar's worth of Japanese money for fifty or sixty cents.

Club life plays a very prominent *rôle* in Yokohama,

partly owing to the fact that so many of the residents have no family ties. The English Club is affiliated with similar organizations in other cities in Japan and in China and India, whose members are admitted to all privileges while visiting Yokohama. The German Club is thoroughly Teutonic, being partly social, partly musical. Here, in winter, they have a series of concerts, theatricals, and balls, at which, however, the fair sex is always in a grievous minority. The scarcity of women is the moral bane of these foreign communities in the East. It leads to concubinage and greater evils. The local " Yoshiwara " contains the finest buildings in the city. The road to Mississippi Bay also is lined with tea-houses, where merry girls invite passers-by to a cup of tea or rice wine.

The residences of the well-to-do foreigners at Yokohama are picturesquely situated on the Bluff, many of them being surrounded by luxurious gardens, with glorious views of the blue ocean on one side and snowy Fuji on the other. These three main parts of the foreign settlement — the Bluff, the Bund, and Main Street — are as sharply marked off from the Japanese division of Yokohama, by far the greater part, as the brown river Ottawa is for miles after it enters the green St. Lawrence. Will the European current ever visibly alter the color of the broad Asiatic stream? Possibly, for the Japanese are wonderful imitators and assimilators. Centuries ago they borrowed most of the oddities and all of the idiotities (if I may coin the word) of their customs from the Chinese, and they have during the last forty years learned an enormous amount from Europe and America; witness, for instance, their amazingly modern war against mediaeval China. Nevertheless, one can to this day spend hours in the native part of Yokohama without being reminded of the foreign invasion and the neighboring European and American settlement. The homes and habits, the dress and food, the employments and amusements, of the natives are here almost exactly what they were before Commodore Perry awakened the country from its long slumbers. They have not even become accustomed yet to the sight of foreigners, especially if women are of the party. We found that if we walked along with the crowds of men and women that fill the main street till midnight, every one stared at us, and many stopped to look after us. If we stood still a moment to look at anything, they immediately formed a circle about us, which soon became so dense, that it was difficult to break through it. There was no rude staring or jostling, no insulting comment, but simply the childish curiosity with which we gaze at a monkey or an elephant. But we had not expected this in the oldest and largest foreign port in Japan.

The only real annoyance came from the young begging children. It has been said that there are few or no beggars in Japan, and that the government and private charity allow no one to starve. I have also read of raids being made on beggars, and their being sent back by the police to their homes in other towns. All I know personally is that these young beggars were numerous, and that they had an exasperating obstinacy and pertinacity that a Spanish beggar might have envied. They repeat their monotonous request a hundred times, and if you lower your umbrella on one side to shut out the sight of them, they run to the other side and plague you another few minutes. Here, as else-

where, the offensive beggars are not those who deserve alms.

Japanese Yokohama has a street which might be compared to the Bowery of New York, or even to its Coney Island counterpart. It is a sort of dime-museum and cheap theatre street, crowded all the evening by natives of the lower class, newly arrived foreigners of all classes, and foreign sailors with their girls. The Japanese pay only one cent for admission, while foreigners are charged ten, without being accorded superior accommodations; nor is there any injustice in this, for we earn ten cents as easily as these people earn one cent. The nature of the show is sometimes indicated by pictures outside, while in other booths a method is resorted to like that of our sensational story-papers of which one number, breaking off in the midst of a blood-curdling scene, is distributed free, with the notice "to be continued in the next number," which is not free. One man raises a curtain till some striking scene within is half-revealed, whereupon the curtain is quickly dropped, while a noisy crier tells what is going on within. We entered some of the shows. In the first we saw the common circus trick of men balancing themselves on moving globes of various sizes. In another, a large woman was put into a small barrel, whereupon four swords were run through it in all directions, and a spear down through the middle. After these were withdrawn the woman popped up fresh and smiling, as badly painted and powdered as before. In one of the shows the wonders of electric light, telephone, phonograph, and so on, were exhibited to gaping natives. We also saw a poor crippled girl, without hands or feet, sitting on a table, holding in her mouth a pencil, with which she drew very fair pictures of ships and animals. Then she took a stick in her mouth and, with the aid of her stumps of arms and legs, made a paper-boat. After her came an idiotic-looking individual with a heavy sack on his shoulders, spinning around like a top, evidently having not enough brains to get dizzy with. The funniest of the sights was a wrestling match between a young boy and a girl, whose legs were as fat as the waists of ordinary boys and girls of their age. They knocked each other over every time, to the great delight of the audience.

The music accompanying these performances was much more of a novelty than the tricks. We heard a blind samisen player, who evidently adapted his style to his usual audience, indulging in all sorts of vulgar tricks with his banjo-like instrument. After playing awhile in the proper way, he would invert the instrument and continue the tune; then he put the plectron under the strings to shorten them, following this up with some glissando effects. Finally, he played with a short bow, which sounded much more musical than when he plucked the strings. He was frequently applauded, hand-clapping being one of the foreign customs readily adopted by the Japanese. In the larger shows there was a regular band, on a platform nearest the street. The players were mostly females, and their instruments were as picturesque as the noises they made were unique. Usually there was a sort of drum, a piccolo, a samisen, with a similar instrument, having a larger body and a shorter neck (biwa). Of the bowed instruments, one had a body like a very small drum, with a neck two feet long; it was played with a bow a foot long, and much wider than our double-bass bows.

The Japanese "harp," or koto, was evidently too refined and aristocratic to be used in such a place. The general effect of this music was somewhat Moorish in tone-color and in the monotonous repetition of the same melodic phrase. The showman held a stick in each hand with which he rapped to indicate the end of a number; sometimes, too, he emphasized the rhythm by pounding the floor rapidly with them, a rap for each tone.

After these samples of unmitigated Japanese music, it was interesting to hear what these people can do with European music. On Wednesday evening we found the hotel dining-room so crowded that there was hardly room for the regular guests. On this evening the band plays every week, and many residents take the opportunity for a social gathering and feast. After dinner the band played on the piazza, and many Japanese, mostly women and children, gathered in front to listen. What they thought of the music I do not know; probably they considered it very funny and meaningless. The band consisted of about twenty Japanese youths, who, I was told, had played together only ten months. Making allowance for that, and considering how utterly different their music is from ours, their performance of marches and waltzes was not bad; from any other point of view it was crude and barrel-organy. While the band was playing, several jugglers exhibited their tricks on the lawn before the hotel: swallowing swords, performing balancing feats, and so on. These came almost every evening. With the aid of the large telescope on the piazza one can observe other Japanese scenes at ease — families in fishing boats, or out for a picnic; boys and girls bathing naked in the bay, on a promontory to the left; or, without telescope, the various passers-by, who will usually reciprocate your curiosity.

Before leaving Yokohama, one feels tempted to investigate one of the large godowns, or one-story stone buildings which attract attention by their length and by their odor of tea, which you can smell several blocks off, like the malt odor of our breweries. Admission to them is not readily obtained, but the inside is worth seeing. At the door you hear a babel of feminine noises, recalling the cigar factories of Spain. Here are nearly a thousand women and girls, with bare arms and bosoms; but they do not, like the cigareras of Spain, hastily cover up their charms when a man enters. Each of them bends over a kettle holding five pounds of tea, which she stirs with her hands about ten minutes, after mixing a chemical powder with the leaves; then, taking that portion out, five more pounds are put in, and the stirring is resumed. The summer heat in Japan is great outside; in a building it is greater still, and as there is a fire under every one of these kettles, you can imagine the result. But the Japanese are salamanders; heat has no terror for them. These women and girls look healthy and contented, though they work ten hours a day, and receive only ten or fifteen cents for it all. They used to get twenty-five cents a day; but the price of tea fell, and wages were reduced. The employers told me that they never have any trouble with these women, some of whom have stirred tea-leaves in the same hot kettle for ten years. Strikes are practically unknown, and would be absurd in a country where, for every striker, there would be a dozen to take her place at almost any wages. A cent an hour seems low, even for an Oriental country; but they manage to live on it, and, strange to say, would probably all agree that life is worth living.

In reviewing my impressions of Yokohama, I have come to the conclusion that its attractions are usually underrated by tourists. Is not the native part of the city as quaintly Oriental as any other Japanese town? Is not the harbor the finest in the country? and could you find anywhere more picturesquely perched residences than those on the Bluff? In the matter of excursions, too, Yokohama is blessed beyond any other harbor town. To name only two, which no globe-trotter omits: Kamakura, "the Japanese Babylon," once a city of a million souls, now a village noted for its Daibutsu, or statue of Buddha, fifty feet in height, a grand work of art; and Enoshima, the "Japanese Capri," noted for its shells, divers, sponges, monstrous lobsters, its sacred cave one hundred and twenty-four yards deep, and its legend of Benten, the dragon goddess. It would be foolish to attempt to describe these places again, after it has been done so poetically and artistically by Mr. Griffis, Sir Edwin Arnold, Mr. Robert Blum, Mr. John La Farge, and others.

But the most interesting excursion is from Yokohama to Tōkyō, the new capital of Japan; and this every one is at liberty to write about, as its kaleidoscopic views of Oriental life are inexhaustibly novel and varied, presenting fresh aspects to every fresh pair of eyes.

RAILWAY AND KURUMA

AMERICA IN JAPAN — LOCOMOTIVES AND NATIVES — A TYPICAL STATION — CLOG DANCE — A EURASIAN HOTEL — A POLITE CLERK — A PLEA FOR LEMONS — A QUIET CITY — BIRD'S-EYE VIEW — HILLS AND PARKS — TRAITS OF KURUMA COOLIES — WHAT IS DEGRADING WORK?

BEFORE 1872 there were no railways in Japan, and trips to Kamakura, Tōkyō, and so on, could be comfortably made only by kuruma or on horseback. To-day Japan has almost two thousand miles of railroad. The first built was the short line of eighteen miles between Yokohama and Tōkyō. It carries us to the capital in less than an hour. By taking it we miss the busy multiple scenes of Japanese life which the kuruma rider could formerly enjoy on his leisurely run along the old road known as the Tōkaidō. But the view from the car-window includes Fuji on one side, the Bay of Tōkyō studded with sails on the other, and there are plenty of genre pictures of village life near the stations, while the rural stretches are varied with orchards, vegetable gardens, rank bamboo groves, and flooded rice-fields with stooping men and women pulling up the weeds or transplanting the young crop. To foreigners residing in Tōkyō a few weeks or months, this railway is a great convenience, as they somehow seem to find it necessary to run over to Yokohama every other day, either to replenish their purses at the banks, or to procure some of the conveniences and luxuries to which they are accustomed, and which are less accessible in Tōkyō, where the number of foreigners is not large enough to be specially catered to. To return to Yokohama after residing in the capital a week or two, seems almost like annihilating the ocean and dropping into one of our own cities. After an absence of a month in the interior, this illusion is so intensified that one experiences quite an American or European emotion on seeing Main Street or the Bund again. To me this was one of the pleasantest experiences in Japan, because it constantly kept alive and fresh the contrast between Occident and Orient.

As for the Japanese, they took readily and eagerly to the cars, as to everything that is new and practical. The railroad to Tōkyō was built by foreigners, and was at first run by them, the engineers and conductors being English, the ticket-sellers Chinamen. To-day everything is in Japanese hands, and all runs smoothly, thus nullifying the foolish fears of those foreigners who, when the Japanese first began to take hold of some of their own engines, chose those which still remained in foreign hands whenever they took a trip. It is related that a Spanish peasant, on seeing for the first time a train in motion, looked on in amazement and finally exclaimed, "But where are the mules?" Many similar scenes occurred when the Japanese peasants first sighted a locomotive. The women used to crowd around, and then run away screaming when it began to puff and move. Here was a monster more terrible than all the dragons described in their weird legends! Every one has heard of the man who, after a late dinner, was sent home in a cab, and as soon as it had started, took off his boots, opened the cab door and threw them out for the porter to blacken. The topsy-turvy Japanese of course do soberly what we do when we are drunk; at any rate, it is related that one day a peasant, on entering a car, took off his wooden pattens and placed them carefully on the station platform, expecting to find them all right on arriving in Tōkyō.

Every kuruma-puller in Yokohama understands the word "station," which has been adopted into the language like many other English words. If you should happen to be late for the train, take two pullers, tell them "hayaku," and you will be hurried along in your "baby carriage with adult wheels" almost as fast as a horse could take you. If you are wise, you will at least have memorized the phrases relating to travel, printed in the little book which some enterprising curio dealer has probably left at your hotel door. But even if your ignorance of the language is still exhaustive and symmetrical, you will have no difficulty at the station, as the civil ticket-sellers know more English than is necessary to understand your demand for a first, second, or third class ticket to Tōkyō.

The station itself is worth inspection. The third-class waiting room is very large, with plain benches. The first-class is very small, but has upholstered chairs and sofas. The second is of medium size, and has a table in the centre, with Japanese and English newspapers. Although first-class is here as cheap as third is in Europe, almost all the Japanese travel third-class. The first is used only by a few high dignitaries, while the second takes most of the foreigners and a considerable number of the well-to-do Japanese. In one of the waiting rooms I saw an automatic weighing machine in the form of a seat, and with a nickel-in-the-slot "cashier"; but as the numerals were in Japanese characters only, I could not ascertain whether the climate had begun yet to reduce me to the dimensions of the miniature natives. The second-class cars are very stupidly arranged with seats along the sides, like our horse-cars. Many of the natives squat on these seats, with their legs curled up under them, instead of letting their feet dangle down as we do. There is no bell rope connecting the cars, and the guards, who look like boys in their foreign uniforms, though they are men, call out the names of stations with genuine imported rapidity and indistinctness.

The first vision of Tōkyō, as we near the station, suggests the railway yards and belching factory chimneys of a western American city, rather than the capital of esthetic Japan, and recalls Ruskin's tirades against railways as the greatest uglifying agency of modern civilization — an agency which makes most American towns and villages hideous with horrid sights and noises. As soon as the train stops, a most extraordinary clattering and shuffling sound assails the ear — a sound which we had heard at the way stations, but only as a mere hint of what was to come at the Shimbashi station, where several hundred third-class passengers were dumped at once on the platform and hobbled over the stone flooring with their clogs, which, held fast by a thong passing between the big toe and its neighbor, constitute their foot gear. It sounded like a clog dance on a large scale, except that there was no rhythmic accent, but mere clattering, deafening chaos. It is a sound that can be heard only in Japan, nor would it be greatly missed there. These miniature stilts may be a great convenience in muddy streets, and to facilitate quick entrance into clean-matted houses without foot gear; but they are exceedingly ugly, and they give the Japanese the most ungainly gait of all nations in the world.

Outside the Shimbashi station there is a stand where you can buy a kuruma ticket to any part of the city at a fixed rate — a great convenience for greenhorns who cannot bargain with the coolies. I took one for the Tōkyō Hotel, which had been recommended to me as convenient and well kept, and so I found it. Tōkyō has several kinds of hotels — purely native, purely foreign, and hybrid. The Tōkyō hotel is modelled largely after the foreign hotels in Yokohama, yet has more Japanese features. After leaving the capital, I made it a habit to go to Japanese inns, even where hotels in foreign style were available, because I wished to study the ways of the country; but in Tōkyō there are so many other things to see than hotels, that it seemed wiser to stay where I could feel sure of a real bed and foreign food, as I did not yet know how Japanese food and beds would agree with me. It was a wise decision, which I found had also been reached by Mr. Henry Norman, who was a guest at this hotel while collecting notes for his graphic and truthful volume entitled *The Real Japan*, and by Mr. Robert Blum, who was there to illustrate Sir Edwin Arnold's articles and one of his books on Japan, and who has also contributed a fascinating account of his impressions to *Scribner's Magazine*, showing Japan, like Mr. John La Farge's admirable articles in the *Century*, through an artist's eyes.

Although partly arranged after foreign models, the

Tōkyō Hotel contrasts pleasantly with American hotels in the courteousness of all the employees. One day I sat down on a bench in the office to talk with the clerk, who immediately got up and brought me a comfortable bamboo chair. Imagine an American hotel clerk doing such a thing! *Can* you imagine it? Our Japanese clerks — there were two — were always ready to give us information and hints, to give the coolies directions where to take us, to write out addresses or telegrams for us in Japanese, and so on. Not that it is necessary to send telegrams in the vernacular; English, German, or French may be used, but then the charges are five cents a word, counting the address, while in Japanese the address is free, and the despatch costs a mere bagatelle.

In the dining room there is the same prompt attention to all wants. It is un-Japanese to have male waiters; but the waiters here are, of course, Japanese, and they are among the best it has ever been my good luck to be served by. My own waiter was particularly prompt and attentive, and one day I could hardly repress my indignation when an American bully, engaged in the silk business, sat down at my table, swore at the waiter, bossed him like a slave, and actually made him run, though there was absolutely no occasion for hurry. In this case the Asiatic menial was infinitely more of a gentleman than the American merchant. However, I swallowed my indignation, with the aid of a quart bottle of Bass's ale, which always goes to the right spot in a hot climate, and, if taken conscientiously twice a day, obviates all danger from the Tōkyō drinking water, in which often lurk the microbes of typhoid, cholera, dysentery, and other murderous microscopic beasts. I have often marvelled at the ignorant inconsistency of tourists in Spain, Italy, and other warm latitudes, carefully shutting out the salubrious night air, but eagerly quaffing the suspicious water on hotel tables, or even such as is offered by street carriers, whose habits and sources are unknown. I have not seldom been in places where I thought it prudent to use Apollinaris even to brush my teeth with. Japan has fortunately a substitute for Apollinaris, and a very good one, which is, in fact, almost identical with it. It is called Hirano water, and is so highly charged with its own gas that the bottles have to be carefully handled. It makes the most delicious lemonade; but, unfortunately, lemons are so scarce that one has to pay twice or thrice as much as in America. Indeed, the scarcity of lemons seemed to me the most deplorable of all the material shortcomings of Japan. I say this in all seriousness. The sultry summer climate of Japan makes the craving for a refreshing sour drink almost irresistible. In the absence of cheap lemons, the Japanese eat sour green fruit, at the expense of their health. He who would truly benefit these people, should make lemons — or, better still, Mexican limes — abundant and cheap. They would save thousands of lives, too, every year, as the acid of limes and lemons is a great germicide.

Tōkyō is anything but a pleasant summer resort. All those who can afford it, leave for the mountains or seashore, but as the number of those who can do so is very small indeed, the city can hardly be called deserted in July and August. The Tōkyō Hotel is one of the few three-storied buildings in the city, and I took my room on the third, so as to catch any stray breezes from the bay. But they seemed to go astray in other directions, or not to exist at all, and I repeatedly "awoke after a sleepless night" to find myself in a bath of perspiration, at a temperature not much lower than that of the hot bath to which the attendant summoned me early in the morning. What lemonade, tea, or beer is esoterically during Lotos-Time in Japan, hot water is exoterically, and luckily the Tōkyō Hotel has given up the communistic tank in favor of the more civilized individual bath tub.

Apart from the sultry nocturnal heat, there is nothing to prevent sound sleep in Tōkyō. I believe that Richard Wagner is not the only brain worker who chose Venice for a temporary residence, largely because the absence of horses makes it so quiet at night. In Tōkyō horses are almost as scarce as in Venice, and there is this farther advantage that the streets are unpaved. The only sound that rises on the air is the melancholy whistle of the strolling blind shampooer, seeking a victim to knead like a lump of dough; or, perhaps, early in the morning, the voices of coolies, passing under your window on their way to their daily tasks. Fiendish factory whistles, the blatant signals of American uncivilization, never murder sleep and kill invalids in Japan.

When the wind blew from a certain quarter, I could faintly hear the military buglers, practising their fanfares in the barracks not far away. One of them would blow the melody, whereupon twenty others would try to imitate him, continuing till success was achieved.

After the morning bath and breakfast, — or, better still, before, — the first daily act should be to go to the roof of the hotel, and see if Fuji is visible. One of the great charms of Tōkyō is the purity of the air and its clearness, due to the fact that charcoal is almost the only fuel used, wherefore there are no thousands of chimneys belching out black smoke. But mountainwards there is usually a summer mist; and unless you look daily, morning and evening, you may fail to see the sacred mountain at all from this point of view.

To get a bird's-eye view of the mountainous surroundings of Tōkyō, the bays and the city itself, the best way is to ascend the "men's staircase" or the "women's staircase" to the top of the hill called Atago-yama, on which a tower has been built. Looking down on the ocean of monotonous gray roofs, covering countless one-story wooden buildings, one misses, most of all, the picturesque towers and large buildings which give variety to our cities. Obviously, architectural wonders are not to be prominent among the things that will attract our attention, apart from a few Buddhist temples with their Chinese pagodas. From this elevated view-point the city itself is, indeed, far less attractive than its surroundings and its site. Washington has been called a city of magnificent distances; but our American capital is in extension a mere village, compared to the Japanese capital, whose 1,400,000 denizens inhabit an area of no less than a hundred square miles, while the 5,000,000 Londoners live within an area of no more than 120 square miles, and the 2,000,000 New-Yorkers manage to find elbow room within forty square miles. Yet we always fancy these Asiatic peoples to be crowded together to suffocation.[1]

[1] Greater New York will cover an area of 317 square miles. According to Professor Supan of Gotha, there are now in the world twelve cities with over a million souls each, ranking in the following order: London, Paris, New York-Brooklyn, Berlin, Canton, Vienna, Wuchang-Hanggang-Hankan, Tōkyō, Chicago, Philadelphia, Siangtan, Singan. Thus Tōkyō city ranks eighth. The Tōkyō province had 1,857,000

From our tower, the difference between these cities is obvious at a glance. In Tōkyō, every family has its own house, however humble, in New York, hundreds live in a single building, and many of our larger downtown buildings have room for a thousand busy men and women. One of our sky-scraping fifteen-story New York monsters, suddenly dropped into the middle of Tōkyō, would look a good deal like an ostrich in a chicken yard, or a whale in a school of herring. Japan is a land of small things, — a fact impressed on us every minute during our sojourn. The settled part of Philadelphia covers more space than that of New York, because it has fewer high buildings and more private residences. Tōkyō is a Philadelphia greatly exaggerated. It has 342,000 houses, — one for every four or five inhabitants.

There is another reason for Tōkyō's vast area. New York has one great park, Tōkyō has many, — I don't know how many, certainly a great many more than even London. The city was originally a collection of villages, gradually subsumed under one name, and luckily still separated by hills, gardens, and groves. On one of these wooded hills, which make up a great part of Tōkyō, you might fancy yourself miles away from all the sights and noises of a city. I remember riding in a kuruma one day for a whole hour without passing through a single business street! Surely, in this mingling of country and city, Tōkyō is prophetic of what our own cities will be when our esthetic and hygienic wisdom teeth are cut, and we begin to value

souls in 1894. The death rate was only 19.95 as compared with New York's 23 per thousand. The new waterworks now in course of construction will still further lower the mortality.

life and nature more than the eager chase of the unenjoyed dollar.

For the sight-seer, the magnificent distances of Tōkyō are not an unmixed blessing, for they imply a great expenditure of time. Steam railways, underground or elevated, there are none within the city itself, and the one street car line, with wretched mules and irregular time, is not noted for its fast time or convenience. Carriages of any kind are an anomaly in the narrow, crowded business streets, and can only progress very slowly. There are plans for widening the streets and introducing electric cars, but that is for the future. At present we must content ourselves with the kuruma, which I am sure is by far the most convenient and comfortable of all conveyances for seeing an Asiatic city. In Yokohama one has little use for the jinrikishas except for excursions in the neighborhood, but in the streets and groves of vast Tōkyō you need them all day long, and soon look on them as a self-evident mode of conveyance, which must have existed ever since the days of Adam.

Most of us, even if we know Japan only superficially through books and pictures, are apt to fancy that of all things the kuruma is most Japanese. But the kuruma was unknown in Japan a quarter of a century ago. It is even probable that it was invented by a foreigner. But the Japanese immediately saw its superiority to other modes of conveyance, and to-day Tōkyō has about 40,000 of them,[1] which are used by all who can afford to do so, while to foreigners, who would be foolish to risk walking in the hot sun, they are indispensable.

---

[1] The official figures in 1892 were 38,265 kurumas. In the same year Tōkyō had 71 tram cars, 15 carriages for hire, and 110 vehicles plying in the streets, employing in all 1136 horses.

Many improvements have been made in the kuruma since its first invention. To judge by early pictures of them (see, *e.g.*, Griffis's *Mikado's Empire*, p. 335) they were not only differently shaped, but less easy to get into. In place of the stuffy, unfragrant hoods of oiled paper, used to keep off the rain, of which Miss Bird complained so frequently, the improved kuruma has a regular diminutive carriage cover, making it look somewhat like a miniature hansom without a driver, and with a man between the shafts. It takes some little time to get over the mixed feeling of pleasure and humiliation one experiences at first in these little vehicles; they are so comfortable, and yet one fancies himself presenting a rather ludicrous figure riding through business streets in a baby hansom, drawn by a half-naked coolie. But, as already intimated, that feeling soon passes away, while the pleasure remains (provided the road is smooth). An American lady said to me that on her first ride she felt as if she were on the back of an ostrich, or some other two-legged animal. The kuruma might also be compared in its effect to a bicycle; but the seat is more comfortable, the force is supplied by another man's muscles, and all responsibility for collisions is shifted on his shoulders. One might call it the lazy man's bicycle, and if you are no more particular about personal attitude and comfort than the Japanese are, you may even take a nap in it on the way home after a dinner or an exhausting outing. I frequently saw natives thus dozing away, with head hanging limp over one side of the kuruma.

Like our cabmen the kuruma pullers have regular stands at railway stations and street corners, and in their habits and morals they are not unlike the jehus of our cities. These horse-men are apt to be "heavy chargers," and their tendency to ask more than the legal fare has already been referred to as a connecting link between America and Japan. Another trait which the kurumaya has in common with our cabmen is that when he sees a tourist trying to go sightseeing on foot, he follows him in the hope that the sun will soon bring him to terms; nor does he often err in his calculations. This frequently happened to me. When several were in the party, the same number of coolies followed us. If they failed in their still hunt, they bore their disappointment with Asiatic complacency.

The Tōkyō kuruma is as unique as the Venetian gondola, and it might, perhaps, be called a land gondola. The gondolier always insists that two rowers are necessary, till he hears your *basta uno!* The kurumaya looks at your girth and weight in simulated dismay (though you may not weigh over 180), and tries to make you understand that for such a heavy fellow two runners are absolutely necessary. If you consent, the second man pushes from behind, or, attaching a rope to the shafts, he precedes the man between the shafts, tandem style. On country tours, where hills are apt to occur, it is always well to take two men, unless you are willing to walk up the slopes; but in the city one man is quite enough, unless you are in a hurry. You feel, indeed, that you are heavier than the natives, but as you constantly see two, three, or even more of these natives crowding into a kuruma pulled by one coolie, you soon become indifferent to that fact. Besides, there are some people who have to study economy. Compared with a cab, a coolie is always cheap; he charges only ten cents an hour going, and three cents waiting, or at the rate of three cents a mile. For sight-seers this is cheap enough, but for daily use it would be expensive. A New York business man pays ten cents to go from Harlem to the Battery and back — about ten miles each way; in Tōkyō the cost would be sixty cents with one runner and $1.20 with two.

It is probable that the kuruma will be ere long superseded by electric tricycles and cars; all the more as there seems to be a feeling that it is a sort of "degradation" to the country. I fail to see why it should be more degrading for a coolie to draw a gentleman or lady on a clean little wagon through the streets, than to carry the city sewage in buckets to the rice fields, as thousands of them do in spring, or to work knee-deep in the malodorous mire of these fields, as millions of peasants and their wives do all summer long. I am sure the kurumayas would not willingly change places with these peasants.

Let us now entrust ourselves to one of these coolies for a ride through the streets of Tōkyō. There are always half-a-dozen of them waiting at the hotel entrance, in company with several stray dogs, who are charitably taken care of, and who sometimes follow us; but some find the sun too warm, and return. If Taro is there, do not fail to engage him; for Taro is a jewel among the kurumayas of the capital. Not only is he a good runner, who knows his Tōkyō as well as Dickens did his London (either of which requires a big brain), but he speaks a little English, and thus enables you to dispense with a guide. Whenever Taro is disengaged for an hour, he sits by his kuruma, with a little book in hand, busily memorizing English words and phrases; and he has his reward, for he is more in demand than any of his colleagues. He has one fault. His national and individual politeness is so great that whenever he does not understand one of your questions, he says, "Yes," fearing that a negative might cause disappointment. One day, to test him, I asked if I might cut the throat of a pretty girl who was serving the tea, whereupon he promptly and cordially replied, "Oh yes!"

STREET SCENES IN TŌKYŌ

RECENT CHANGES — DAIMYOS AND SAMURAI — YASHIKIS AND MOATS — POLICEMEN — ATTACKS ON FOREIGNERS — SAFETY IN CITY AND COUNTRY — SHOPS AND HOMES EXPOSED TO VIEW — BAZAARS — TRADES FLOCKING TOGETHER — COMIC SIGNBOARDS — UNGRAMMATICAL COSTUMES — BRUNETTES IN BLUE — MODEST EXPOSURE — JAPANESE CHILDREN — BOWING — HOW THE POOR LIVE — FIRES AND GODOWNS

PERHAPS no city in the world has ever undergone so wonderful a change as has the capital of Japan within little more than a quarter of a century. The Japanese, says Professor Chamberlain, "have done in twenty years what it took Europe as many centuries to accomplish." Descriptions of Tōkyō street scenes made by Laurence Oliphant and Sir Rutherford Alcock three or four decades ago are, in some respects, as antiquated and inapplicable to-day, as the accounts of life in mediæval Europe are to modern London, Paris, and Berlin. For example, take the following from Alcock:

"Every hundred steps, more or less, we pass a ward-gate, which at night they can close if an alarm of thieves is given, or by day if any disturbance should arise, while a sort of decrepit municipal guard is kept in a lodge at each, supposed to be responsible for the peace of their wards, and to be ever vigilant! Some, as we pass, rush out with a long iron pole, to the top of which rings are attached, and make a distracting noise when the lower end is struck on the ground. This is considered an honor," etc.

When Oliphant visited Tōkyō, in 1858, crowds of men, women, and children ran after his party, politely staring, till one of these barriers was reached.

"The moment we pass this, the gate is shut, and the old crowd is left behind to crane through the bars, and watch with envious eyes the new crowd forming. All the cross-streets entering the main street are shut off from it by ropes stretched across them, under or over which the people never attempt to pass."

To-day you would look for these ropes, barriers, gate-keepers, and pursuing crowds, as vainly as in New York. In vain, too, would you look for the clumsy and horribly uncomfortable norimons and kagos — the more or less complicated Sedan chairs, litters, palanquins, or whatever you choose to call them — with two or more bearers, that used to be the mode of conveyance for the well-to-do. They have been superseded in the cities by the kurumas, and banished to mountain regions, where these modern two-wheelers are useless. Will Adams, the shipwrecked English sailor who resided in Japan from 1600 to 1620, writes, in one of his quaint letters, of "sixe men appointed to carrie my pallankin in plaine and even ground. But where the country grew hilly, ten men were allowed me thereto." To-day one or two men do the work which then required six or ten, and iron wheels hold the weight which then rested on human shoulders. Whatever may be the "degradation" implied in the use of the kuruma, it certainly has proved a blessing to the poor coolie; and what the well-to-do populace thought of the change, may be inferred from the rapidity of its adoption and multiplication.

In vain, again, would you look in modern Tōkyō for the samurai, or two-sworded soldiers, looking like "some new species of biped adorned with two tails," who used

A KAGO

to swarm in the city by the hundred thousand, and who, in their drunken fits, made the streets unsafe for inoffensive dogs and coolies, on whom they loved to try the temper of their steel, so that it was often unsafe to venture into the streets after dark. Gone are the daimyos, or provincial nobles, the barons of feudal Japan, three hundred in number, who used to bring each from a few thousand to as many as 30,000 of these burly samurai as retainers to the capital, where the daimyos were compelled by law to spend half the year, leaving their families as hostages and pledges of good behavior during their residence at home the rest of the year. Luckily some of the buildings in which they lived are still in existence, constituting one of the oddest of the street sights, puzzling to the globe-trotter unless he knows at least as much of Japanese history as is conveyed in this paragraph.

It cannot be said that these yashikis add anything to the beauty of Tōkyō. They are low, unpainted, interminable buildings which might be taken for Asiatic tenement houses, were it not that most of them seem utterly deserted. Many have been demolished or destroyed by fire, and others converted into government buildings, but enough remain in their primitive state to astonish the visitor, like the endless moats and walls along which he passes on the way to the business centres. Mr. Griffis has graphically compared these yashikis — literally "spread-out houses" — to military tents, made permanent in wood and stone. The plan of the city of Yeddo (as Tōkyō was formerly called), when it was made by the Shogun Iyeyasu, at the beginning of the seventeenth century, was, as he says, "simply that of a great camp." "This one idea explains its centre, divisions, and relations. In the heart of this vast encampment was the general's headquarters—a well-nigh impregnable castle. On the most eligible and commanding sites were the tents of his chief satraps. These tents were yashikis. The architectural prototype of a yashiki is a Japanese tent."[1]

Even more than these yashikis, the moats surrounding them and the great castle, together with the numerous canals that intersect the city, and their bridges, attract the attention on one's first rides through the less populous parts of Tōkyō. There are miles of broad moats, steep on one side, with sloping banks on the other, leading up to massive stone walls, usually adorned with green creepers or a row of evergreen trees on top, spreading out like large oaks. The moats are always filled with sluggish water, almost stagnant, and are the home, in winter, of water fowl, secure in the protection of the law; in summer, of the pink lotos. But even the sacred lotos, symbol of purity, rising triumphantly from the mud, would not, perhaps, be able with its faint fragrance to overcome the foul odors which arise from some of these canals, and which constitute one more reminder of Venice. On my first visit to the capital these stenches made it unpleasant to cross the bridges, but on my return from Yezo, after an absence of several weeks, I found that the moats and canals had been disinfected by the sanitary authorities, regardless of expense, to check the ravages of the cholera, which had in the meantime made its appearance.

The bridges over these canals are the best places

[1] A vivid idea of life in one of these buildings is conveyed by Maclay's romance *Mito Yashiki*.

to observe the miscellaneous and crowded boat traffic which in the capital (and still more in the commercial city of Osaka) largely takes the place of horses and wagons. The canals are supplied by the river Sumida, which flows through Tōkyō, and on them you will see at any time of the day, hundreds of roofed boats and barges laden with merchandise from or for steamers, or vegetables from farms or suburban gardens. The men who load and unload them seem to have a liking for the direct rays of the sun; for in fair weather their sole garment is a loin cloth, whereas the rain is often warded off by a grotesque coat of straw suggesting a porcupine on the warpath.

On one side or the other of a bridge we usually passed a policeman, whose peaceful aspect gave no intimation of the fact that he belonged to the former warrior class of the samurai. The Japanese samurai have been pronounced unique by the historians, because they were at the same time the soldiers and the scholars of their country. But are not our scholars also noted for their pugnacity? Do they not dearly love a fight, even though they utilize the discovery that the pen is mightier than the sword? The samurai had not learned this lesson when they lost their occupation through the abolition of the Shogun and the daimyos, and the restoration of the Mikado, in 1868. And when the new law compelled them to give up their two swords many of them joined the police force, where they could wear at least one sword.

Thus it came about that the new Japanese police force is the most intelligent, courteous, and efficient in the world. Of the old-style policeman we get a glimpse in the pages of Oliphant, who describes them as wearing a sort of harlequin costume of many colors, and carrying iron rods, six or seven feet long, with iron rings attached to them, which they jingled to inspire awe in the crowd. To-day, the policemen are the most foreign-looking class of all Japanese. They wear, in summer, white linen trousers and sack coats of foreign cut, and white hats, with white crepe hanging behind to prevent the sun from striking the neck.

It is this foreign costume that helps to make the Tōkyō policemen seem so small compared with our Irish giants in New York. To us, too, it seems odd to see policemen wearing spectacles, as 30 per cent of the Japanese are said to do,—an inheritance from their studious ancestors. They are still fond of reading. In Netto's beautifully illustrated quarto there is an amusing illustration (p. 77) of a policeman guarding some convicts at work. The prisoners have things pretty much their own way, for their erudite and spectacled guardian is sitting on a campstool, reading a big volume, with his feet not resting on the ground, but tucked away under him on the stool. Yet I fancy that if one of those convicts attempted to escape, he would find that that samurai had not forgotten the ancestral art of wielding the two-handed sword. During my summer in Japan I never saw a policeman's sword drawn, nor, apart from having to show my passport in rural regions, was I ever accosted by one of these scholarly guardians of the peace except once, when my man-horse (not Taro) had forgotten to take along the lantern, which is prescribed by law at night, to avoid collisions. For a moment it looked serious for the runner, but when I produced my official invitation to the exposition, the policeman smiled, bowed low, and allowed us to proceed in peace. Whether he took my puller's number and fined him afterwards, I could not find out.

Such is the Tōkyō policeman — intelligent, courteous, and sufficiently brave to enforce order even were his countrymen a hundred times less peaceable than they are. I have been asked repeatedly, "Is it perfectly safe to travel alone in Japan?" A perusal of Alcock and even more recent books would create a suspicion that such a tour would not be without its risks to life. Between 1859 and 1870, it is estimated, about fifty foreigners were killed in Japan, and at the latter date the government still deemed it necessary to protect the foreign preachers in Tōkyō by an escort of fifty men. "During my stay of nearly four years in Japan," says Mr. Griffis, "several Europeans were attacked or killed: *but in no case was there a genuine assassination or unprovoked assault.*" An impartial investigation of all the attacks made on foreigners has convinced the best authorities that in most cases the foreigners themselves brought on the tragedy by insolent or reckless conduct. There were, indeed, some exceptions — a few assassinations by patriotic fanatics, who believed they would serve their country and its ruler by murdering a hated foreigner; but even these ceased at once after the Mikado's proclamation in 1868, declaring that he regarded such attacks as infamous and detestable, and that samurai guilty of them would be degraded, their swords taken from them, and their dishonored names erased from the rolls of the samurai; that, further, they should be beheaded by the common executioner (instead of being allowed the honorable privilege of hara-kiri), and their heads be exposed for three days.[1]

[1] Black's *Young Japan*, II. 190, 191.

The Japanese kindliness and courtesy inspire one with such boundless and immediate confidence in the whole population, that I cheerfully followed Taro on day and night excursions through dark suburban lanes and alleys — houseless regions, with a ditch on one side, a high wall on the other — such as I would never dream of passing alone and unarmed at night in New York, London, Paris, or Berlin. I may also quote the testimony of Miss Bird, who wrote: "I have . . . travelled twelve hundred miles in the interior and in Yezo, with perfect safety and freedom from alarm, and I believe there is no country in the world in which a lady can travel with such absolute security from danger and rudeness as in Japan."

Turning to the left, after crossing one of the bridges, we suddenly find ourselves in a street crowded with kurumas and thousands of men, women, and children, moving on in a calm, Oriental gait that would make a New York business man nervous and wild with impatience. It is in wending his way through these sluggish crowds that the kurumaya shows his skill and tact. He misses collisions with his colleagues as narrowly, but as unfailingly, as a London 'bus or cab driver, and, like the Londoner, he always passes to the left, while he differs from the Englishman in constantly emitting a warning "Hi! hi!" We are not sorry that he cannot go fast, for here there is so much to see that the countless eye lenses of a fly would hardly seem too many for a tourist.

In American or European cities, we understand by "street scenes" the sights in the streets and on the sidewalks, including, at most, the few wares exposed in the windows. In a Japanese city, the whole contents

of the shops or stores are included in the street scenes.
It is true that the dealers in silks, works of art, and other
valuable articles, keep most of their stock locked up in
their fire-proof *kura*, or godowns, bringing them out only
as wanted by customers. But these seem to be the exception; and the surmise that most Japanese merchants
have their whole stock in trade visible from the street
is probably not far from the truth. The merchants and
their clerks are, of course, visible too, and so are the
customers, who, if they have expensive purchases to
make, take off their clogs and squat on a mat inside,
partaking of the tea and tobacco offered by the merchant; but ordinarily the buyer simply sits on the foot-high projecting part of the shop floor, with a sloping
roof over him, and his feet in the street, for there is
not even a sidewalk. On sunny days, screens shut out
part of the view; but ordinarily, as you ride or walk
down a Tōkyō street, you can see all the goods and all
the transactions of the clerks, the buyers, and the boys
who are hauling the things wanted from the godowns;
not to speak of the domestic scenes in the interior rooms
and the garden — of persons sleeping, eating, drinking,
bathing, dressing, gossiping — all of which are visible
from the street, since all the movable partitions between
the rooms are removed in the daytime to let in daylight and fresh cool air, if there is any. It has been
suggested, with some appearance of probability, that
one reason why the Japanese of all classes are so courteous and refined is that all their doings, domestic as
well as public, are constantly exposed to the eyes of
neighbors and strangers — even at night; for when the
sliding screens are put back in their places, the oiled
paper on them, which takes the place of window panes,

serves as a stereopticon screen, on which are shown amusing shadow pictures of whatever goes on within.

The average Japanese merchant likes to bargain, and is apt to charge foreigners much more than he expects to get. Strangers, therefore, in purchasing articles of everyday use, will do well to patronize one of the large bazaars in Shiba Park, or on the Broadway of Tōkyō; the Ginza, the widest avenue in the city, in which the price of each article is plainly marked; yet even here it is well to look out for tricks, especially on the part of the kuruma men, who like to get their "squeeze," or percentage. These bazaars are interesting, too, in giving one a convenient bird's-eye view of everything that goes to furnish Japanese sitting rooms (kneeling rooms would be a more correct term), bed and dining rooms, libraries, and kitchens. Here you will see tobacco pipes and pouches in endless variety; Japanese paper in all colors, for a hundred different uses, some of it as tough as linen; toys, lacquer ware, rice bowls, chop sticks, wooden pillows, wooden shoes, foot mittens; leather trunks and bags, in foreign style, wonderfully cheap; umbrellas, Japanese and foreign; ornamental screens and fans; kimonos, obis, and other articles of dress; and so on, till the eye is bewildered, and you beg your Taro to take you back to the kuruma; for alone it would not be easy to find one's way out of the commercial mazes of these national museums.

Although New York bankers still flock together on Wall Street, and the newspaper and publishing houses favor special quarters, as a general thing our Occidental cities have outgrown the mediæval habit of monopolizing certain streets for certain trades. In Japanese cities this custom is still largely in vogue: you will

SILK STORE

ride through streets where everybody is selling paper lanterns; others, where hairdressers ply their loquacious trade; others, where lacquer ware or curios are sold, or bamboo furniture, or baskets, or fans, or new and second-hand clothing, or books, and so on. In the Ginza, however, the various trades and commercial branches are strung together at random, as in our own Broadway. Here, too, you may see evidences of foreign influence, — leather shoe shops, tailors using sewing machines, and the like. Foreign telegraph lines introduce a dissonant element in the street views which does not please the eyes of the natives, and the newspapers plead occasionally to have them put underground.

Times are hard in Tōkyō, as elsewhere, and enterprising merchants make efforts to attract all the foreign customers they can. To this end they put out shop signs, many of which are amusingly "Eurasian." Here are a few samples: "Several Woolen Cloths and Tailor Shop." "French Infections." "Great Sail of Man-of-War Beer, Wine, Spiritual Liquors." "The Improved Milk." "Carver and Gilder for Sale." "Wine, Beer & other Medicines." "Best Perfuming Water Anti-Fleas." "Washins and Ironins." "Bible Shop."

The costumes of the natives are sometimes quite as ungrammatical as these shop signs, — a ludicrous mixture of Europe and Asia. Many of the educated Japanese we meet in America and in Tōkyō wear foreign clothes with such ease and elegance that one might think they had never known any other. The policemen, too, seem to take kindly to clothes of our pattern, and the soldiers are becoming reconciled to them. But in the street crowds one meets the oddest mixtures of evening dress and bathing suits, — naked legs with a blouse and a foreign hat, high boots with a kimono, legs and head Asiatic, trunk European, or *rice versa*, with endless combinations and variations. As a rule, the Japanese men, like the women, go bareheaded; and when they do manage to secure a foreign hat, they do not usually improve their appearance. If the Duke of Wellington could have lived to visit Tōkyō to-day, he would confess that his exclamation, "I never saw so many shocking bad hats," was no longer applicable to the first Reformed Parliament. Trousers too long or short, unbrushed silk hats, and a general awkwardness in European clothing, prove that Japanese taste in dressing is an inherited instinct which has great trouble in accommodating itself to our present ugly costume.

It would be a great mistake to suppose that such evidences of foreign influence are abundant in the capital. On the contrary, you may force your way through crowded miles of natives without seeing a dozen men in foreign clothes or a score in the hybrid masquerade just described. As for the women, they represent here, as elsewhere, the conservative element. They tried Parisian costume, a few years ago, and found it odious, ugly, and uncomfortable; a reaction set in, and to-day you may spend a whole afternoon or evening in the streets of Tōkyō without meeting one of them in foreign attire. Bareheaded, smiling, armed with parasol and fan by way of protection against the sun, they seem like those very familiar figures on screens, fans, and vases, touched by a fairy's wand and changed into living beings, — except that their eyes are not so absurdly oblique as in those conventional scenes, nor their gowns so picturesque. To-day it is only the little girls who wear brightly colored gowns. As the maidens grow older, they discard these, and the initiated can tell the age of every Japanese girl by the increasing sombreness of her dress, as well as by the increasing elaborateness of her coiffure; an expert can also tell whether a young woman is married or single, respectable or otherwise, whether from the country or city-bred.

It is a maxim of Western esthetics that brunettes should wear some shade of red, while blue is most becoming to blondes. It seems strange, therefore, that the Japanese, the esthetic nation *par excellence*, a nation of brunettes, should have chosen blue as the almost universal color of their everyday gown. There are other things I cannot admire about their female costume. The kimono is so tight below the waist that the women are obliged to shuffle along on their hideous clogs, with short, clumsy steps, ruinous to grace. Above the waist the kimono is a thing of beauty, and an ideal dress for this climate. The women have a comfortable way of leaving it open, so as to give the air free access to the bosom. It is curious to see how Japanese boys will draw their skirts together over their legs, and the young women their kimonos over the chest, when they pass a foreigner. Among themselves they feel perfectly innocent, and they are innocent, — much more so than some of their foreign visitors with their prurient ideas regarding exposure. Complete nudity in public is now forbidden by law, but the men still freely expose the lower half of the body, the women the upper.

Although Japanese women are not chaperoned so zealously as in other Oriental countries, but mingle freely with the men in the streets, they usually keep together in a way which suggests the separation of the sexes in the promenades along a Spanish alameda.

There are of course mixed family groups, in which the centre of attraction is made by the "wee ones," about whose cunning ways whole books have been written. I believe I have already mentioned several things as the oddest and most characteristic of all Japanese sights; but I must take all those back and give the first place to these tots. Perfect Lilliputian ladies and gentlemen, they smile as sweetly and bow as courteously as their elders. I had been in the country three weeks before I heard an infant cry. Many of the children are extremely pretty, and most of them are useful as well as ornamental. Of her first child the mother has to take care herself, which she does by tucking it away in the back of her dress, thus leaving her hands free for work. The second child is cradled on the back of its elder sister, where it lives, taking in all the sights with its black bead-eyes till it gets sleepy, when it lets the head drop and dangle as it pleases, while the elder sister continues her walk or play regardless of her sleeping burden. This sight, which is repeated at every street corner, is even more Japanesy than the kuruma, kimono, or paper lantern.

You cannot spend an hour in the streets of Tōkyō without coming to the conclusion that the Japanese are indeed "the very pineapples of politeness." When we meet a friend we say "How d'you do?" or "Hello," and perhaps we shake hands. To the Japanese of the old school such conduct appears both foolish and rude. Hand-shaking is unknown to them, and so is kissing among friends or even by lovers. In the house, a Japanese greeting consists in getting down on the knees, spreading the hands on the mats and quickly and repeatedly lowering the head till it touches the

CARRYING CHILDREN

floor. In the street there are no clean mats to kneel on, wherefore a different method is adopted. Two acquaintances, on meeting, stop, bend over, rub their knees with their hands, at the same time sucking in the breath audibly; this is done several times, and the one who keeps it up longest feels proudest of himself. It takes time, but time is not money in the East. I noticed that my kuruma man, though he might be all out of breath, never neglected to nod to a passing acquaintance. If he happened to be resting, he would take his big white umbrella-hat in his hand and make several bows. Imagine *our* "cabbies" bowing to each other three times!

Among the hundreds of thousands you may pass in the streets of this capital, you will rarely see any with the nervous, busy, preoccupied mien which is stereotyped on our street crowds. Though most of them are poor, their faces wear a mien of placid contentment with their fate. Evidently these Orientals get more solid enjoyment out of life than the jostling, eager, worried, and hurried populace of our Western cities.

In my daily rides through all parts of Tōkyō, I looked in vain for those shocking contrasts between extreme wealth and extreme poverty that are such a disgrace and reproach to our "Christian" cities. A Tōkyō paper published in June, 1890, the results of an official investigation into the extent of destitution in that city. Altogether 5423 cases were found. Of these, 163 stood face to face with starvation, 584 were living on roots and potato rinds, while 4600 were too poor to buy rice, but lived on millet and buckwheat meal. This is not a cheerful record, but it would be absurd to compare it for a moment with the horrible wretchedness and starvation in the slums of our large cities. Moreover, however ill-provided Japanese paupers may be in the matter of food, they are, at all events, not huddled together like hogs in deadly, unventilated tenement pens. The poorest family usually has its own house, nor is it customary to take in boarders. This implies a great many houses in a city of nearly a million and a half souls, and explains why Tōkyō gives the impression of being an immense and rather mean-looking village — an impression heightened by the fact that the rich do not usually display their wealth by adorning the street side of their houses, but reserve the interior and the back garden for whatever artistic or floral display they may desire.

The cheap appearance of most Japanese houses is simply a consequence of the frequent fires. There was one in 1879, which destroyed 11,000 houses, making 50,000 people homeless. In his book on earthquakes, Professor Milne says: " In one winter I was a spectator of three fires, each of which was said to have destroyed upwards of 10,000 houses," — together about a tenth of all the houses in the city. These fires follow regular tracks, like cyclones; and were it not for the fact that Greater Tōkyō is practically a conglomeration of villages, retaining all the intervening hills and groves and fields, they would be still more disastrous. A large proportion of the city's population depends for its living on building up new houses and streets, and these strenuously oppose all efforts to improve the fire-extinguishing service. In case of fire, the victims generally succeed in saving their few garments, mats, and kakemonos. Their more valuable things are kept in fireproof kura, one, two, or three stories high, made of mud or clay, and closed airtight like safes. Hence a fire is not so very great a calamity as elsewhere, and is apt to be made the occasion of a picnic. The houses are soon rebuilt; and they say it often happens that one man's house is burned down twice in one day, because after rebuilding the shifting wind brings back the flames in his direction. This sounds like a "California story"; but it may be true, since some of the Japanese keep in stock the material for complete houses, nicely fitted and finished, so that they need only to be put together and raised like tents.

The most ornamental features of Japanese streets are fortunately easily replaced after a fire. I allude to the shop signs,—not the comic "Eurasian" ones, already referred to, but the large Japanese and Chinese ideographs, drawn—up and down, of course—on door posts, screens, paper lanterns, and on the backs of coolies. These are real works of art; but as every Japanese is an artist in chirography, the supply of such decorations is limited only by the demand. They are usually in black, but sometimes gold or another color is used. Perhaps, after all, it is these signs that are the most Japanese thing in Tōkyō.

FROM MORNING TILL MIDNIGHT

TŌKYŌ AT ITS TOILET — DOGS AND CHICKENS — FISH MARKET — DANGEROUS WELLS — NAP TIME — A FOOLISH LAW — COOLIES VERSUS HORSES — STREET SPRINKLING — PLANED ICE — STEWED TEA — A CARRIAGE DRIVE — WHERE MISSIONARIES LIVE — SCENES ABOUT A BUDDHIST TEMPLE — RELIGION AND FUN — ARCHERY GIRLS — A NIGHT CROWD — FLOWER SHOW — RIVER FESTIVAL — DAY AND NIGHT FIREWORKS — THE CITY BAND

In Lotos-Time the habit of early rising has not much to commend itself in sultry Tōkyō, where refreshing sleep is attainable only in the cool hours of the morning dawn. Yet it would be a great mistake not to set out at least once at six o'clock, in order to see the city waking up and at its toilet. As Taro trots down the deserted streets you have a good chance to notice how uniformly clean they are kept, how free from disagreeable odors. The law compels every man to sweep regularly before his house, and if he fails to do so, the police swoops down on him. As there are no sidewalks, everybody walks in the streets and wants them clean, while the absence of horses makes it comparatively easy to keep them so.

Riding along leisurely in your kuruma, you will be startled every moment by the rattling noise of the amado, or rain doors, being pushed aside to let air and light into the windowless houses. We have something similar over some of our shop windows, but as we push ours up and down, the Japanese of course draw theirs to the right or left, the noise alone being the same in both cases. In other houses the amado have already been pushed aside for some little time, and you behold a merchant arranging his goods or a family group drinking thimble cups of tea and demolishing bowls of hot, snowy rice with the aid of wooden chopsticks; or a man stretched on his back, knocking the ashes out of his early pipe, making mien to get up from his hard couch; or a young girl kneeling before her metal mirror arranging her toilet, stripped to the waist and seeing no more impropriety in the fact than the passers by do; besides other domestic scenes which in our houses are enacted only behind curtains.

In the streets, at this hour, you will see few human beings, except, perhaps, some women sweeping the street before their houses, or a policeman, or an occasional coolie, with or without a kuruma. Yet the streets are not deserted, for this is chicken hour; every street is being scavenged by hens, whose eggs are doubtless a welcome addition to the scant larder. We have been followed by one of our harmless hotel dogs, and at one place he scares the hens and their lordly rooster into a noisy panic, which brings out the owners, with anxious faces, to see who is disturbing their pets. All this in the centre of Tōkyō.

A glance at the pocket dictionary, and a word to Taro makes him turn about. Ere long we find ourselves at the fish market. Fish and rice being to the Japanese what beef and potatoes are to the English, I felt sure that the Tōkyō fish market would present a large variety of odd piscatorial sights. Experts say that no part of the ocean has so rich an assortment and such large numbers of fish as the Japanese waters, which harbor about four hundred species. I did not count the species exhibited, but I saw many odd fish and other sea-animals; some of them small, ugly, slimy beasts, which it takes as much courage to taste as the man must have had who ate the first oyster (he was probably a shipwrecked sailor); yet I afterwards in my travels tried many of them, and while some were as tough as snails, others were a welcome addition to my gastronomic experiences. Some of the fish were kept alive, as they all ought to be in every fish market, and have to be in Berlin; others were dried or smoked. Eels seemed to be in special demand. There was a tough-looking devil-fish, of which you could buy slices, either raw or boiled. A large shark was also among the delicacies offered, the carcass being divided into sections commanding different prices, like the sirloin, tenderloin, and round steak of an ox. But the strangest thing about this market was the utter absence of women. All the buyers and sellers were men. Possibly this absence of fish-women may account for the fact that the Japanese language has no terms of abuse and no oaths.

Among the objects likely to attract one's attention in the morning, when the streets are deserted, are the wells. Although Tōkyō has a system of waterworks, it is still full of primitive wells, with plain wooden enclosures, around which the women assemble to gossip, fetch water, or wash their rice. It seems strange that in a city where sanitation has made so much progress, these wells have not all been closed up. The dust from the street can settle down into them all day long.

and this, during cholera or typhoid time, when microbes float in the air, dried but still alive, may mean death to hundreds of families. Artesian wells would be safe, but there are only a few of these in the city. Fortunately the Japanese are not addicted to cold water; they make tea of it before they drink it, and the mortality of the city is not remarkably high, notwithstanding these wells, the contents of which have been shown by chemical analysis to be very impure.

In the early afternoon Tōkyō is as drowsy and deserted as Andalusian Seville. At that hour Taro is not anxious to take you out; he knows that you would suffer even more from the sun while riding in the kuruma than he would in pulling it. He knows, too, that there is comparatively little for you to see, for the blue awnings are down, hiding the goods in the shops and the domestic scenes in the houses, while the streets themselves present no human panorama for your study. The glare of the sun, as thrown back from the unpainted sides of the houses, is less painful than in whitewashed Cadiz or Tangier, yet it tires the eyes and begets a desire to sleep; for, strange to say, the same heat which keeps us awake at night compels slumber in the daytime. Even the kuruma runners take their nap, stretched out on the shady side of the hotel; they are probably dreaming of the good old times when a tattoed skin was considered sufficient clothing, whereas now they must wear their blue jackets and trousers in deference to law and the prejudices of foreigners. It does seem a cruel and foolish law, as any one must admit who has seen how the perspiration runs in streams from these coolies, and how, every now and then, they have to take the cloth tied around the head (with a knot in front) and wring it dry, like a washerwoman standing over her tub.

At four o'clock the sun is still merciless, but we may as well start, as the distances are great. Pity for Taro is apt to be mitigated both by his own cheerfulness and by the sight of other coolies whose task is twice as hard. Man-power is applied to freight as well as to persons, and a frequent sight is a cart heavily laden with stones, slowly pulled and pushed along by two or three coolies, whose veins on the forehead are swelled to the point of bursting, and who keep on shouting "ho! huida!" when one would think they ought to have sense enough to save their breath for the work. Perhaps the rhythmic noise assists them, like sailors. These men are often bareheaded in the broiling sun, and in this respect are less merciful to themselves than to their beasts; for those who are lucky enough to possess an ox to do their work, rarely neglect to protect him from the sun by means of a mat suspended over him on a long pole. This may be either Buddhistic kindness to animals or an enlightened utilitarianism. But why do we see so few oxen and dray horses in Japanese cities? Probably because the coolies are too poor to buy and feed them. It must be remembered that their wages are extremely low, and that fodder for animals must be comparatively high in a country where all level ground is used for rice or other agricultural crops, leaving no margin for pasturage.

Occasionally a horse is seen dragging along a primitive water-cart for sprinkling the streets — an occupation in which I sometimes thought half the population took more or less part, in one way or another. Besides the horse-carts there were smaller carts drawn by coolies. Then there were men armed with buckets attached to long poles, with which they dipped the water from the green roadside ditches and dashed it into the streets. Elsewhere several men would carry a large tub of water into the middle of the street, and then, with small buckets, scatter it about in a circle. The women also assisted in various amateur ways in laying the dust, to prevent it from flying into their houses, and to keep the air cool. Millions of gallons of water must be used up in street sprinkling on a midsummer's afternoon, and I fancy that so much of it as comes from the green ditches is a prolific source of disease; for it is thus that the dried microbes of malaria, typhoid, cholera, dysentery, etc., get into the dust, and with it into open wells and open mouths.

Compared with the watering cart and other freight-coolies, Taro is an aristocrat. To them his income of seventy-five cents to one dollar a day must seem princely; he can have all the rice and fish and saké he wants; he can even indulge in the buying of an occasional glass of kori. Kori is one of the latest midsummer fads in Japan. It is planed ice, served in heaped, big tumblers by smiling girls, in special shops. When artificial ice was first introduced, not many years ago, these shops sprang up like mushrooms on all sides. Everybody ate or drank kori greedily, and the craze threatened to develop into an epidemic of dyspepsia, when the warning voice of Dr. Baeltz of the Tōkyō University was raised. He intimidated some, but the kori shops still flourish; and it was amusing to see men, women, and children crowding around them, eagerly waiting for their glasses to be planed full, and greedily devouring the noxious stuff, either plain, or, if they could afford an extra cent, with a little fruit syrup added for flavoring.

Kuruma runners are crazy for this icy beverage, and if you treat them to a glass they are ready to take you round the world on a continuous trot, and with a perpetual smile. Dripping with perspiration, and all out of breath, they gulp it down as fast as a Neapolitan beggar does a plateful of free scalding-hot macaroni, in order to show a tourist what *can* be done in that line. The result to teeth and digestion must be the same in both cases.

The Japanese also injure their health with hot drinks. They undeniably drink tea oftener than is good for their nerves, and one kind of tea that they favor must be decidedly injurious. My Japanese friend, Mr. Shugio, took Mr. Blum and me one afternoon to one of the most famous tea houses, where we had a taste of that aristocratic variety which is made of the most delicate leaves of the most expensive plants. The neat but airy little building was surrounded by shrubs in a garden representing a miniature landscape, with a reed-bordered "lake" in the centre, and a number of large stones for visitors to step on. After walking in our stocking feet through the tea house, we sat on the verandah facing the garden, where we were entertained by the hostess. In the meantime, a young girl was preparing in the kitchen a purée of tea leaves of which Laurence Oliphant thus describes the process of manufacture: The leaves "are first stewed, then dried and ground in a handmill into a powder; this is mixed with hot water and whipped with a split bamboo until it creams. It is served up hot and looks like physic. Altogether, I thought it more palatable than senna. This delicacy is called koitscha or thick tea." He adds that it is "a beverage peculiar to the upper classes of Japan," and I am sure the lower classes ought not to envy them this prerogative. I would as soon eat a salad made of green hops as drink another cup of that tea, or, rather, eat it, for you swallow it, powder and all. Now, I believe that while the phlegmatic Turk may not be hurt by drinking the dregs of his coffee, the delicate and weakly upper classes of Japan are much injured by eating nerve-shattering boiled tea leaves. However, they take it only on special occasions, the daily, or rather hourly, beverage being a weak infusion of ordinary tea leaves. This, if properly made with water that has not reached the boiling point, is comparatively harmless. If made with boiling water, it becomes a nasty decoction of tannic acid, strong enough to tan leather. I tasted such stuff occasionally at wayside inns and wondered no longer that statistics attribute one quarter of all deaths in Japan to nervous diseases. Another thing wherein Japanese differs from Chinese tea is that whereas in the latter, made with boiling water, only the first infusion is good, in Japanese tea the second infusion is less bitter than the first, and is accordingly preferred. I once remonstrated with a Japanese journalist, who was travelling with me, for his supposed economy in pouring water a second time on the same tea in the pot; but he laughingly explained that that was better than the first, being less astringent.

So far all our excursions had been made by kuruma, the most convenient and cheapest of local conveyances. But there is one objection to the man-power cab: it is unsocial. When several friends go out together it is difficult to talk on the way, as there is seldom room for two kurumayas to trot side by side. Accordingly, for a change, and to see what it was like, I accepted an invitation one afternoon for a carriage ride down the river and a call at Tsukiji, the foreign concession of Tōkyō, which it seemed proper to visit in a foreign conveyance. We drove some way along the river, but found it the dullest part of the city — rows of commonplace houses, with nothing to break the monotony except an occasional tea house perched high for the sake of the view and the breeze. We had, besides the driver, a runner, who always got off and ran ahead when we came to a corner, in order to clear a track for us in the crowd. That a carriage is still a rare sight here was shown by the curiosity with which every man, woman, and child stopped and stared at us. The horses, too, were evidently not used to the rapid pace associated with a carriage drive, for they easily got out of breath and sweated profusely.

Tsukiji is hardly worth seeing, except as a historic curiosity. As the name implies, this corner of Tōkyō is "made ground," — an embankment made on the tidal soil near the mouth of the Sumida River. It has the reputation of being a not particularly healthy part of the city, though it has been greatly improved of late. It certainly must have been unhealthy at the time when it was selected for the foreign colony's place of exile. Like the site of Yokohama, it was originally a swamp, a coincidence which might suggest the suspicion that perhaps the Japanese officials chose these spots in the hope that malaria would help them to get rid of the then unwelcome foreigners. To this day no foreigner can buy property or rent a private residence in any part of the city excepting Tsukiji, unless he happens to be a government employee, in which case he can at any rate rent a house wherever he pleases. The streets in Tsukiji are wide and clean, and the foreign-style but low houses are surrounded by gardens and shady trees. Here live principally merchants and missionaries, who are not usually on the most amicable terms. A missionary will perhaps tell you of merchants who keep several mistresses and change them every month, while a merchant will retaliate by telling you of a missionary who lives at a certain hotel paying twenty-five dollars a day for himself and family—"money which was sent here for the conversion of the Japanese to Christianity."

Christian Tsukiji is simply a slice of Europe or America on Japanese soil, as "Chinatown" is a section of Pekin dropped in the centre of San Francisco. To the sightseer from abroad it therefore offers no special attractions, whereas the Buddhist Asakusa in Ueno Park demands at least one afternoon. It is like a free theatrical performance, partly in temples, partly in the grounds around them, representing Japanese life in some of its most picturesque aspects. I have no desire to describe once more what has been done so vividly and comprehensively by Mr. Griffis; but what an extraordinary spectacle it is! what a deference to the world, the flesh, and the devil in the very temple of religion! A New Yorker might get a faint idea of it by imagining a Chinese pagoda and temple in Central Park; inside the ceremonial of a Catholic Cathedral, and midsummer Coney Island in full blast on the outside. Within the temple there are officiating priests, with their idols, candles, and incense; demons to be propitiated; votive tablets and colossal paper lanterns; devout worshippers calling the gods' attention to their prayers by striking a bell, and clapping their hands to let them know when they are through; others writing their prayers on slips of paper which they chew and spit at the idol, hoping that it may stick, which indicates that the prayer has been heard; others again touching some idol and then themselves at a corresponding spot, in the belief that a local disease will thus be cured (whereas in truth nothing could be better calculated to spread disease); and so on through the whole gamut of superstition. The Buddhists are even more liberal than the Catholics of southern Europe in allowing sightseers to walk about admiring the treasures of art even while the service is going on. Outside of the temples there are flocks of sacred pigeons and other birds; old women selling peas and beans to feed them with; rows of booths where you can buy charms, toys, hairpins, photographs, and things to eat; monkey shows, theatrical stalls, singing and dancing exhibitions, shooting galleries — all these having been from time immemorial the surroundings of great Buddhist temples, although in Tōkyō the "Coney Island" features appear to have been somewhat repressed in recent years. I must add that there is perhaps nothing in the Buddhist temples of Japan which seems more odd and incongruous to us than the electric light which has found its way into some of them.

Following the example of the Japanese, we went straight from the temple to an archery gallery, in a region where there was a whole street of them. As we were taking off our shoes preparatory to crawling in and squatting on the clean mats, an old woman in rags planted herself before the booth and sang a song as ugly as her face, accompanying herself with the Japa-

nese "banjo," or samisen. We gave her a few pennies
(enough to support her for several days), not for her
music, but in view of the fact that thirty years before
she may have been as pretty as the three young maidens
of fourteen or fifteen who brought us tea and smoking
materials. After we had refreshed ourselves they
handed us light bamboo bows and tiny arrows, wherewith we so successfully and continuously missed the
mark, that ere long we adopted the lazy Oriental way
of letting the girls do the shooting for us. Why not,
since we had to pay for it anyway? It was fascinating
to see how gracefully they shot the arrows, and how
often they hit the mark; nor was it in the least uncomfortable to recline and have one girl fan you while the
other shot the arrows. They were so sweet and winsome, and smiled so bewitchingly, that it seemed cruel
not to be able to talk to them except with the aid of
Taro's very limited vocabulary. While we were there,
only one Japanese guest came in. He looked solemn
and stolid, smoked his thimble pipe and sipped his
yellow tea in silence, while the girls, after supplying
his simple wants, paid no further attention to him —
possibly because he would pay only a few cents, while
we paid a dollar, of which Taro, I fancy, pocketed one-
half; but since he was interpreter as well as guide, he
deserved an extra fee. When we left, the maidens
prostrated themselves on the mats, and there was no
end to their sayonara (good by) and irasshai (come
again). It was here that Taro informed me so promptly
that I might cut the girl's throat.

Evening excursions are in midsummer Tōkyō more
interesting than afternoon rides and calls. In the cool
night air some of the avenues are crowded till mid-

night. On account of these crowds, it is advisable for two sightseers to go out together, with two kurumas and runners. Taro and his companion had an ingenious method on such occasions. There are streets where the crowds are so dense that kurumas are not allowed to enter, a policeman being on hand to enforce the rule. As we wanted to mingle with this populace, we got off, one of the men took the empty kurumas through another street to a place where Taro arranged to meet him, whereupon he played the rôle of guide and steered us to the various points of interest. In one street where there were small theatres similar to those we had seen in Yokohama, we had positively to squeeze our way through the crowd; and this was an ordinary night, not a holiday. The shows were a little bigger and more numerous than at Yokohama, but the sights were similar, and need not be described again. Everything was on a more metropolitan scale than at Yokohama, and the variety of sights in shops, tea houses, and open-air booths proportionately greater. The shops were lighted with gay paper lanterns, while the booths that were erected in two rows in some of the wider streets, were illuminated with torches. An endless variety of fancy toys for the children, and hairpins for the women, seemed to constitute the principal stock in trade of these stalls.

One of the incidents I remember is a woman buying a glass globe no larger than an orange, with a small goldfish in it. She looked happy over her purchase, but it did not seem quite in accordance with Buddhist principles to give a poor fish so little elbow-room — or tail-room, one ought perhaps to say. I bought a few toys for some children who were looking at them longingly, and was abundantly rewarded by their grateful smiles and graceful bows. I wish American children could bow so prettily. One of the clerks at the hotel had two little girls, apparently twins, to whom I never failed to bow whenever I saw them, and they always returned the bow with the most fascinating girlish grace and Oriental gravity.

During a whole evening thus spent in the most populous streets, we did not see a single foreigner, and very few Japanese in foreign costume, and those invariably men. Almost all of the men and women walked bareheaded, not one in a hundred having a hat. The men rarely took any notice of us, while many of the women turned to stare in a surprised and almost startled way. Women being more conservative than men, many of them doubtless still look on foreigners as being the fiends and ogres they were supposed to be during Japan's long seclusion from the world. It is said that in the country even now some Japanese children scream and run away in terror at first sight of a foreigner. This never happened to me, doubtless because I am somewhat less ferocious and diabolical in appearance than most of my compatriots.

One narrow street was given up almost entirely, for a long distance, to a flower show, being lined on both sides with pots containing flowering plants or feathery ferns, or small pines resembling ferns in softness of texture and delicacy of structure, or trees dwarfed and cut into various fancy shapes, illumination being supplied by lamps stuck on bamboo sticks. The owners kept the plants fresh by frequently taking a mouthful of water, as a Chinaman does in his laundry, and sprinkling them with a fine spray. (I have heard of a Chinese cook being detected in making biscuits that way.) Down this street men and women walked slowly, stooping every now and then to examine a choice flower or arrangement of twigs and leaves. On the exhibition grounds, the day before, I had watched a floral expert arranging some of the potted plants, which he did with the same care and attention to detail that an artist would use in putting a flowering plant on his canvas. He would give this leaf or that flower a different inclination to one side, or up or down; then he would step back a yard or two and take a critical look at it; one more twist of a twig or leaf, and the plant looked as if it had grown up in nature's garden, untouched by man.

If the Japanese are not remarkably devout in their attitude towards the gods of their pantheon, they make up for it by their worship of flowers and other phenomena of nature, especially the mountains and the rivers. In a preceding paragraph I spoke rather disrespectfully of the Sumida River, but I discovered that during Lotos-Time there is an annual festival in honor of this river and its deity, when it presents a scene more fairy-like and suggestive of another planet than even the streets of Tōkyō ever do. I was lucky enough to be in the city at the proper time and gladly accepted an invitation from Mr. Blum to this river picnic, which proved to be one of the most picturesque and unique of my experiences in Japan. Hiring a barge, — which had to be secured days in advance, so great is the demand for boats on this popular occasion, — we secured two coolies, one to steer, the other to push us with a long pole, and thus moved down a canal, past dingy warehouses and rather Venetian-looking staircases leading up to the street through high walls from the water.

Dusky figures were lounging or sleeping at various places, enjoying a greater degree of agreeable nudity than would be allowed in an Italian city. We passed under a number of bridges, arched and massive, and the further we got, the more numerous became the boats of all sizes, some two-storied, and all of them filled with happy, expectant Japanese, so that when we finally reached the river itself it required careful steering to make our way through them.

It was still broad daylight when we came to our anchorage, and hardly had we reached our destination when surprise number one was let loose in the shape of fireworks. We perverse Occidentals associate fireworks with night: consequently the Japanese have them in the daytime, as a matter of course. Up goes a rocket with a whish-h-h; and as it explodes in the air a large bird emerges from the smoke and slowly circling, sinks to the ground. Other rockets carried up bits of paper which on exploding in the air took the form of a flock of pigeons, or of a horse, or of two boxers, or of a dragon unfolding its long tail. The birds were in five colors, and among them were of course the irrepressible crows, which infest the whole country. As the twilight deepened, the exhibition changed to regular fireworks, as we understand the word. Some of these were very fine, especially a golden weeping willow, and a medley of various colored ribbons floating away slowly; but as a whole the nocturnal fireworks were not equal to our best, possibly because such displays are very expensive. Who paid for those we saw I could not find out, as we paid no admission fee, and apparently no one else did. Asiatic patience had abundant opportunity to manifest itself, for the intervals between rockets were from five to ten minutes. Imagine how impatient an American or an English audience would get under such circumstances, not to speak of Spanish spectators, who like to have their fireworks go off all at once, like their own impetuous passions. The Japanese prefer to dally with their pastimes, and they are wise. We are too apt to gulp down our pleasures as a dog does his dinner.

For the Japanese the show was principally in the air, but to us the centre of attraction was the river, with its thousands of boats, the bridges and the river banks jammed with spectators, who also crowded the overhanging tea houses, which were gaily decorated with colored paper lanterns. As it grew darker, the upper rows of these lights seemed to be suspended in the air without support, as they emitted just enough light to make the surrounding darkness visible. Each of the boats, too, had from one to a dozen or more colored lanterns, which dotted the darkness as far as eye could see. Surely the canals of Venice, in the palmiest days of Oriental trade, never witnessed a more striking scene; and surely the suggestion for those "Venetian nights" must have come from the Far East.

In calling this festival a river picnic, I meant exactly what I said. All about us the Japanese (we saw no foreigners) were picnicking. In these diverse supper scenes, it was curious to see the mixture of foreign with native elements, less in the food, however, than in the implements. Chopsticks were universal, no knives, forks, or spoons being in use on any of the boats we passed. The food was in lacquer boxes, but in place of the pretty lacquer saké (or wine) cups and saké jars, coarse foreign glass bottles and tumblers were in use

PLEASURE BOAT

everywhere. Our own boatmen had a large bottle which they rinsed in the dirty river water (we had just passed a dead dog), and then had it filled with some mysterious liquid by a man who came forward in a sort of buffet boat with all sorts of supplies, solid and liquid. Their *pièce de résistance* was green beans boiled on the stalk and eaten from the pods, as we eat green corn.

One of the larger boats was provided with two ropes meeting at the top, like an inverted V, and adorned with the flags of all nations in picturesque confusion of colors. The Japanese flag was on top, and after it came the American, but upside down, as a matter of course. It must be extremely annoying to the Japanese to see us float our flag wrong side up, with our usual Occidental topsy-turviness. This boat belonged to the city band, which played Japanese and European music alternately. They played all of our cheap national tunes, the vulgarity of which probably escapes their notice at present. During an intermission the leader of the band came over to us in a row boat, presenting his card, on which we read in English that these musicians can be hired three hours for $15, and a whole day for $30. The Japanese crowd, while it applauded the best effects of the fireworkers, paid little attention to the band, but some of them had on their own boats music more to their taste; namely, pretty geishas singing to the accompaniment of their samisens. On one boat there was a pretty pantomimic dance by geishas, and in another, a regular theatrical performance, to judge by the gaudy costumes and the peculiar Chinese intonation of those who took part in it. On some of the boats, a simple drum or horn supplied the needful noise. The Japanese love thus to transform their boats into temporary tea houses, with all that the name implies. Netto relates that the river (here about a thousand feet wide) is sometimes so densely crowded with boats that it forms a favorite sport of some young men to cross it dry shod by stepping from boat to boat. "They seem in no great hurry, and if they should happen to come upon a particularly merry party, with plenty of wine, pretty girls, and clever dancers, they are not at all averse to accepting the polite invitation to remain."

We happened to be moored next to the boat of a Japanese nobleman, who introduced himself, and gave us his card, — Japanese on one side, and Le Baron X. on the other. He spoke French; and, after some general remarks, expressed his opinion that the Japanese got all their civilization from us, against which I protested vigorously, insisting that in their love of art and nature, their avoidance of any display of wealth, and their courtesy and refinement of manners, they were infinitely superior to us as a nation; adding that there was danger that our civilization, imposed on them so abruptly, might make them less contented and happy. I called his attention to the utter absence of ruffians and rude actions in this picnic crowd, as compared with scenes to be witnessed near New York, London, and Paris; emphasizing especially the excellent behavior of the young people, and the absence of scenes of vulgar flirtation such as would make a nocturnal water picnic in those cities an occasion to be avoided by refined people. The Baron told me he had a son in our naval school at Annapolis. Another of his sons was with him, and spoke English; while his daughter, a winsome but delicate looking girl of about seventeen, spoke French quite well, and seemed to be not at all averse to conversation with a foreigner. She informed me, however, that it was more usual for young ladies of her class to learn English than French. She herself would have been glad, she said, to finish her education at one of our female colleges, but her father did not wish more than one of his children to be across the ocean at the same time. One of her friends was then at Bryn Mawr.

WINE, WOMEN, AND SONG

BEAUTY OF JAPANESE WOMEN — BRUNETTES ONLY — WAITING MAIDS AND SINGING GIRLS — LIKE THE ANCIENT GREEKS — AN ESTHETIC BANQUET — MUSIC AND BANTER — FIRE BOXES — RICE WINE — SOUP AND FISH — CHOPSTICKS — DANCING AND DRUMS — GILDED VICE — A SLAVE MARKET — TRAP FOR CRIMINALS

Two hundred years ago Kaempfer, who first described for Europeans the manners and customs of Japan, wrote that the women of Saga, on the Inland Sea of Japan, were "handsomer than those of any other Asiatic country." In 1876 Mr. W. E. Griffis was led to declare that, "the fairest sights in Japan are Japan's fair daughters." In 1892 Mr. Henry Norman, in describing the "Real Japan," said that "if Japanese women generally adopt foreign dress, the stream of foreign visitors will turn aside from Japan"; thereby implying that these women, with their picturesque costumes and ways, are the principal attraction to tourists. I quite agree with him in this, as well as in his assertion that "prettiness is the rule among Japanese women." Every one interested in this topic knows of the rhapsodies of Sir Edwin Arnold over the Japanese *musumé*. It is true that tastes differ; some tourists have blatantly declared that there is absolutely no female beauty in Japan. I can understand these critics, but cannot sympathize with them. If a man's taste leads him to look upon a tall, buxom, queenly, Scandinavian, English, or German blonde as his ideal of beauty, he will be disappointed in Japan, for such women do not exist there. But if his ideal of beauty is the graceful, elegant, petite brunette of Andalusia, his eyes will be constantly delighted in Japan by visions of loveliness and grace. I frankly confess that what made me plan my visit to Japan was the knowledge that all the women are built after this type. And I confess, too, that after a few weeks among these graceful, miniature beauties, the few large foreign women I saw seemed angular, ungainly, plain, and masculine. Nowhere on four continents have I seen eyes, black and brown, more lovely in color and shape than in Tōkyō and Kyōto; nowhere hands and wrists more delicately moulded; nowhere arms and busts more beautifully rounded; nowhere lips more refined and inviting, though they are ignorant of the art of kissing; nowhere more perfect grace of attitude and gesture, above the waist. Their gait alone is clumsy, because of their clogs and their fashion of turning in the toes. I object also to the prevalent use of paint and powder on cheeks and lips, and to the national habit of combing back the hair from the forehead. Were these objectionable habits amended, the obvious proportion of beauty would be still greater.

Unless he is a teacher or a missionary, a foreigner in Japan finds it difficult to become acquainted with women of the better classes, who are kept more or less in the background by their lords and masters. It is not customary even for Japanese men to make calls on the women of other families, and when a Japanese friend invites you to dine with him, he takes you, not to his house, but to a restaurant, where his wife and daughter do not accompany him, as he does not wish them to associate with the possibly frail beauties who help to enliven tea-house dinners. For, while the Japanese have never been cannibals, it must be confessed that the principal ingredients in their tea-house meals are tender young girls — pretty waiting maids to serve the dishes, and educated geishas to sing, play, dance, and enliven the conversation with their spicy wit and merry laughter.

Under these circumstances, foreign visitors — those who reside in the country a year or two, no less than tourists — are apt to get their ideas and impressions of Japanese women principally at the tea houses. Nor, from some points of view, is this a disadvantage: for the waiting maids are chosen for their beauty, while the geishas, like the hetairai of ancient Greece, are not only trained in all the arts of personal beauty and artistic fascination, but are so carefully educated that in wit and intelligence they usually surpass the domestic women in the quiet family circle. The geishas are the brightest and most accomplished of all Japanese women, and in making their acquaintance one meets, therefore, favorable specimens of the country's womanhood, except in the matter of frailty of character. Yet this trait must not be exaggerated, as it is by superficial observers, who confound the geisha with the joro. As a class, geishas are perhaps no more frail than European or American actresses, and the most respectable men, native and foreign, never hesitate to have their meals spiced by their beauty and art.

In such matters women are much severer judges than

men; yet Miss Alice Bacon says, in her thoroughly reliable book on *Japanese Girls and Women*, that —

"The geisha is not necessarily bad, but there is in her life much temptation to evil, and little stimulus to do right; so that, where one lives blameless, many go wrong, and drop below the margin of respectability altogether. Yet so fascinating, bright, and lively are these geishas, that many of them have been taken by men of good position as wives, and are now the heads of the most respectable homes. . . . The problem of the geisha and her fascination is a deep one in Japan."

The geishas, after having received a long and careful training in the art of making themselves agreeable to men, usually live at home with their families. They are engaged, as musicians and other social entertainers are engaged by us, usually two or more together, at so much an hour or evening; and the place selected is almost always a tea house, where tea, food, and rice wine serve as accompaniment to the feast of smiles, wit, and music. The combination cannot but be considered a happy one.

I said in a previous chapter that one could live a year in Japan without ever tasting any of the dishes peculiar to the country; and here I may add that this is possible even in travelling in the interior, where "foreign" hotels do not exist; for in every town of a few thousand inhabitants, you can now buy Chicago canned meats and California canned fruits, besides bottled beer or ale, condensed milk, jellies, and crackers. But a sensible person would no more think of limiting his gastronomic experiences to these canned goods, and such fresh meats and eggs as he can get, than he would of confining his tours of observation to Tsukiji and the foreign settlement in Yokohama. An educated palate delights in new varieties of local flavor just as much as an educated pair of eyes delights in fresh local colors.

A real Japanese banquet is, therefore, from the gastronomic as well as the geisha point of view, an indispensable item in the Tōkyō program, and I may as well add that although the Japanese do not usually take their own families to such dinners, there is no reason whatever why foreign women touring in the country should not attend them. They need not fear the slightest breach of propriety, and they may be amused at the eager curiosity with which the geishas will examine their earrings, finger rings, and bracelets, and the childish delight they will show if allowed to try them on. To see these girls at their best, it is needless to say that one or two Japanese who speak both their and our language should be among the guests.

My first experience in the realms of esthetic Japanese gastronomy was a lunch or dinner given to Mr. Blum, myself, Mr. Shugio, and another Japanese gentleman, by some unknown benefactor whose identity I suspect but have not been able to discover. We rode in kurumas to a restaurant in Shimbashi, and were received at the door by half-a-dozen pretty and smiling maidens. Leaving our shoes at the entrance, we were escorted, by two of the girls, upstairs, where they had reserved for us a large room, two sides of which faced a garden full of flowers, ornamental stones, and trees. Here, at the outset, we had the keynote of Japanese gastronomy, which is not merely an indulgence of the palate, but quite as much, or even more, a matter of esthetic enjoyment. For here we were surrounded by trees and flowers on the outside, while within the house there were trees and flowers and birds painted on the

GLIMPSE OF AN INTERIOR

screens that formed the walls of our room. Still more of an esthetic treat were the girls in attendance, especially the youngest one, O Haru, or "Springtime," who was quite a beauty, with regular features, refined lips, and large black eyes with the merest suspicion of obliqueness; just enough to give them a piquant touch of Orientalism. Her smile was as sweet and enchanting as that of a Houri in the Mohammedan paradise, and it would have been difficult to avoid falling in love with her at first sight had she always remained on her knees, for from the waist up she was the perfection of grace; but the effect was marred whenever she got up and walked; for her gait, like that of all Japanese women, was ungraceful, the knees being too far apart, and the toes turned in, while her loose slippers flapped along on the floor without ever quite leaving it, — all these things being prescribed by topsy-turvy Japanese etiquette, with one of those strange inconsistencies in taste of which I shall have occasion to point out not a few in later pages.

There were, of course, no chairs or tables in our tea house, and if we had asked for a tablecloth we would have been looked on as being even greater greenhorns than we actually were. As Sir Edwin Arnold has pertinently remarked of the Japanese, "they do not make streets of their homes." They do not walk with dirty boots on their floor mats, any more than we stand on our chairs and sofas. The mat is their only seat and tablecloth, and every meal is a sort of picnic. We accordingly found no visible preparations for our banquet, except a square section of the floor marked off with four soft leather cushions for us to kneel on. We were prepared for any further amount of topsy-turviness, and it began with the serving of tea first, apparently because *we* serve coffee *last*. In Japan tea is the beginning and end of all things, and it need not be said that it is the esthetic beverage *par excellence*. With the yellow tea were served tiny wafers, so thin and unsubstantial that they might be called esthetic too. These wafers were sweet (because *we* reserve sweets for the end of a meal), and of course they were round, because *our* wafers are not round.

The next course was again esthetic. It consisted of two hibachis or fire boxes, for lighting our cigarettes. The Japanese use matches as freely as we do, but not at meals, where they would be voted vulgar. The hibachi is made in many varieties, the most popular being a round vessel with live charcoals in the centre, around which are heaped ashes in the shape of a crater. This poetic arrangement enables the imaginative Japanese to fancy that they are lighting their cigarettes or pipes at the original fires of their beloved Fuji, once a volcano, now a snow peak lifting its summit above the hills and dales of the main island, as a cathedral spire rises above the streets and houses of a city, and doubtless visible from our tea house on a clear day.

Again the course following was esthetic: it consisted of the singing girls and samisen players who had been hired to supply the music and smiles. They were of a somewhat more intellectual type of beauty than the waiting maids, and also a few years older, and less given to giggling. That they were bright, and saucy too, we soon found out. The waiter girls, who had left us the moment the music girls entered, now returned with small lacquer tables, five or six inches high, and a foot in length and breadth, one of which was placed before each of us.

together with a dainty porcelain bottle containing about
half a pint of hot saké or rice wine, and for drinking it,
a tiny cup of thin porcelain, which looked as if it were
meant to hold our cigarette ashes — mind, I do not say
cigar ashes, for one must not exaggerate in talking of
things Japanese. The geishas filled these cups for us,
and after drinking their health we touched them to the
napkins, handed them to the girls, and filled them up
for them to drink to our health. To fill your own cup
would be considered bad form, but with so many geishas
and waiting girls to vie with each other in keeping the
cups filled, there was no danger of violating the laws of
etiquette in that respect. I need hardly point out the
Orientalism of drinking the wine at so early a stage of
the proceedings, and hot. Rice wine is not even as
strong as ordinary claret or Rhine wine, but being taken
hot, and before eating, it produces an effect sooner than
it would otherwise, especially on the Japanese, who are
much more easily affected than we are, and who are,
therefore, in refined circles, usually moderate in their
cups.

While the saké was being sampled, the geishas tuned
up their long-necked samisens, and gave us some of
their vocal and instrumental music, which must be an
acquired taste, to put it mildly, and which I shall not
attempt to describe in words, since it cannot even be
reproduced exactly in our notation. Piggott says that
the samisen is "irreverently called by some the banjo
of Japan, an instrument with which it has no affinities."
But it certainly looks a good deal like a banjo, and
sounds not so very unlike one. Unlike our banjo, its
body is square; but there is the same parchment face,
and an even longer neck. The samisens played by our

geishas had three silk strings, which they were forever tuning, sometimes in different intervals; and it must be admitted that they had an excellent ear for pitch. They did not pluck the strings with the fingers, but with a plectron, which produced a twangy, disagreeable, hard tone, mingled with a faint drum sound. The sides of their instruments were adorned with green velvet, and they carefully wiped the strings before playing. So they sang and strummed away, usually without any rhyme and reason discoverable to a foreign ear; but ever and anon they fell into a polka-like rhythm and a distinctly defined melody, which my memory was able to retain. Their music was all melody, no chords; and when I took one of the samisens and played a few of our simplest harmonies, they frankly confessed that they could hear nothing pleasing in them. When plucked with the fingers, I found that the Japanese samisen has a better tone than our banjo; but the girls always use the harsh plectron. Among the songs they sang I remember one of a lively nature, in which a comic effect was produced by means of very high glissandos on the instrument. The faces of the geishas brightened up, and their eyes sparkled, as they became interested in their music; but their voices were not so musical as when they spoke or laughed. They were, in truth, as nasal and twangy as the tones of their instruments. Nor was there any change in loudness.

So it must be confessed that to us the geishas were more interesting personally than musically, nor was this an unusual situation; for Professor Chamberlain says that the Japanese men, too, "send for singing girls chiefly in order to ogle and chaff them, and to help along the entertainment by a little noise. To ask the name of the composer of any tune the girls are singing is a thing that would never enter their heads." During the intermissions we plied the girls with questions, and they kindly gave us their opinion of ourselves. They wanted to know if Mr. Blum and I were twins, as they could hardly tell us apart, although we do not in the least resemble each other, except in both being blond. "One cannot distinguish those foreigners, anyway," said one of them, "they have all such prominent noses."

One of the girls asked me how old I was. "Sanjiu-go," I replied. "Thirty-five?" she echoed, with a mischievous smile, adding something which went beyond my knowledge of the vernacular, but which my Japanese friend interpreted as "I thought you were at least forty." Mr. Shugio thought this was a "good one" on me, but he, too, was fated not to escape. The girls were trying to recall the words of a certain song, but did not succeed, and finally appealed to Mr. Shugio, who, by the way, was only thirty-six.

"Why do you ask me?" he inquired.

"Oh," was the answer, "it is a very old song, and we thought you might remember it from your youthful days."

Perhaps I should add, in elucidation of this conversation, that a person's age is a favorite topic of conversation in topsy-turvy Japan. On being introduced to a lady, you ask her age, and, paradox of paradoxes, she not only is not offended, but makes no secret of it, though it may be ever so much above twenty.

Nothing seemed to please both the geishas and the

tea girls so much as to hear a few Japanese words from foreign lips. They, too, seemed to know a few English words, such as, "Thank you," "Good by," "I love you." Pretty O Haru laughed till she had to cover her face to hide her tears, when one of us looked at her with an inverted opera glass. Her laughter was one of the most delightful and contagious musical sounds I have ever heard. When one of our Japanese friends threw a back somersault to amuse the girls, they were convulsed with merriment. Obviously, table etiquette is not very rigid on such occasions.

But I must hasten on to the solid part of our repast, lest the reader should fancy that a Japanese banquet is entirely a matter of esthetics, — of trees and flowers and pictures, of yellow tea, red wafers, and miniature craters, laughing black-eyed tea girls and geishas with pretty poses, saucy wit, and Oriental music. On the contrary, it is apt to be a most substantial affair, consisting of several compound courses, each of which includes soup (we perversely have soup only once). Each course was brought in on a separate tray for every diner, and placed on his table; and when the other courses were brought in, the earlier ones were not taken away, but remained, so that we could, after sampling all the dishes, come back to those we liked best. There was only one drawback to this arrangement, — everything got cold, — a result aggravated by the constant chaffing and laughing, which made of the eating a mere side-show, though there were not a few tempting things on our trays. We had fish (cooked, raw, and smoked), several kinds of seaweed, vegetables (warm, cold, or pickled), radishes, mushrooms, boiled bamboo and lotos roots, potatoes, chicken and mutton, and several kinds of mysterious salads. I sampled every dish, and survive to tell the tale.

The soup was served in small lacquer bowls, black outside, and red inside, and had slices of hard-boiled eggs, or omelette, or seaweed, or fish floating on top. These solids we fished out *more Japanico* with our chopsticks, while the soup was drunk out of the bowls. The girls at first laughed at my attempts to use the chopsticks, and said that I ate like a baby, but they kindly and gladly instructed me how to hold and ply them. This was my first lesson, and before the end of the meal I made considerable progress: but I never quite acquired the skill of the natives, who use their sticks as deftly as storks use their bills in fishing solids out of the soup, in corraling the coy rice, and in picking a small fish clean to the skeleton, which seems the most wonderful feat of all. The apparent difficulty of eating chicken or mutton is solved by having all meat cut up into small morsels before it is sent to the table; the Japanese being of the opinion that all carving and cutting should be done by the servants in the kitchen, since we consider it more aristocratic to have the joints and chickens set on the table whole, and carved and cut by the host and the guests themselves.

I had read so much about rice as forming the substance and last course of all Japanese meals, that I was surprised not to find it included in our menu at all. It is, in fact, not served at expensive dinners unless specially ordered. I am sure it was not missed on this occasion, for of all unappetizing desserts, rice without cream and sugar (which are never served with it in Japan) seems to me the most insipid.[1] The rice wine, on the other hand, I found much better than its reputation among foreigners, many of whom, I am afraid, tried it once at an inferior tea house, and never had the courage to repeat the experiment. Ordinary wayside saké is indeed quite as bad as ordinary American beer, but the more expensive brands are much superior in taste and less heady. Japanese brewers are all rich men, but their products differ as widely as those of our beer brewers. When Miss Bird says that saké is "faint, sickly, and nauseous," she speaks for herself only. Rein compares it to the flavor of weak sherry. In truth the flavor is unique, and can no more be described than the taste of wine could be described to one who has never had any. It is said that Japanese experts look for five distinct tastes in good saké: "sweetness, sharpness, sourness, bitterness, and astringency, with a flavor of fusel oil in addition."

When we left the tea house, at a late hour, all the girls belonging to it accompanied us to the street, where, with many low bows, they united in the usual musical chorus of irasshai and sayonara — "come again," and "good by." We had enjoyed a typical Japanese banquet, from which only one customary ingredient had been omitted, — dancing. A few evenings later, I made up for this omission by attending, with some American friends, an entertainment specially arranged for us by one of the hotel clerks, and which

[1] I must add, however, that, after some experience, I found that plain Japanese rice has a pleasant, if faint flavor, which, I fancied, might so grow on me that after a while I should prefer it to our sweet and flavored rice puddings, even as I preferred their plain tea to our tea and cream. Expert rice tasters can tell, like tea and wine tasters, just what section of the country a sample of rice comes from.

consisted solely of music and dancing, the gastronomic element being represented only by saké, tea, and cake. There were again two geishas, ready with song and samisen, two dancers, and two other young maidens whose duty consisted in smiling and perpetually banging away at two small but noisy drums. The dancing girls never left their place, and hardly moved their feet, their performance being, in Oriental fashion, not saltatorial, but pantomimic. By means of facial expression, word, and gestures, and the use of fans, they enacted several tales, all of which would not have been approved by missionaries.

As for the drum girls, they were at first a comic curiosity, but soon became a decided nuisance, for, armed, each, with two sticks, they belabored their queer, obliquely placed drumheads fortissimo, until my tympanum rang in sympathy. For half an hour at a time, without a second's intermission, they rapidly beat the following rhythm : —

and so on *senza fine*. Since drumming seemed to be a necessary feature of the entertainment, we did not wish to interfere with the program; but, remembering that a room filled with tobacco smoke is less offensive when you light a cigar of your own, we tried to apply this nasal experience to the realm of tone, by taking charge of the drums ourselves, to the amusement of the girls. We found drumsticks much easier to master than chopsticks; and the noise really did seem less offensive when we contributed to it ourselves. But the combined din of the drums, samisens, and falsetto geisha voices — when we got up a grand ensemble — was delightfully barbarous and picturesquely diabolical. The Chinese, whenever there is an eclipse, try to frighten away the devouring shadow with their noisiest drums and tomtoms. Had there been an eclipse visible in Tōkyō at that moment, I am sure the shadow of the moon would have slunk away in dismay, with its tail between its legs.

A little of this sort of thing goes a great way, wherefore we broke up early in the evening in order to get a glimpse of the Yoshiwara on the way home. The singing, dancing, and tea-house girls whose acquaintance we had so far made were, as previously intimated, of a class the members of which may be entirely respectable or partially so, in comparison with a more degraded class of girls and women who are now, as they were two centuries ago, confined by law to a special district known as the Yoshiwara. Here vice is indeed gilded. Property is said to be worth four times as much as in most other parts of the city, and nowhere else are the houses so high and so costly in appearance. Besides some shorter streets, there is one long avenue, consisting of two rows of palaces, brilliantly illuminated at night. In the case of the largest and most sumptuous of these buildings there is nothing to indicate their character from without, whereas in the more humble ones the ground floor, elevated a couple of feet above the street level, is open to the view and presents the appearance of a human menagerie. These ground floors are literally cages, wherein hundreds of imprisoned girls sit behind rows of bars every night, some of them stolid looking, others smiling or chaffing the passers by. No

Oriental slave market could present a more pitiable and loathsome sight. These poor girls have been sold for a term of years to the owners of the palaces of vice, and there is no escape for them except through suicide or the very rare chance of being ransomed by a rich admirer, and elevated to concubinage or possibly even to marriage.

In Japanese novels the heroine is not infrequently a girl who has been sold by starving parents into this horrible life, or has voluntarily offered this sacrifice of her chastity to rescue them from debt. But it is the opinion of those best informed that, except among the very poorest or in famine times, such cases mostly belong to the realm of romance and rarely occur in real life — perhaps not more frequently than in Europe or America. Foreigners usually get erroneous ideas on this subject by confounding the Yoshiwara victims with the geishas or tea-house girls. These are often refined and beautiful, but in the Yoshiwara cages one rarely sees a face that could be called pretty; and what little beauty there may be is utterly marred by the disgusting daubs of paint and powder with which the faces are rouged and whitewashed. Most of the girls are in Japanese garb, but some of them seek to attract attention by sitting on chairs, wearing ill-fitting foreign clothes, crowned by vulgar Parisian hats. They are the most offensive ingredient in this whole repulsive spectacle, the one redeeming feature of which is that by thus collecting all of the women in a special region, the other streets are kept undefiled by certain nocturnal phenomena which are a disgrace to the "Christian" cities of Europe and America.

The Yoshiwara is the only part of Tōkyō where a

foreigner who behaves himself is liable to insult. Here, as we rode and walked along, we encountered now and then the sneering looks and taunting words of members of the former samurai or the criminal classes. Every reader of Japanese novels or police records knows that the Yoshiwara is the haunt of the vicious — of libertines, thieves, forgers, murderers — who come here to drown their pangs of conscience and spend their dishonest gains in carousals. Hence it forms a convenient trap for detectives, who usually find their game here without the trouble of hunting it. Here, too, for the first and only time in Japan, I saw the spectacle of a drunken man.

A THEATRE AND A SCHOOL

ONLY SEVEN HOURS — BEHAVIOR OF THE AUDIENCE — SOCIAL STATUS OF ACTORS — TRAILING TROUSERS — THE KNEELING NATION — EXPRESSION OF EMOTION — CHINESE FALSETTO — SCENERY AND MUSIC — STAGE ILLUSIONS — COUNT OKUMA'S SCHOOL — SPEECHES AND PRIZES — LUNCH IN THE COUNT'S GARDEN

DURING the hot lotos months the theatres of Japan, as of most countries, are closed. On July 7 and 8, however, there happened to be, for the benefit of sufferers from the failure of the rice crops, a special charity performance by the Danjiuro Association, at the Shintomi Theatre, to which foreigners were able to purchase tickets at two dollars each, and which was on no account to be missed, for Danjiuro is the greatest of Japanese actors. It was expected that a great many foreigners would be present, and for their benefit the principal play to be given had been abbreviated so that it would last *only* seven hours. For the same reason the performance was begun at three P.M. instead of at six o'clock in the morning, which is the orthodox Japanese hour for beginning a play that usually lasts till six in the evening, — sometimes like our newspaper serials, "to be continued" next day.

It was raining when we rode up to the theatre, which we found to be somewhat larger than ordinary Japanese buildings, but without any pretensions to architectural beauty, which would be too expensive a luxury in a city where destructive fires are as frequent as in Tōkyō. Being already provided with tickets, we were able to dodge the custom indulged in by well-to-do Japanese, of securing their seats in an adjoining tea house, instead of at the box office. These tea houses also provide lunches during the intermissions of the play, and in various ways absorb a large share of the general theatrical profits, to which fact the frequent collapse of managers has been attributed.

Kurumas by the score discharged their foreign or native occupants at the door, while hundreds of other natives came along on clogs, that lifted them stilt-like above the mud of the unpaved streets. Before entering they left these clogs near the door, where a pile of at least a hundred pairs had accumulated, which servants were rapidly carrying to a corner within. Leaving our umbrellas — but not our shoes — in charge of an attendant, we were ushered up a flight of stairs to a gallery facing the stage, and provided with chairs — luckily, for it would have been torture to sit or squat for hours on the mats, as the natives did in the side galleries and in the parquet. This parquet was divided into small square boxes, somewhat as we divide the floor of a church into pews; there were, of course, no benches or chairs, but everybody knelt on mats during the whole performance.

On a first visit to a Japanese theatre the audience is quite as interesting as the play, for the reason that the family groups in the parquet behave very much as they would if they were between the paper walls and screens of their own homes. No one is so rude as to disturb others by coming or going during the continuance of an act; but between the acts the scenes in the parquet constitute an entertaining side-show. Every family group is provided with a lunch, which has either been brought along, or is ordered from an adjoining tea house. Two gangways, right and left, called hana-michi or flower paths, on a level with the stage, run from it to the other end of the hall, and from these gangways (which are also used sometimes for special entrances of the actors or for processions) male attendants distributed tea, cakes, and other refreshments to the audience. A number of the spectators took their lunch unceremoniously on the stage, in front of the curtain. Almost every man and woman was smoking a thimble-sized pipe, and this indulgence was not limited to the intermissions, but continued most of the time, except when the tears over a tragic situation threatened to put out the pipe.

Although many Japanese plays are very immoral, according to our notions of propriety, boys and girls of all ages are taken to them by their parents of the lower classes; but in justice to the Japanese, it must be added that until recently, on account of the coarseness of the stage, the upper classes did not frequent the ordinary theatre, but only certain ancient and highly respectable, unintelligible, and tiresome performances — *quasi*-operatic — known as *Nō*. The actors of these were honored in society; but ordinary actors were held in such contempt that, as Professor Chamberlain tells us, "when a census was taken, they were spoken of with the numerals used in counting animals. . . . Those to whom Japanese is familiar will," he adds, "appreciate the terrible sting of the insult." The strictness of Japanese etiquette on this point is illustrated by the account given, only a few decades ago, by Sir Rutherford Alcock of a visit to a theatre, which he made in Osaka, prefaced by this information: "In Yeddo I had never been able to gratify my desire to see this illustration of national manners, because no person of rank can be seen in such places; and it would have been a breach of all rules of propriety for a minister to visit a theatre." Within recent years there has been a change and improvement, in consequence of which theatres and actors are no longer tabooed, which is a fortunate circumstance, for the reason that, to quote Chamberlain once more, the theatre is "the only remaining place where the life of Old Japan can be studied in these radical latter days."

Apart from us foreigners seated on chairs in one gallery and our method of applause, which the Japanese have adopted in their public places, there was nothing in this theatre that could not have been seen in Old Japan. The dresses of the spectators may have been less sombre in former days; but this sombreness only served to enhance, by contrast, the beautiful colors and patterns of the accurate historic costumes worn by the actors. I cannot add "and actresses"; for even yet women are not considered to be fit to appear in a first-class play, and their parts are still taken by men — admirably taken by them, it must be confessed, with a grace truly feminine. Of the men's costumes the oddest were the trailing trousers — those most extraordinary garments, which were part of the court costume until a few decades ago, and which amazed Sir Rutherford Alcock when he was received by the Shogun. He relates that facing him were fifty officials, "all in gauze and silks. . . . The most singular part of the whole costume, and that which, added to the headgear, gave an irresistibly comic air to the whole presentment, was the immeasurable prolongation of the silk trousers. These, instead of stopping short at the heels, are unconscionably lengthened and left to trail two or three feet behind them, so that their feet, as they advanced, seemed pushed into what should have been the knees of the garment."

These trailing trousers played a conspicuous rôle in the drama we saw at the Shintomi. It has been suggested that, as such a garment must make its wearer clumsy and helpless, it was prescribed by the rulers to ward off the danger of assassination. But when I asked Mr. Shugio what he thought was the original object of this strange costume, he replied that it was to give the impression that the Shogun's subjects were *on their knees even when walking.* The Japanese are indeed always on their knees, both for courtesy and comfort, except when walking or sleeping, and it would not be inappropriate to entitle a book on them, *The Kneeling Nation.* If one of them wrote a book on us, he would probably be tempted to entitle it, *The Sitting Nation;* for kneeling and walking are fast becoming lost arts among us.

Our performance consisted of a tragedy in four acts, a short comedy, and a dance in four acts, in which last the Misses Fukiko and Jitsuko, daughters of Danjiuro, took part — models of elegance in appearance and grace in gesture. An English program was distributed, containing the "dramatic (*sic*) personae" and a brief sketch of the tragic plot, the scene of which was placed at the beginning of the seventeenth century, and which had a good deal to do with fighting and plotting and poisoned cakes. I have never seen better acting than that in the poisoning scene of this play. However much the Japanese may differ from us in customs and etiquette, in the expression of grief and joy their faces are like ours, and their actors have such wonderful mimetic powers that I found no difficulty whatever in following the plot, both in the tragedy and the comedy. Danjiuro might come to America and act in his own language, as Salvini has done; he is the Salvini of Japan, and would be a popular idol anywhere. One of our party had intended to return to Yokohama at six, but I heard him say that he liked the play (of which he could not understand a word) so well that he had decided to stay to the end — four hours more, including an hour's intermission for supper.

The only disagreeable feature of the performance was the tone in which the actors spoke their parts. In ordinary conversation the Japanese speak in a low, musical voice and with natural inflections, but on the stage they have adopted the idiotic Chinese sing-song, squeaking falsetto, unearthly yells, and other extraordinary sounds which make a Chinese theatre seem like an improvised lunatic asylum. Almost everything that is really absurd in Japan comes from China, and prominent among the absurdities which ought to yield as soon as possible to Occidental influences is the stage falsetto. I was surprised by another peculiarity of the theatrical diction. My grammars had told me that the Japanese have practically no verbal or oratorical accent, every syllable and word having about the same emphasis. But it seemed to me that these actors positively swooped down on certain syllables and words, with an emphatic *sforzando*. I had also noticed previously that railway guards often accented one syllable much more strongly than the others; for instance, Kamákura.

In its scenic features the Japanese stage has gone far beyond the Chinese, which is still in the primitive condition of Shakspere's time when a board with "This is a Forest," or whatever else was to be suggested, took the place of real or painted trees, mountains, and so on. It would be strange, indeed, if, with their passionate love of nature, which makes them paint a maple branch or a Fuji on every fan, screen, and teapot, the Japanese had been willing to dispense with a scenic background on the stage. Episodes of street life, domestic interiors, dogs, horses, boats, moats, and castles, forest scenes — are all painted, or bodily introduced, with an art that is thoroughly realistic, and illusory in its perspective. What is more, to save time, or rather, to shorten intermissions, the Japanese were the first to invent a revolving stage, which makes it possible to set up one scene while another is in use, thus facilitating rapid changes. The curtain is sometimes raised, as in our theatres, sometimes dropped out of sight, or again pushed aside and closed, as at Bayreuth. The Shintomi has two ornamental curtains, — one Dutch, the other the gift of a Hawaiian monarch.

But again, just as the splendid acting is marred by the silly Chinese intonation, so the scenic illusion is destroyed by incongruities. One might forgive the gangways running from the stage across the parquet, and the occasional appearance of actors on them, especially when they are arrayed in their most gorgeous costumes, genuine works of art which have few counterparts at the present day, and which can be better seen this way than on the stage itself; but one fails to understand how the Japanese can tolerate the Chinese nuisance of allowing stage attendants to walk about among the actors, light up their faces with candles, prompt them from an open book, bring on or remove furniture, etc., in an obtrusive manner which destroys all illusion. What is amusing about this farce is the Oriental naïveté of supposing these attendants to be invisible, as is indicated by their wearing black garments and veils. An explanation of this absurdity may perhaps be found in the fact that until recently the Japanese theatre was frequented only by the lower classes, whose illusion is not easily marred.

Shall I attempt to describe the music which accompanied the tragedy? It must be admitted that the Japanese, as well as the Chinese, anticipated Wagner in the idea that a tragedy needs a musical accompaniment. It is their way of carrying out this idea that Western ears object to. I frankly confess that I found a certain charm in the barbarous music of the Chinese theatre in San Francisco after I had heard it four or five times. If this Japanese dramatic music gave me less pleasure, it may be owing to the fact that it was too deep to be understood at first hearing. I will give it the benefit of the doubt,—the more willingly as I did subsequently hear samisen and koto playing which was truly musical in its way. What was surprising in the play at the Shintomi Theatre was the variety of musical effects and groupings. To the left of the stage was a sort of menagerie cage with bars, the occupants of which kept up a monotonous strumming on their samisens in accompanying the dialogue. In a row on the back of the stage there were some flute players and more samisenists, whose performance sometimes assumed a well-defined rhythmic form. In a sort of proscenium box on our right, ten feet above the stage, there were two more samisen players, besides two doleful vocalists, looking, with their shaven crowns, like Buddhist priests. Their song consisted of an occasional melodic bud, with a great deal of garnishing that it would be impossible to indicate in our musical notation. But the prima donna of the occasion was the fellow with the big drum. He had his innings when a ghost came on the stage, and again, when the ghost made his exit. That drummer could give points to a thunderstorm in the Alps. It is said that the Japanese do not stand in real awe of ghosts, but look upon their possible appearance with a certain kindly interest; yet I fancy that when accompanied by such an unearthly drum solo, a ghost must be awful even to them.

If I have neglected to mention the name of the play or its writer, that is not my fault. No name or author was given on the playbill, it being the custom to ascribe new dramas to the manager who produces them. Many of the plays are the result of the co-operation of a writer with the actors, scene painters, and carpenters, and there is much improvisation during the performance. Such a thing, after all, is not unknown in our own theatres. I have been told that of the original "Black Crook" nothing whatever remains but the name; yet the author still draws his royalty.

One great advantage of travelling in a country so much like another planet as Japan is lies in this, that it is really not necessary to go to a theatre in order to enjoy novel and entertaining sights. Here everything is novel, the audience as well as the play, and to us the oldest is the newest. At the same time what is new to them cannot but interest us too, as showing what success has attended their efforts to graft foreign ideas on Japanese stock. Bearing this in mind, I welcomed an invitation, secured for me by my ever-obliging friend, Mr. Shugio, to attend the seventh graduating exercises of the school of political science and law, the Tōkyō Semmon Gakko, organized and supported by Count Okuma. This school had 800 students, 182 of whom were to receive their degrees on this occasion. The exercises were held in a large, airy building, provided, like all Japanese schools to-day, with desks, benches, and chairs, the old kneeling attitude being apparently considered incompatible with the modern educational spirit. Chairs had been placed on one side for the invited guests, while the rest of the hall was densely packed with students, no two of whom were dressed alike. The majority were in Japanese attire; others had foreign trousers or a shirt, oddly combined with native garments, while a few were completely attired in foreign dress. The President wore the national costume. The order of exercises, as kindly translated for me by Mr. Shugio, was as follows:—

> Enter the students with their relatives and guardians.
> Enter the guests and the faculty.
> Music.
> The President distributes the certificates.
> The President distributes the prizes.
> Music.
> Speech by the President.
> Mr. Teuda responds for the graduates.
> Music.
> Speeches by guests.
> Music.

The prizes consisted of books given to about twenty of the best students. The speeches were apparently most eloquent, being often interrupted by laughter and applause. Before the exercises we had been taken to an anteroom, where we found fans, cigarettes, and ice water on tap, free for everybody. After the exercises we all adjourned to the garden of Count Okuma, where the band played foreign music with real swing and expression. Having partaken of an open-air lunch of cold meats, ice cream and cake, beer and claret lemonade, we inspected the beauties of the garden, which is widely famed for its conservatories and rare flowers and shrubs. We then visited the house, which is of Japanese construction, except that there is glass instead of paper in the sliding screens serving as walls. Within, some of the rooms are furnished in Japanese style, while others have foreign chairs, tables, and carpets, so that one can enter with boots on. But the artistic decorations even in these rooms are Japanese, showing how a Japanese gentleman of taste can blend Occidental features with Oriental art as successfully as we do the reverse. It was on the verandah of the Japanese entrance to the house that I had the pleasure of a personal introduction to the Count, who, as the reader knows, has long been one of the most prominent of Japanese statesmen, noted for his foreign sympathies, which had not long before this led to an attempted assassination by a patriotic fanatic. The Count was still suffering from the effects of his wounds, but was in a most affable mood. I realized that he was up even in foreign slang when, on pouring brandy into my tumbler, he looked at me and exclaimed, "Say when!"

We had a chat on international topics, one of his remarks being that the Japanese were like the Americans, inasmuch as they borrowed what was best from all other countries — "a privilege of young nations."

THE MIKADO AND THE EXHIBITION

A VAST CURIO STORE — VISITORS — SEMI-FOREIGN PICTURE GALLERY — A GASTRONOMIC INSULT — AN IMPERIAL PRISONER — THE MIKADO'S FIRST OUTING — INVISIBLE NO LONGER — EDITORIAL PUNISHMENT — A REMARKABLE MONARCH — PERSONAL APPEARANCE — EVENING DRESS IN THE MORNING — JAPANESE JOURNALISTS — EMPEROR OR MIKADO? — A FOREIGN DINNER.

SHORTLY before leaving New York, I had a conversation with Mr. John La Farge, who remarked that he felt very much tempted to revisit Japan that summer, were it only to attend the third National Exhibition, which would bring under one roof many choice works of art ordinarily scattered all over the country, and belonging to wealthy ex-daimyos, to whom one must get letters of introduction, and then submit to various time-robbing ceremonies. There certainly was a great advantage in having so many art treasures collected in one building; and one reason why Tōkyō proved so fascinating to me, in the sweltering lotos months, was that I could spend a few hours every day in the Exposition grounds.

Three national expositions have so far been held in Tōkyō, the government taking an increasing interest in them, as is shown by the appropriation of $100,000 for the first, $180,000 for the second, and $500,000 for the third. The buildings erected for this last one covered about eight acres of Ueno Park. The manager had visited several European expositions, and modelled his buildings and interior arrangement in accordance with his foreign experiences, so that at first sight the general impression was European rather than Japanese. But on closer inspection, it became apparent that, with the exception of some models of electric cars, suites of rooms furnished with chairs, tables, and sofas, and a few other things, unknown to Old Japan, everything on the stands and in the showcases had a purely Japanese coloring and origin. The whole exhibition building seemed like a vast curio store, containing not only art works, but illustrations of all branches of industry; and in passing along these miles of exhibits, the thought that most frequently recurred was that in modern Japan, as in ancient Greece, art is largely industrial; that is, works of art are not created as things apart from daily life, to be preserved in galleries and museums, but form an integral part of the vases, fans, tea sets, and screens, that adorn the homes and throw an esthetic glamour over domestic life. Here was room after room of the finest lacquer goods, Japan's specialty; vases of all sizes, of the most exquisite texture and realistic or fanciful ornamentation; tiny teacups, so beautiful and delicate that the most infatuated lover would deem them fit to touch his sweetheart's lips; screens, fans, and pots, on which scenes of Japanese life, or landscapes, trees, and flowers were illustrated with an art which foreign artists cannot approach — and most of these at prices that would have made connoisseurs and bargain hunters elsewhere wild with delight.

There were about a million visitors in all — a daily average of over 8000, including foreigners holding special invitations, and other deadheads; but as the season tickets were only $2, and a single admission only seven cents (fifteen on Sundays), the income did not meet the expenditures. The higher admission price asked on Sunday was to give the fastidious classes a better chance to see the exhibits at leisure, without mixing with the crowds, for whom Saturday was the principal day. I may add here, in parenthesis, that the Christian Sunday is not recognized in Japan, where work goes on, and stores are open as on other days, except in treaty ports like Yokohama, where the custom house and the foreign shops are closed.

The one disappointing feature of the Exhibition was the semi-foreign picture gallery. Both the old and the new schools were represented, but the screen-shaped pictures still predominated over the modern square canvases. Birds and flowers have always been the most successful province of Japanese artists, but there were also a few good landscapes and scenes from domestic life. The oil paintings, with few exceptions, did not indicate that the genius of Japanese artists finds ready expression in oil and canvas and foreign methods. Comparing the whole collection of pictures with a similar one in America or Europe, the most striking difference, as regards subjects, lay in the entire absence of the nude. Female beauty unadorned is the favorite subject of Occidental art, but in this gallery there was not a single undraped female (or male) form, and in the Japanese wood and ivory carvings and bronzes shown in other rooms, the figures were also fully clothed. The cause of this will be discussed in a later chapter.

One afternoon I had cause to blush for my country. Sitting down at a refreshment booth, I asked for a cup of cha, expecting, of course, to receive a tiny sample of Japanese tea in a dainty cup. Instead of that, the sophisticated attendant brought me one of those heavy, thick cups, without a handle, which are used in our Wild West hotels to prevent breakage; and, horror of horrors, he had put in milk, taking it for granted that I, being a foreigner, would prefer tea in that form. If I could have talked Japanese, I should have told him that I would as soon put lager beer in my tea as milk or cream. I fancy that our unspeakable gastronomic solecism arose from the prevailing Occidental ignorance how to make tea properly. If tea is boiled, or allowed to stand too long (as it almost always is in America and Europe), it becomes so bitter that not only sugar but cream are welcomed to modify its astringency; but when tea is properly made, it has a bouquet like that of a choice old wine, which it is simply a crime to spoil with cream. Would you put cream in a glass of Tokay?

One of the great events during Exhibition time was the chance it gave me to see the Mikado. When the newspapers announced one morning that the Emperor would preside over the distribution of prizes at the Exposition, no one was in the least surprised. Yet twenty-five years previous to this the appearance of such an item in the newspapers — if there had been any at that time — would have created more incredulous surprise than would the announcement in a Berlin paper of to-day that Emperor William had consented hereafter to sweep the street in front of his palace. European monarchs sometimes travel incognito for a few days; but in Japan, for many centuries, the monarchs remained always unknown and invisible, and Mutsuhito is the first Mikado in hundreds of years who has shown his face to his subjects. Every one interested in Japan knows that for more than seven hundred years the Mikados, though the nominal rulers of the country, were in reality little more than puppets in the hands of the generals, or Shoguns, the real rulers of the land. Many of the Mikados were mere boys when they were made to abdicate, to be succeeded by other boys, whom the Shoguns found it easy to keep in subjection. Others abdicated voluntarily, and retired to a monastery, preferring the religious meditations on nirvana to the actual "imperial nirvana" of their palace prisons.

For prisoners they practically were. They lived at Kyōto, then called Miaco ("the metropolis"), and were supposed by the people to be too holy to trouble themselves with worldly matters, the popular belief about the Mikado being that "he lived in a state of sublime abstraction, occupying himself from morning to night, at all times and seasons, in prayer to the gods, his ancestors, for the welfare of Japan." He never left the palace grounds except in a closed palanquin, or a covered cart drawn by bullocks.[1] Some of the Mikados were refined patrons of art and literature, others were effeminate voluptuaries, but all were powerless to affect the destinies of their country; nor were they particularly wealthy, depending for their income on what the Shogun deemed fit to allow them, the real imperial pomp and display of wealth and ceremony being at the

[1] One of these clumsy imperial bullock carts, with enormous wheels six feet in diameter, is still on exhibition at the Ueno Museum.

Shogun's court in Tōkyō. As late as the year 1868, the Japanese statesman, Okubo Ichizo, drew up a memorial to the Government, in which he thus graphically described the Mikado's peculiar position:—

"The residence of the sovereign is called 'above the clouds,' his nobles are styled 'men of the region above the clouds,' his face is compared to a 'dragon's countenance,' as something not easily to be seen, and his 'gem-like person' is spoken of by excess of respect as something which must not touch the earth; so that he begins to think himself a more honorable and illustrious being than he is until high and low being alienated from him, his condition comes to be as miserable as it is now." [1]

These were bold words to speak of a monarch who was considered as sacred as a mediaeval Pope, and whose descent was traced back directly to the gods through Jimmu Tenno, the first of the "historic" Mikados, who is supposed to have flourished in the seventh century before Christ; bold words to speak in a country where, as late as 1890, two editors of the *Nohi Nippo* were sentenced to four years in prison with hard labor, a fine of $100 each, and police supervision for a year and a half after liberation, for having spoken disrespectfully of this Jimmu Tenno, who died in 585 B.C.[2]

It seems surprising that the present Emperor should not have pardoned these editors, since he himself set the example in demolishing the mythical and sacred

---

[1] To this day it is said that there are, in remote country villages, old men and women who believe that to see the face of the Mikado would be a fatal honor. Among the legends current about him were such as these, that all the rice he ate was picked over by hand to prevent any imperfect kernels from getting into the imperial stomach, and that all his dishes were dashed to pieces to prevent others from using them.

[2] The case was appealed, but the higher court confirmed the sentence, on June 21, 1890.

nimbus about the Mikado's head. He ascended the throne in 1867, aged only fifteen, the Shogun having been forced by his enemies to abdicate. Thus the Mikado was restored to his true position, as not only nominal but actual ruler of Japan. But the conservatives, who had hoped that with this change Old Japan would be restored and the foreigners (whom the Shoguns had protected) expelled, were doomed to grievous disappointment. For, whereas the former Mikado had opposed the efforts of foreigners to establish themselves in the country, Mutsuhito and his advisers changed about and became the foreigners' friends, having come to the conclusion that in the Europeanization of Japan, as far as government affairs are concerned, lay the only hope of escaping the fate of India and other Oriental nations now subject to European powers; a conclusion, the wisdom of which has been proved by the successful war made by Japan on China with modern methods.

The Mikado now gradually became like any European emperor, human, visible, and accessible. Black vividly describes the transition stage when, on April 15, 1868, he went to Osaka : —

"Up to this period he had probably never seen a green field. Born in the palace, he was kept strictly within its domain, and there he had remained, only being removed to another equally secluded residence, a short distance from it, when it was destroyed by fire, and until it was rebuilt. Outside of Kyōto he had never been; and to a lad sixteen years of age, and some spirit and intelligence (which he has shown himself to possess), it must have been a great pleasure to see something of the beauties of nature and the active life of men in town and country. Even now he was not allowed to gaze upon them freely, nor was the eye of any loyal or curious subject permitted to fall upon him. In a norimon of exquisite finish — made of the purest Kiri (*Paullownia Imperialis*) without an atom of either paint or varnish — he sat. Fine bamboo blinds divided him from the world, allowing him to see without being seen . . .

"He had never been seen except by a few of his more immediate family and attendants, and even by his courtiers his face was never seen; a screen falling between him and them concealing the upper portion of his body."[1]

All this Orientalism and mediævalism was rapidly done away with by the bright young monarch as soon as he felt himself his own master. Three years after the first outing just described, he adopted European clothes for himself and his courtiers, and has never worn the Japanese costume in public since. He issued a severe edict against patriotic fanatics, which at once put an end to attacks on foreigners. He approved and fostered the introduction of foreign methods of education, manufacture, agriculture, and trade. He abolished odious class distinctions and gave human rights to the previously degraded class of *Eta*. He removed his capital to Tōkyō, where he gave receptions not only to his own courtiers and nobles, but to representatives of foreign governments, gradually extending his hospitality to all ladies and gentlemen who had influential friends to introduce them. But his greatest act was his voluntary resignation, in 1889, of his absolute monarchic power, and the creation of a parliamentary form of government with upper and lower houses, representing all classes of voters.

Surely this remarkable Mikado will be recorded in history as the most interesting monarch of the nineteenth century. No other has had such a romantic

[1] Black's *Young Japan*, II. 195, 196.

career; no other has had the privilege of abolishing mediaeval feudalism and Oriental despotism with a stroke of the pen, and thus placing his country in a line with modern European nations. This was the monarch I was to see one morning in July. My guardian angel, Mr. Shugio, had secured an invitation for me; and in his company I entered the large pavilion which had been erected in the park, capable of holding several thousand spectators. The Mikado's throne was at one end, and a slightly sloping platform covered with white matting led up to it. On both sides of the throne a few rows of chairs had been placed for the Japanese ministers, the foreign ambassadors, and members of the press. The thousands outside of this charmed circle had to stand.

I found my colleagues of the Japanese press, as on several subsequent occasions, extremely affable and courteous. There were about a dozen of them; and before the proceedings began, we all met in an anteroom, where programs, paper, tables, and chairs had been provided for our use. Several of the journalists spoke English, and kindly offered to help me in any way they could. Their courtesy to each other was equally remarkable. Imagine two American reporters bowing each time they meet till their heads are on a level with their lowest coat buttons! With the exception of the Oriental ambassadors, who wore their national costume (the Coreans were a sight to behold), and the Japanese officers, who wore dark blue uniforms with yellow stripes, all the spectators in our section, including the newspaper men, were in full evening dress — swallow tail, white tie, and high silk hat — although the performance began at nine o'clock in the morning. Indeed, that morning I was arrayed in evening dress as early as six o'clock, writing a letter home, in which I naturally had to explain that the American inference, that a man who is seen in that attire at such an hour has not been in bed at all, did not apply to antipodal Japan. There is at present a reaction and a decided prejudice against our evening dress, but for some years it has been *de rigueur* in Tōkyō society on all ceremonious occasions and at all hours. We laugh at the idea of appearing in full dress at nine A.M.; but if we put aside our traditional notions, and look at the matter without prejudice, we must acknowledge that the time of the day has little to do with the question, and that the ridiculousness of the swallow-tail coat lies in its own cut and shape. To the under-sized Japanese this costume is particularly unbecoming. One of their own papers has argued that the Japanese figure is too dumpy and the legs too short to appear to advantage in this foreign dress; and I have seen the statement somewhere that the marginal note, "Wear your dress suit," is no longer customary on invitation cards. If the Japanese fully realized how European and American artists detest the swallow-tail coat, they would banish it as unceremoniously as they did, not long ago, the trailing trousers of the court dress. At any rate, if they will persist in wearing our most absurd costume, they ought to be more careful to secure a good fit, and to keep their silk hats brushed in the right direction. Professor Chamberlain says that "it seems scarcely credible, but it is true, that the Japanese imagine their appearance to be improved when they exchange their own costume for ours; and they are angry with people who tell them the contrary. In this, as in many other matters, their former exquisite taste has died a sudden death."

As the Mikado was now expected to make his appearance at any moment, we went into the large hall and took seats on the chairs placed for us, to the left of the throne, and quite near it. Where there was such a mixture of national and foreign things, it seemed less barbarous than it would have seemed otherwise, for us to walk with our boots over the clean white mats that floored the hall. The arrival of the Emperor, in the fine carriage (for which he long ago exchanged his palanquin) was heralded by the royal brass band, which played the Japanese national hymn with German harmonies, on German instruments, and followed it up at intervals with European dance music, a curious preference being shown for polkas. I was curious to see how the Emperor would be received by the thousands of spectators. Would they prostrate themselves, as they were formerly obliged to do, whenever his Majesty passed in the street? Probably not, since the people were notified, as early as 1868, that the *shitaniro* (bow-down) would no longer be enforced. Would he be received with a foreign hurrah, or *hoch*, or *Vive l'Empereur!* or with the old-fashioned audible drawing-in of the breath, resulting in a prolonged f-f-f-f sound? The spectators, apparently, did not quite know, themselves, what they ought to do. As the Mikado walked up to his throne, they all bowed their heads, but not as low as in ordinary salutations. When he sat down, and again after he had made his address, an attempt was made to applaud him by clapping hands; but this did not meet with the approval of the majority, whose sentiment seemed to be that solemn silence was the most becoming way of receiving the monarch.

The Mikado's address was preceded by one delivered by the president of the association, both being read in so low a tone as to be almost inaudible, even to us who were so near. The exhibitors who had received the principal prizes now came up in couples to receive their diplomas. They bowed before his Majesty, received a huge roll (containing certificates for their whole section), whereupon they retreated a dozen steps backward, lobster fashion, before etiquette allowed them to turn their back on the Mikado. The ceremony lasted about an hour, after which the Emperor drove off in his carriage to the sounds of the national hymn. While he was sitting on his throne we had an excellent opportunity to observe his face. It was solemn, almost stern, but there was something majestic in his bearing which was prepossessing; nor could one fail to read in that countenance the firm will and the keen intelligence which have made Mutsuhito the most remarkable ruler of Japan since Ieyasu. He has a high forehead, dark complexion, and rather thick lips. In height he is somewhat above the Japanese average — 5 feet 9 inches. In former years, according to Black, his walk was not good, as he turned in his toes and shuffled along; but now he walks in the natural way approved by us, and has a fine, manly gait. He wore a foreign uniform.

Throughout this chapter I have taken the liberty to retain the word "Mikado," although I know that the Japanese themselves no longer consider it good form to use it, "except in poetry and on great occasions." Ordinarily he is referred to as Tenshi, Tenno, or Shujo, which Chamberlain translates, "the Son of Heaven," "the Heavenly Emperor," "the Supreme Master." In the English press of Japan, and in official documents, he is usually referred to simply as the Emperor. But there is absolutely no reason why foreigners should give up the use of such a characteristic word as "Mikado." The Japanese have a foolish custom of constantly changing names of classes and cities. The samurai are now called shizoku, Yeddo is Tōkyō, and Miako became Kyōto, and later still Saikyo, which last change foreigners have refused to accept. "Mikado" is not only a better sounding word than any of its new substitutes, but, like "Czar," it has a definite national significance which the word "Emperor" lacks.

A few days after the distribution of prizes I had the honor to be invited to a banquet given at the Ueno Hotel by Mr. Hanabusa, Commissioner-General of the Exposition. Although it was a dinner in foreign style, I found that I was the only foreigner invited, except Mr. K. M. Schroff of India. The dinner was cooked in the best French style and washed down with French wines; and although several Japanese of high rank were present, the national courtesy was shown by always serving the two foreign guests first. Most of those present spoke English, and one gentleman astonished me by his idiomatic accuracy and fluency of speech. But my principal reason for mentioning this dinner is that it provided another illustration of the vexed dress problem in the present transition stage of Japanese etiquette. I had put on a brand new light flannel suit, just made by an English tailor at Yokohama — clean, stylish, the very thing, it seemed to me, for a midsummer, early afternoon dinner in a hot climate. To my consternation, on entering the reception room, I found that every one wore his swallow-tail suit. Fearing that I had sinned against etiquette, I apologized to the host, who smiled and said it made no difference whatever. However, I felt guilty until the door opened again, and in came Mr. Schroff attired in an informal white linen duster. I am convinced that our entertainers secretly envied him his cool coat.

OFF FOR JAPANESE SIBERIA

CLIMATE OF JAPAN — MONKEYS IN THE SNOW — SKATING IN TŌKYŌ — YEZO VERSUS HONDO — DAMP DAYS — CLIMATE AND LITERATURE — PROFESSORS AT HOME — A LITERARY COMPANION — UNUSUAL PRIVILEGES — MULBERRY PLANTATIONS — AN INN AT SENDAI — TRANSFORMING A ROOM — QUILTS AND PILLOWS — THE BILL

IF an American were asked, "What is the climate of your country in the region between New Orleans and Halifax?" he would laugh at the absurdity of the question. "My dear sir," he would reply, "New York alone has several climates every other day; and as for New Orleans and Halifax, you might as well ask what is the temperature between Peru and Alaska." Yet the question is asked every day, "What is the climate of Japan?" when a glance at the map would show that (even if we omit a few of the northernmost small islands) its southern and northern extremities are as far apart as New Orleans and Halifax. If we made the comparison on the Pacific coast, the range would be from Northern Mexico to Northern Oregon. Thus the Japanese Empire is longer than California; but, being less broad, its area is about 12,000 square miles less than that of the most favored State in the Union.

Monkeys in the snow — in these four words the climate of Japan might be summed up. Monkeys are found near the northern extremity of the main island, in places where, according to Professor Chamberlain, "the snow often drifts to a depth of fifteen or twenty feet." Monkeys are always associated in our minds with a tropical climate; and when we think of Japan, we always have in mind silk and tea, camphor, rice, and other products of tropical or sub-tropical regions. In truth, however, the general climate of Japan is too cold for bananas, or even for oranges and lemons. The summers are, indeed, warm enough for tropical plants; but the winters are fatal to them, so that it is useless to look here for a luxuriant palm vegetation like that of the Hawaiian Islands.

Even as far south as Tōkyō (latitude of Raleigh, N.C.), there are, on the average, nearly seventy frosty nights between November and March. Snow sometimes covers the ground for a few days, and the thermometer may fall eight or nine degrees below freezing point. The ice is seldom thick here; but in January, 1868, as Holtham relates, "foreigners were able to offer the natives the spectacle of skating, which they had never seen." At this time the Japanese are wrapped in as many coats as the core of an onion, and sit shiveringly around their charcoal fireboxes; for their frail houses have no stoves or fireplaces, and the wind comes howling through the holes made by fingers or rats in the paper panes of the sliding screens. In the northern parts of the main island, the snow is often so deep that the villagers have to make steps up to its surface from their houses, unless they wish to dig tunnels or snow cañons.

It is not in Hondo, however, but in Yezo, the northernmost of the three main islands of the Empire, that winter snows and blows its worst. For although Yezo occupies the latitude of that part of Italy which lies between Rome and Venice, its climate is such that it may be properly called Japanese Siberia. Geographically, too, Yezo is a part of Siberia rather than of Japan; for there is reason to think that it was formerly connected with the northern island of Saghalin, which Japan ceded to Russia in 1875, and which itself is practically a peninsula of the Siberian mainland, as it can be reached on foot in low tide at one point, whereas the great depth of the Tsugaru straits make it seem probable that Yezo never was a part of the main island of Japan — a probability changed to certainty by zoölogical facts. "Japan [Hondo] has monkeys, which Yezo has not. Yezo has grouse, which Japan has not. Even the fossils differ on both sides of the straits."[1]

To these climatic, geological, and zoölogical reasons for calling the northern island "Japanese Siberia," must be added the coincidence that to Yezo the dangerous Japanese criminals and convicts are sent, just as from Russia they are exiled to Siberia.

But why this essay on Yezo and its climate, while we are still in Tōkyō? If you had ever been in that city at the beginning of August, you would not ask such a question, for you would know that then the mere thought of going to an island from whose mountains you can catch a glimpse of Siberia, acts on the nerves like a refrigerator. I decided to go to Yezo because Tōkyō was becoming daily more glaring, drowsy, damp, and uncomfortable. Shoes left under the bed, or clothes packed away in the trunk a few days were

[1] Chamberlain, *Things Japanese.* See, also, Blakiston's *Japan in Yezo*, and the writings of Professor Milne.

covered with green mould, and the whole city seemed as clammy as the inside of a bivalve. About the middle of July there had indeed been a few cool days and nights when an overcoat by day, and a blanket at night, were comfortable; but on other days my room and the air outside were like a Turkish bath. It is the dampness that makes the Japanese heat so depressing in summer, the cold so chilling in winter. In dry California it is cooler with a temperature twenty degrees higher; in dry Colorado it is warmer with the thermometer twenty degrees lower. Japan is a climatic resort for foreigners in China, which is damper yet; but it will never be a climatic resort for Californians. I have frequently seen statements in the reports of missionaries that they could do only half as much brainwork in Japan as at home. My own experiences confirmed this statement.

It was not the cooler climate alone that invited a visit to mountainous, river-netted Yezo. There are cities like Hakodate, the "Japanese Gibraltar," and Sapporo, the centre of American agricultural and industrial experiments, to tempt the tourist, and, much better than that, there are vast gloomy forests, and numbers of the aboriginal Ainos who have been driven north by the Japanese, as we have driven our "Ainos," the red Indians, west. On the way, moreover, there was a chance to see the east coast of Japan, and the famous Pine Islands.

Before starting I had a few calls to make. Mr. Kneisel, concert master of the Boston Symphony Orchestra, had kindly given me a letter to Mr. Dittrich, director of the Imperial Academy of Music in Tōkyō. Like other foreign employees of the government, Mr. Dittrich had the privilege of renting a house of his own in any part of the city; a privilege of which he had made good use by selecting a site on one of the numerous hilltops included within Greater Tōkyō, where he had a view and a breeze. We had a long conversation on the prospects of European music in Japan, which then seemed bright, although there has since been a reaction, Mr. Dittrich himself having resigned in April, 1894. I was introduced to one of his pupils, who was in his parlor, not to take a lesson, but to make a social call. She had been there several hours, in accordance with Japanese etiquette, which makes long visits good form — probably owing to the immense distances and slow means of locomotion which discourage frequent calling. She was a violin pupil, spoke a little English, and told me that she liked our foreign music better than their own. After she had left, Mr. Dittrich asked me if I thought she was beautiful; a question which I gently but firmly answered in the negative, whereupon he laughed and replied that she was considered a beauty by his Japanese friends, who, on the other hand, saw little to admire in those of their countrywomen who approached types that would be considered beautiful in Vienna or New York.

Mr. Dittrich did not seem alarmed at the prospect of a cholera epidemic in the capital. He said that his native cook was, in fact, rather hoping there would be one, on the ground that the rice crop was short; wherefore there would not be enough to go round unless the population were reduced. Some time previously, this reprobate had informed his employer that he would not mind if his wife died, as he could easily get another, but that he should be very sorry to lose his son. This cook's predecessor was a man who knew a little German. One day he failed to come, but sent a note to Mr. Dittrich in which the dictionary had played him false. He explained that his mother-in-law was dead, adding, " Morgen werden wir das Aas begraben" (to-morrow we shall bury the carcass). Mr. Dittrich had many things to tell about the marvellous adaptability of the Japanese to foreign ways; and he told a striking story of the efficiency of the postal arrangements. An Austrian lady of his acquaintance, having heard that he was living in the capital of Japan, consulted an old encyclopedia in which she found Kyōto put down as the capital. So to Kyōto she forwarded her letter, which nevertheless he received all right in Tōkyō. Forty years ago it would have cost about twenty-five dollars to get that letter from the old to the new capital by express runner. To-day the cost is two cents; modern Japan having one of the best and safest postal systems in the world.

My next call was on Professor Milne, who had lived in Japan fourteen years, studying the phenomena of earthquakes, for which that country has afforded him such frequent opportunities that he is to-day, perhaps, the leading authority on seismology in the world. He, too, had chosen an elevated spot for his residence, which was a pleasant mixture of Japanese coziness and British comfort. He gave me valuable points regarding the interior of Yezo, and presented me with a copy of the Transactions of the Seismological Society of Japan, Vol. IX., Part I., which is brimful of interesting and quaint information about the hundred volcanoes of Japan. Mr. Shugio had suggested that instead of taking a professional guide, who would cost me a dollar a day and travelling expenses, not to speak of his "squeezes" on every hotel bill. I might be able to secure a student who would accompany me for the pleasure of the trip, without asking more than the payment of his expenses. Professor Milne thought this was an excellent idea, and promised to see if he could find a candidate among his pupils.

On the following evening a young man called with the professor's card, but in the meantime I had already made arrangements with a young man named Yabi, whom Mr. Shugio, with his usual painstaking kindness and courtesy, had found for me. He was not a student, but, what was better still, a young author and journalist, on the staff of the *Mainichi Shimbun* (Daily News), one of the leading Japanese papers. He had lived in San Francisco several years and spoke English quite well. A year or two before I met him he had been imprisoned for writing an article in which the government was censured. The prison was not in good sanitary condition, and poor Mr. Yabi was taken ill with typhoid fever. He escaped with his life, but had never fully recovered his health, wherefore he welcomed an opportunity to get a free outing and vacation, and at the same time a chance to see parts of the country which his scant salary, and the necessity of helping to support his orphaned brothers and sisters, had never allowed him to visit. The proprietors of the *Mainichi Shimbun* readily granted him leave of absence for a month, without stopping his salary, on the understanding that he would write up our trip for its columns. Thus the inhabitants of Tōkyō were kept duly informed of our movements on our exploring trip into the virgin forests of Yezo.

In describing the garden party at Count Okuma's

residence I forgot to mention that Mr. Shugio introduced me to various notabilities, one of whom was Mr. Kitabatake, chief justice of Japan, a venerable-looking gentleman, with a long white beard, such as I never saw on any other Japanese. On hearing that I was about to leave for Yezo, this gentleman, with the spontaneous courtesy characteristic of all the Japanese I have ever met, asked me if I should like a letter of introduction from him to the Governor-General of Yezo. The offer would have been gratefully accepted, even without Mr. Shugio's explanation that it would mean much in the way of superior attention, privileges, and comforts. On the following morning a messenger brought the valuable document to my hotel. I had also the government invitation, previously referred to, which enabled me to secure a passport allowing me to roam at will all over Japan — a very unusual privilege, as ordinary passports are for routes which have to be minutely specified beforehand. A further advantage conferred by this invitation card was, that on presenting it at government railway and steamship offices I was entitled to a twenty per cent reduction in fare — quite an item in a trip as far as Yezo. At the Tōkyō station the same privilege was extended to my companion, but not in the interior, where the agents seemed to be uncertain as to what they should do in such a case.

The simplest way to go to Yezo is to take the train to the northern end of Hondo and cross over the Tsugaru Strait to Hakodate; or else to take a Yokohama steamer direct to Hakodate. But as we wanted to see the famous Pine Islands, we took the train only as far as Sendai, which we reached after a few hours' ride through rice-fields, varied by an occasional lotos pond, and mulberry

TEA PLANTATION

plantations, looking like California vineyards, as the mulberries are not allowed to grow up as trees, but only as clusters of tender young shoots and leaves, for the benefit of the silkworms. Sendai, a city of 90,000 souls, is not in any way remarkable, but to me it remains memorable because, although I had been in Japan several weeks, it was here that I spent my first night in a purely Japanese inn, destitute of beds, chairs, tables. However much one may have read about such things, the real experience always comes as a surprise. Our dinner was good enough, although the chicken was spoiled for me by being flavored with soy, the everlasting national sauce, which I found more unendurable from day to day. We had raw sliced fish, which was delicious and tender, melting in the mouth like butter. A young girl knelt opposite us and refilled our lacquer bowls with rice till we cried "enough."

Japanese inns have no separate dining rooms, every guest taking his meals in his own room. In fact, apart from the kitchen, there is no "division of labor," among the rooms of a house, be it public or private. The space assigned to us was first our parlor, then our dining room, and finally our bedroom. The absence of furniture makes these transformations easy enough. For a sitting room nothing is required but clean mats to kneel or lie on, and a picture screen or kakemono (hanging picture painted on silk) to look at. When you feel hungry you clap your hands (as they do in the old Arabian tales to call the slaves), and at once all the waiting maids within hearing answer with a long drawn hé-e-e-e (hai), while one of them comes shuffling along as nimbly as possible, gets down on all fours, and asks your honorable desires. Having received the order, she touches the mat once more with her forehead, goes out and presently returns with miniature tables and trays of food — one table and one girl to each diner. After the meal, the parlor is restored by simply removing the trays and tables. When you are ready to retire, you clap your hands again, the girl returns, brings out some wadded quilts from a closet, spreads them on the mats, rolls up another for a pillow, fastens a large green mosquito net to the corners of the room so as to completely cover the bed with a reticulated tent, and there you are, the whole performance being almost as simple as opening a folding bed.

Red Indians call us "tenderfeet," because we cannot walk barefooted or in thin moccasins. The Japanese probably feel tempted to call us "tenderbacks," in view of the fuss we are apt to make over their beds. Accustomed as we are to soft springs and mattresses, we find their mats and quilts so hard that in the morning it would be easy for us to give a lecture on the anatomy of the back, locating every bone. Sleeping in a Japanese bed is a good deal like sleeping in a tent, with a handful of hay, fern, or moss for a substratum. But the Japanese are kind-hearted and considerate. Mindful of our pampered backs, they mercifully give us two or three quilts to lie on, where one suffices for their backs, hardened from infancy. In the larger towns the innkeepers are supplied with sheets for the use of foreign guests. As for their makura, or pillows, they know that it is useless to offer them to us. They are crazy little flat wooden boxes, about the size of a cigar box set on edge, but with a "rocker" bottom and shaped on top to receive a roll of paper stuffed like a doll, for the head, or rather the neck, to rest on. They look more like the ground floor of some Oriental guillotine than like an arrangement for courting sleep. Men gave them up long ago, but women still use them, to prevent their hair from needing an elaborate dressing every day, and the pomade from soiling the quilts. Instead of makura we simply had a couple of quilts rolled up and put under the sheets. This rotund pillow had a detestable habit of getting away from the rest of the bed, in spite of the valise I had placed against it, but that did not make much difference, as I was kept awake anyway by countless black bed-fellows and by the noise and conversation in adjoining rooms, which lasted till long after midnight. I could not stop the noise, but I got up several times during the night to shut the door leading to a part of the house whence issued those foul odors which I soon found to be the greatest drawback toward the enjoyment of travel in Japan.

In the morning I found that the bill for two persons, including dinner, lodging, baths, breakfast, and kuruma to and from the hotel, was only $2.18. Seeing my look of surprise, Mr. Yabi said, "They don't charge journalists much." Here was a decidedly un-Asiatic touch, proving the "power of the press" in the very antipodes. Having settled the bill, we departed amidst a shower of *sayonara* from the host and his wife and a dozen maids, all of whom had come out to bow their farewells.

ON A COAST STEAMER

THE FAMOUS PINE ISLANDS — THE ISLAND EMPIRE — MELONS AND EELS — JAPANESE STEAMERS — HIGH FARE — MEALS IN "FOREIGN" STYLE — YANKEES OUT-YANKEED — PASSENGERS AND CARGO — A LARGE FISHING VILLAGE

If Japanese taste in scenery was reliable, we were now about to see one of the "three most beautiful views" in the country; for that is what the Matsushima Archipelago and the Pine Islands of Shiogama are reputed to be. Proceeding from Sendai to its port Shiogama, we took a small steamer which on its way to the fishing village Oginohama (where we were to wait for the Yezo-bound steamer from Yokohama) was to take us through this famous archipelago.

There are places in Japan — among which I should class Lake Biwa — that hardly deserve the fame which attaches to them for their scenic charms, but the Pine Islands are quite up to their reputation. They are all small, but unique and beautiful. The Japanese claim that there are 808 of them, and if they count every isolated rock as a separate island, we can understand how they make out that their Empire consists of 3800 islands. If we were to count every detached rock along the coast of Alaska as an island, that Territory would include, perhaps, 38,000 islands. But the size or number of these Pine Islands is a matter of small importance; it is their picturesqueness that cannot fail to fascinate even the most travelled tourist.

A few of the smallest islands are bare rocks, looking strangely like Japanese junks and other craft, but most of them wear a green vegetable dress, and, no matter how small, are surmounted by a few straggling pines (sometimes only one or two) of a peculiar species, which, at some distance, are not unlike palms, the most picturesque of all trees — unless that honor be claimed by weeping willows, which, also, are simulated on some of the islets by small pines gracefully overhanging their sides. One island is a regular cone-shaped tower, with a few pines on top, and others, seemingly horizontal, sticking out on the sides. The guide book says that, "Each of these, down to the least, has received a separate name, many of them fantastic, as 'Buddha's Entry into Nirvana,' 'Question and Answer Island,' 'The Twelve Imperial Consorts,' and so on." It adds that the islands are formed of volcanic tufa, into which the sea makes rapid inroads, especially during the violent southwest gales; but it does not mention a feature which seemed to me quite as striking and as characteristic as the pines; namely, the caves or archways which the waves have worn through many of them — in some cases perfect tunnels, through which small boats could easily pass, as the water on the other side is visible through them. One island, though only about three hundred feet long, has four of these tunnels, side by side. Floating islands some of them seem, and one can easily fancy that a strong wind would blow them away like rafts, or like the floating icebergs in Glacier Bay, Alaska. But from the islands which one sees on the way to Sitka they are quite different; for their green dress consists chiefly of young firs growing down to the very edge of the water, whereas in these Pine Islands the lower part is always a precipitous wall of yellow rock, beautifully marked and carved by the waves, and this rock is fringed with low vegetation and crowned by one or more pines.

When we arrived in the pretty little harbor of Oginohama, we were received at the wharf, a projecting pier, by a bevy of smiling and chattering tea girls, — six of them, — who bowed gracefully, seized our valises, and escorted us in style to the yadoya. I was sorry to have these girls carry my heavy bag, but in Rome we must do as the Romans do ; if I had offered to carry it myself, I should have doubtless committed a grave breach of etiquette and forfeited not only their respect, but my chances for a first-class dinner, for which I was more than ready. We were established in a room on the second story, overlooking the harbor, and while the meal was being prepared, Yabi took off the edge of his appetite with a small yellow melon, looking somewhat like a cantaloup, but with no more sweetness or flavor than a raw pumpkin. Among the courses we had for dinner, I remember, as a special delicacy, a dish of eels baked with vegetables. These eels are very small and are raised in the irrigation water of the rice fields.

Having five hours to wait for the steamer from Yokohama, we took an after-dinner stroll through the town and along the water. There was nothing particularly novel in the street scenes, but in a garden I saw a most beautiful white lily of gigantic size, with red spots like a tiger lily, and stamens adorned with anthers almost as large as almonds, neatly balanced in the middle. On the beach, near the wreck of a junk, we found some strange animals, including a species of crabs which first showed fight, and then surprised me by backing off. I had expected that Japanese crabs would, as a matter of course, move forward; but these didn't: probably they had forgotten that they were in Japan.

When our steamer arrived, we found that we had happened upon an old boat, the *Wakanoura*; still, it was comfortable enough, and as all the first-cabin berths were on the upper deck, they were free from ship odors. The captain, first officer, and engineer were Englishmen, and I noticed that not only here, but on the smaller boat that had brought us to Oginohama, on which officers and men were Japanese, orders were always given in English. The modern Japanese practice has been to engage foreigners to teach them their arts and sciences, and as soon as the lesson has been learned, to take charge of matters themselves. Ocean steamers being somewhat more difficult to manage than trains, foreign commanders and officers have been retained on them longer. When we consider that for more than two hundred years the Japanese were forbidden, under penalty of death, to construct or use any vessel larger than an ordinary junk, in order to preserve their isolation from the rest of the world, we can hardly wonder that it should take time to give them confidence as to the management of our huge modern steamers. It is, however, only a question of time for them to equal, possibly to surpass, us; for history tells us that the Japanese are born navigators, who were noted during the Middle Ages for their bold voyages, peaceful and belligerent, to distant lands, their pirates being for a long time the scourge of the extreme East. To-day the principal steamship company already owns about fifty vessels, touching at various Japanese, Corean, Chinese, Russian, and Hawaiian ports. In 1890 the number of steamers that entered Japan was 492 English, 365 Japanese, 225 German, 26 French, 20 American (U.S.), 22 Russian, 26 Norwegian, 4 Corean; while the number of sailers was, Japanese 156 (with 742 junks), British 50, American (U.S.) 33, German 11, Russian 3, Swedish 2. This list, supplied by Mr. Henson of Hakodate, shows that in the sailing vessels Japan is far ahead, and even in steamers is now distanced only by England, which she will doubtless soon overtake.

What I found most extraordinary about the steamers plying between Yokohama and Hakodate was that whereas Japanese railway travel is perhaps the cheapest in the world, the charges made by these steamers were absurdly high. It would have cost us twice as much to go from Yokohama to Sendai by water as it did by rail, whereas in all other parts of the world travel is cheaper by steamer than by railway. The only reason I could see for this is that the Japanese are bound to be contrary. In one detail, however, Yankeeism pure and simple had been introduced on our steamer. When I bought my meal tickets, the purser, who was a Japanese, asked me if I wished to take my meals in foreign or native style. As I wanted to see how the natives manage their eating on a steamer, I naturally chose the latter, — the more willingly as I was told that for the foreign meals two dollars more would be charged for the trip. Moreover, Mr. Yabi had winked at me and said it would be "half-foreign." When the bell rang I went to the dining room, expecting to find mats to squat on and to have my own table and lacquer trays and chopsticks, and a girl all to myself, kneeling opposite, ready to bow and to smile and to fill up the saké cup and rice bowl as often as emptied. But I found nothing of the sort, for there was a regular foreign table and chairs, a table cloth, porcelain plate, knives and forks, and a masculine Chinese waiter, not a bit pretty. The cook, too, was a Chinaman; but at least the food, I thought, will be Japanese. Judge for yourself. Our first course was Julienne soup, French style; the second, roast veal, German style; the third, roast duck, American style. Vegetables: boiled potatoes and green peas, foreign style. Dessert: pie (extremely un-Japanese), American cheese, and finally, plums (ripe, therefore not *à la japonaise*), and Chinese black tea. This being the "Japanese" edition of the dinner, I had considerable curiosity to know what the "foreign" version was like. On comparing notes with the other foreigners, who had paid the two dollars extra, I found that they had exactly the same things, with this difference, however, that they had paid more for them and had had to wait for the second table, when everything was cold and stale. Obviously, these Oriental Yankees are making rapid progress in Occidental civilization! How the great American Barnum would have chuckled over that sly scheme for getting extra dollars out of the foreign devils![1]

Although our purser was, as I have said, of the native persuasion, he had taken his cue from our pursers, for he wore fine clothes (foreign) and affable manners, and

---

[1] Perhaps I ought to add, that in the second cabin and the steerage a real Japanese menu was provided. Our purser, evidently out of courtesy, ate at our table once, but then he deserted us for the Japanese, which was evidently more to his liking.

took care of the ladies, making himself useful, among others, to a native woman, who took down her hair right on deck and put it up again — an elaborate and lengthy process. Another native woman was a nurse, who carried a white baby on her back, just as she would have done her own child. I noticed that when this child walked, it was somewhat bow-legged, and had the native gait, which suggested to me the idea that perhaps one reason why the Japanese turn in their toes in walking may be found in this cramped way of carrying them. It seemed very odd to hear this foreign child of about two speak Japanese to his nurse and German to his father. Most of the foreign passengers were Germans, going North to spend the summer. As for the Japanese passengers, there were not many in the cabin, and those that were, including my companion, were all seasick, although the ocean was almost as smooth as a river, thus bearing out a theory explained to me on the *City of Peking,* by Captain Cavarly, that blondes were usually better "sailors" than brunettes.

The cargo of our steamer consisted largely of numberless baskets of fish, destined for Hakodate, especially a large kind of eel, of which large numbers are caught here, and which is esteemed a great delicacy. On the return trip, these steamers take, among other things, dried salmon and fish manure. The engineer told me these trips were sometimes memorable for their odors. But, in going to Hakodate, one might as well become accustomed at once to ancient and fish-like smells, since that city, though now containing 55,000 inhabitants, remains essentially a large fishing village, its chief source of income being still salmon, herring, sea-ears, fish manure, and edible seaweeds.

JAPANESE GIBRALTAR

SIGHTS IN HAKODATE — NEW BUDDHIST TEMPLE — AN INTERVIEW — A JAPANESE INTERIOR — TOY GARDEN AND FISH POND — BARBER AND TAILOR — HOW TO PLEASE GIRLS — TAKEN TO THE BATH — COURTSHIP AND MARRIAGE — DINING AND CLIMBING — A SEA BATH — ROUND THE ISLAND — "IRISH STEWED" — OTARU PEASANTS — MARVEL OF POLITENESS — A MIXED INN

AFTER a smooth passage of about twenty-four hours, during which we passed precipitous coast scenes that reminded me of Catalina Island in California, we came in sight of Hakodate harbor, and could not help being struck, like Commodore Perry, and many others after him, by its resemblance to Gibraltar. These supposed resemblances often remind one of Hamlet's weasel-and-camel cloud, but in this case the imagination has a real basis of comparison. Although the Japanese "Rock," rising behind the city, is greener than the English, and not quite so high, nor bristling with guns, the general impression given by Hakodate, nestling at the base of this mountain, and built upon its slope, with a flat peninsula (the "neutral ground" of Gibraltar) connecting it with the rest of the island, is strikingly similar to that of the English fortress in Spain; and, what is more, owing to its favorable and commanding position on the narrow strait which separates Yezo from the Japanese mainland, it might be made to assume a military function and importance similar to that at Gibraltar. Another British suggestion was the presence in the harbor of the English fleet, which, as one of our officers informed me, spends the winter at Hong Kong and the early summer at Yokohama, following this up with a visit to Hakodate in search of a cool climate. And why should it not, since the summer heat at Hong Kong is dangerous to foreigners? The officer added that wherever the English fleet arrives, beer shops spring up at every corner as by magic — an observation which I was able to verify at Hakodate.

Leaving our bags in charge of a hotel runner, we walked up to our inn, engaged a room, and then sallied forth to see the town. In Tōkyō we could hardly have done such a thing in these last days of July, owing to the heat and the great distances; but here the sun's rays were tempered by a cool breeze, and it was a pleasure to walk. Kurumas are not so fashionable here as in Southern Japan, and, after all, walking is preferable for sight seeing. We were not surprised to find that every other house was a storage place for fish, dried, smoked, canned, or fresh; but it was odd to see dried fish stuck on poles, invading even the streets. Of course only a small proportion of these fish and other marine products are for the local market; the forty million Japanese of Hondo get a good many of them, and shiploads are also sent to China, where there are ten times forty million hungry mouths to feed.

In the upper part of the city we stopped half an hour to watch some native architects at work on a large new Buddhist temple. Though it was almost finished, the scaffolding still remained, and was gaily adorned with colored flags and bunting. Worshippers were already kneeling inside before the unfinished altar. The steps leading up to the temple were encumbered by a number of old women selling sweetmeats and unripe fruit. The fact that new temples are being built, shows that Buddhism has not yet lost its hold on the Japanese, although the government favors Shintoism, and no longer persecutes the Christians.

Returning to the hotel, we found a reporter of a local Japanese newspaper awaiting us. He had read about our projected trip into the interior in the columns of the *Mainichi Shimbun*, and came to get the bill of particulars, which we gave him as far as it had been made out. In the morning the interview duly appeared in Japanese type, which Mr. Yabi translated for me; it had the effect of bringing another reporter after us the next day. While Mr. Yabi sat down to write a letter for the *Mainichi*, I explored the inn, which was entirely Japanese, although I had been asked whether I wanted foreign chairs and a table. I accepted them at first, but when they were brought into the room, the stiff, angular, painted, vulgar things presented such a painful contrast to the neat, tasteful, Japanese surroundings, that I sent them away in disgrace, and lay down on the soft, clean mats, after kicking off the slippers which I had brought up from the entrance, where there are always several pairs for the convenience of guests who do not wish to walk about in their stockings, although there is, in warm weather, no reason why they should not do that, as there are clean, soft mats to step on in all the rooms and passages. There was now no furniture in our room except a folding screen and the dwarf table on which my companion was writing his strange hieroglyphics, on a long-drawn-out roll of paper. The sides of the room were not disfigured by wall paper, paint, or whitewash, but one of them was adorned with an oblong kakemono, on which were painted long-necked cranes, in those graceful, natural attitudes of flight and rest of which Japanese artists alone have copied the secret from nature. It was not a valuable picture, but it is a peculiarity of Japanese art that it manifests almost as much taste in cheap articles for every-day use as in expensive works of genius.

Our room was on the ground floor and opened directly on a sort of Spanish patio, or small interior court, with a miniature rock-girded pond in the centre. It was inhabited by goldfish, carp, eels, a turtle and a frog; and with a gentle exercise of the imagination, such as one needs in a theatre, one could easily fancy himself gazing at a real lake and landscape, as the Japanese love to do in their toy gardens. I had some curiosity to see how Japanese fish would while away their time, and I found them in a particularly frolicsome mood, playing regular games, as it seemed. I remember in particular a large carp lying perfectly still, but wiggling its tail very rapidly. Presently a small goldfish came alongside, playfully biting the big fish in several places, whereupon the carp suddenly swam away, but soon stopped and again wagged its tail persuasively, seemingly anxious to be tickled again. This performance was repeated over and over again.

After I had seen enough of this, my attention was attracted by a characteristic scene in the room opposite ours. A man walked in, sat down, and produced a razor and other shaving material. In the public barber shops I had seen, the victim was sitting in a chair and the shaver standing by his side, trouserless. But here the victim remained squatting on his hind legs, and the barber managed to polish him off without the use of soap. The scene was hardly as amusing as that in Rossini's *Barber of Seville*, but it had its novel points, and again brought to my attention that in Japan the prophet does not go to the mountain, but makes the mountain come to him. In Tōkyō I had seen clerks carrying whole mountains of assorted goods to the houses of customers, whereas in America the goods are not sent until selected and paid for. Mr. Yabi gave me to understand that it was not good form to go out shopping, and that the proper thing was to have the shop come to you. When I asked him if that would not cost more, he replied, "No; rather less." Now I wanted a kimono, as I was beginning to envy my friend his convenient Japanese gown, which he usually put on after we had reached our room; it seemed as comfortable as pajamas and more easily put on — simply throwing it over the head and dropping trousers and coat. A word to the landlord, and in half an hour a tailor came along with a bundle of samples, which he opened for my selection after he had bounced his head against the floor a few times. The selection was soon made, and the price did not seem prohibitive, — $1.25 for the whole garment, — but presently the tailor began to look perplexed and to size me up, as if I was a Goliath. He said that he had never seen such a big man (I measure five feet ten and a-half), and that the width of Japanese goods was such that he was afraid he would not be able to make the gown large enough. Whereupon he proceeded (not with a tape measure, but with a stick) to ascertain my gigantic dimensions — a process which gave him and our waiter girls no end of amusement, in which I tried my best to join. Finally the tailor said that he could make it *almost* big enough, but it would cost fifteen cents extra. The garment was duly sent on the following day, and when it arrived, Mr. Yabi remarked, " If you wear our costume, Japanese girls will like you." So there was an extra inducement for wearing it, even if it was somewhat short in the sleeves, which was my fault, not the tailor's.

Shortly after my measure had been taken, one of our waiting maidens, a comely lass of about seventeen, returned to inform us that the bath was ready. Mr. Yabi told me to go ahead with her, and I followed meekly as a lamb, ready to be told just what to do, and determined not to flinch at any ordeal. The bathroom was divided into two sections, an inner one, where the bath tub was, and an outer one for undressing, both of them exposed to view from the corridors. Having arrived at the dressing room, I supposed that she would leave me to my fate, but she knew her duties better. She gave me to understand that she would take my coat, so I took it off and gave it to her, expecting her to retreat. But she waited for more, and more I gave her, till there was absolutely no more to give, whereupon she quietly deposited her plunder on a box in the corner, and opened the door to the inner room. The floor of this was very slippery, and I fell flat on it. In a moment she came to my assistance with some pitying exclamations. I was, however, not seriously damaged. She now left me and sent in a young man, who soaped me all over, poured hot water over me, and then took me to the large bath tub, the contents of which had evidently not yet been used. But I was forewarned, and, therefore, forearmed; that is, I put my forearm in and found that the water was about ten or twenty degrees too hot for a foreigner. A few buckets of cold water remedied the evil, and after a few minutes' immersion, I gave myself up again to the young man to be towelled and dried. When it was all over, he hinted gently that a fee would be acceptable. I gave him ten cents, and was then allowed to dress and return to my room, enriched by one more Oriental experience.

The next day I heard about a fussy English officer who stirred up quite a commotion in this inn, by being unable, in his Occidental perverseness, to see why the bathroom should be the only one in the house which had no screen, or curtain, and by angrily sending for one, and refusing any assistance.

Shortly after supper Mr. Yabi clapped his hands. Our girl responded promptly with a long-drawn-out "Ha-e-e-e-e," and when she came, he told her to make up the beds. Although this girl was always smiling, and seemed as merry as most tea-house attendants are expected to be, she was somewhat dissatisfied with her lot. She had been brought up here from Southern Japan, and was longing to go back. When I asked her if she would like to go to America, she said yes, she would like that better still. Then she wanted to know something about American girls. Happening to have the photograph of an American beauty in my valise, I showed it to her. She liked it, and seemed particularly struck by the way the hair was done up, which she admired, although she said she was afraid it would not become herself. As a matter of fact it would have greatly improved her appearance, since, like all Japanese girls, she wore her hair combed back from her forehead — a coiffure which is becoming to very few women.

After she had left, two men came in to put up the green mosquito net, which, covering almost the whole room, would have been too heavy for the girls to handle. It formed a canopy over our two beds, which were separated only two or three feet from each other — convenient for chatting. I told Yabi that I had sometimes thought that the Japanese might be descendants of the Spaniards, or *their* partial ancestors, the Moors and Arabs. Why? Because I had already noticed several points of resemblance. I had seen women in Tōkyō, dressed in European clothes, with a rose in their foreign coiffure, and with sparkling black eyes, that made them look very much like Spanish women. I had noticed, too, that in the streets of Tōkyō, as on the alameda of Madrid, the men and the women walked in separate groups, and here, in this Hakodate hotel, was a sort of patio, which reminded me of Seville. Mr. Yabi replied that the Japanese were doubtless a mixed race, and it was difficult to tell what the ancestral ingredients were. He believed that the separation of the sexes on the streets could be traced back to the laws of the Chinese Confucius, which had been so largely adopted in Japan, and that these extended to the home too; for whereas a married woman might go about freely (especially if accompanied by a servant), it was not proper for her to receive a man at home in the absence of her husband. As for unmarried girls in the upper classes, they were closely watched, and there was no such thing for them as a "harmless flirtation." They might go to picnics and receptions, or perhaps even to the theatre, but only with their parents, and never with a young man alone.

Courtship is not carried on by the young folks themselves, but the engagement is brought about in a business-like way by the aid of a nakodo, or middleman. He admitted that, with all these restrictions and precautions, married women were sometimes faithless, and girls went astray, but not more frequently, in his opinion, than in other countries, and he scouted the notion, current among the merchants of the treaty ports, that virtue is rare in Japan — a notion which simply showed that their experience was limited to one class of women.

No doubt he was right in his remarks on Japan, but evidently he had not deeply studied the subject of love and courtship while in America, for he asked me if it was customary there for an engaged couple to go to housekeeping at once. He said, also, that in Japan there are practically no bachelors and old maids, it being cheaper for men to marry a housewife than to remain single, and in every way pleasanter, as there are no bachelor quarters or even boarding houses. Japanese girls are less pretentious than Americans, and more willing to work; hence all get married between fourteen and twenty, the men between eighteen and twenty-five. Some have a wife and one or more concubines; others hire a girl at five dollars to do all their work and bidding; in which practice many foreigners follow their example. I finally asked him which city of his country was reputed to have the most beautiful women. He said Kyōto; and since Kyōto was on our schedule, I composed myself for slumber, prepared to dream of the belles of Kyōto.

I forgot to mention our dinner, which had consisted entirely of fish and eggs — omelette in the soup and omelette on a plate. Again I relished the raw fish, but by far the best thing we had was an immense eel — one of those our steamer had brought up from Oginohama. It was cooked whole and served in a peculiarly shaped two-story lacquered box. We ate what we could of it, and Mr. Yabi gave directions to have the rest saved for next day's lunch, as it was an extra, not included in the regular fare. The host had come to ask if I knew how to use chopsticks or wanted knife and fork. Afterwards he sent in some "French butter," in an unopened can: I returned it unopened. One of our breakfast dishes was a soup with shreds of seaweed floating in the bowl. The soup was good, but the seaweed was too fishy and tannic to suit my taste. I asked Yabi, if it wasn't of the kind that the poor lived on, but he said no, it was a more expensive kind, and was considered quite a delicacy. It must be an acquired taste.

Having been informed that there was a fine view from Hakodate Head, the peak at the base of which the city lies, we decided to devote the forenoon to climbing it. On the way we ran across an acquaintance of Mr. Yabi, a young merchant who spoke a very little English. We invited him to join us, but he did not appear anxious to exert himself, alleging as an excuse that he had on his native clothes, which would put him at a disadvantage compared with us, with our foreign trousers. He was right; comfortable as is the kimono in the house, it is on the street, and especially in climbing, as great an impediment to a man as her skirts are to a woman. In course of our conversation the young merchant made a funny but perfectly natural mistake. We had exchanged cards, and in addressing me he repeatedly called me Mr. Henry. Evidently he had not yet got to the page in his grammar where he would have found out that we topsy-turvy Americans say and write "Mr. John Brown" instead of "Brown John Mr." as we ought to, and would if our minds were logically constructed.

A pleasant road led us through shady trees up to the peak, which is 1157 feet above the sea, and commands an extensive view, embracing volcanoes, rivers, seacoast villages, and a picturesque lighthouse. The climb reminded me somewhat of a similar ascent of a peak near Malaga, but I missed the intense blue of the Mediterranean. The foreign men-of-war lay like toy steamers below us, but part of the harbor was hidden by a cloud beneath us. The city itself presented a most extraordinary aspect. The low houses, almost all of the same level, looked as if some giant had sat down on them, crushing them flat as boards; and the prevailing hue was as gray as if one of the neighboring volcanoes had strewed a thick layer of ashes and stones over them. Only here and there was the gray monotonous level interrupted by a temple, in one place by a large tank, calling attention to the fact that Hakodate is ahead of most Japanese cities in having an excellent system of waterworks. These were constructed in 1889, and made it possible for the inhabitants to close up their dangerous wells and get their water fresh and pure from a mountain stream seven miles away. The backwardness of Japan in sanitary matters may be inferred from this, that, recent as these waterworks are, Hakodate was preceded by only one Japanese city in adopting this reform.

The afternoon was warm enough to suggest the idea that a bath in Japanese salt water would be a pleasant novelty. So we went to the beach, and found a booth, where we succeeded in getting two towels from an old woman. Bathing suits appeared to be an unknown luxury, nor did they seem necessary in this climate, so I concluded to follow the example of some youngsters who were tumbling about in the waves, and two naked men riding in their horses for a swim. As my companion did not seem to care for a sea bath, I set him to guard my watch and my clothes, and then made for the water, which I found of a most agreeable temperature. The spectacle of a naked foreigner in the breakers attracted a number of boys and girls, who probably marvelled at my white skin (the only thing in a blond which the Japanese admire), and afterwards seemed greatly interested in watching the process of getting into a suit of foreign clothes. Among the spectators was a young woman who had a novel way of holding a baby on her back. Instead of fastening it on the outside of her dress, she had it under her dress, right on her skin, with only its head peeping out — an arrangement which must be pleasanter for the baby in winter than in summer.

This sea bath, combined with the climb up the peak and a bottle of hot saké for a nightcap, gave me a deep and refreshing night's sleep, such as I had not enjoyed since reaching Japan. It began at nine, so that I was not disgusted to be aroused at five by the usual morning racket. Our plan was to leave Hakodate before noon, by one of the steamers which every four days round the island to the left up to Otaru, which is second in size among the seaports of Yezo, and situated only a short distance from Sapporo, the Americanized capital of the island. When mine host presented the bill, on his knees, I thought at first that the only way to square matters was to exchange my letter of credit for it. The bill was as long as Leporello's list of Don Juan's love affairs, every item, including each separate bottle of beer and saké, being marked in admirable Japanese caligraphy. It was really a work of art, and it has since formed one of the choicest ornaments in my bedroom at home. That large eel, I found, cost $1 alone, and the whole bill, two persons for two days, was $8. This can hardly be called excessive, still it seemed to indicate that journalists receive less discount in Hakodate than at Sendai.

The steamer *Takasago* was not so large as the *Wakanura* which had brought us up the coast of Hondo, but it had comfortable cabins. The fare again included Japanese meals, with $2 extra for "foreign style." At dinner I was rather appalled to see "Irish stewed" on the bill of fare, but was relieved to find that it was only Irish stew. For breakfast we had about the same menu as for dinner — coffee, oatmeal and milk, beefsteak, eggs, curry and rice, and "Irish stewed" again, besides American cheese, prunes, and — peanuts! But I must add, in justice, that no one ate these at breakfast. There were ten Japanese at our table, but none of them spoke a word, although they are always talkative and noisy enough when dining in their own rooms.

In the morning we were far up the western side of the island, on the Sea of Japan, of which few visitors to that country get a glimpse, as most of the cities and places of interest lie on the east coast. Numerous fishing boats, each with one or two sails, indicated that we were nearing Otaru, on the north coast of Yezo. We soon reached it, and sending our baggage ahead to the inn, we disembarked for a walk to see the town and its surroundings. It is a dismal place, where life must be monotonous enough for a hermit. The great business of the people is catching herring, and most of the houses are low, decaying fishermen's huts. Far out on a pier a large vessel was loading coal which had been brought by rail from the Poronai mines in the interior, whither we were bound. Our train was not to start for several hours, and as the town itself seemed a pleasant place to get away from, we started up the hill for the woods and suburban gardens. Many peasants passed us with their burdens; most of them were women, with extraordinarily muscular legs, bare to the knee. Others had their limbs swathed in clinging cloth, and with their enormous umbrella hats — like those of the Moorish women of Tetuan — they seemed to belong to a different race from the delicate tea-house girls. The patois of these peasants was so peculiar that Mr. Yabi could not understand their conversation, although he had no difficulty with the townspeople. The Japanese language seems difficult enough without such differences of dialect; still, in this respect China is much worse, for there the coolies from different provinces are obliged to use "Pidjin English" if they wish to converse with one another.

Many of these Otaru peasants were carrying baskets of vegetables, chiefly new potatoes of a lovely, clean, pink color. Yezo potatoes are very good, and the people know how to cook them without making them soggy; at least that was my experience. We soon struck a small village, situated near a brook, which drained the fields sloping from it — fields manured with sewage from the town; yet here the women came with their buckets to get water for cooking and drinking. Turning aside toward the seashore, we came to a place, just outside the city, where a number of men were digging away the hillside, to make room for more houses, in a cool situation, convenient for the fishermen. As we were about to leave for the interior, not to see the ocean again for a week or two, I suggested that another sea bath would be a pleasant diversion, and this time my companion joined me. There was no sandy beach, the shore being disagreeably rocky, but we managed to find a place to undress, and then swam out into the bay. Through the transparent water we had glimpses of various kinds of seaweeds, growing luxuriantly in their marine garden, and swayed by the slow waves as by a gentle breeze. In the shallow places we picked up a number of beautiful blue and pink seastars, apparently the same kinds that adorn the ocean shallows of Oregon. When we were out pretty far, I noticed that some of the workmen approached our clothes; I expressed a fear that they might steal my watch or purse; but Mr. Yabi said there was no danger. When we returned, what do you think we found that these laborers had done? They had spread two clean, new mats over the sharp rocks, so that we might have a place to dress comfortably! In what other country would such an act of gratuitous courtesy enter the minds of common workmen? They looked pleased to see us use them, and I thought that perhaps they expected a fee, but Mr. Yabi said no, they did it to please us, and would be offended at an offer of money. I was now convinced that the courtesy of the Japanese is not a mere surface polish, like that of Occidentals, rubbed off as easily as shoe blacking, but genuine and durable as the lustre of their lacquer.

Our inn proved to be one of those hybrid mixtures of tea house and foreign hotel which are among the curiosities of modern Japan. If you wish to be entertained in Japanese style, you remain on the ground floor, take off your shoes on the verandah, and at once enter your own matted room, with screens and sliding doors. If you choose foreign style, you go upstairs into a general carpeted sitting room, which you can enter with boots on. Nay, more, even in this room you can still have your choice, for on one side there is a slightly elevated platform covered with mats on which those who choose to take off their footgear can squat or recline, while for others there are chairs on the carpeted part of the room. We partook of a simple lunch, and in the meantime the attendants bought our tickets and checked our baggage, as is the custom of Japanese inns, where all such errands are attended to without extra charge. A party of Americans, including a funny man, took lunch with us. One of the ladies was very anxious to ascend one of the Yezo volcanoes, and wondered whether any of them smoked. "If they are Japanese," replied the funny man, "you will find them smoking, as a matter of course."

AMERICAN SAPPORO

NATIVES IN THE OCEAN — CAPITAL OF YEZO — RUSSIAN DESIGNS — AMERICAN FARMS AND FACTORIES — EXPENSIVE EXPERIMENTS — CITY AND SUBURBS — CALLING ON THE GOVERNOR-GENERAL — A EURASIAN HOUSE — BEER AND FRUIT — THE SUPERINTENDENT'S KINDNESS — A UNIQUE MUSEUM — A DAIRY — SEEING THE FACTORIES — TEA-HOUSE GIRLS — LAMPS AND WASHSTANDS — AMERICAN AND ASIATIC CORRESPONDENCE — A COMIC RESEMBLANCE

THE twenty-two mile railroad from Otaru to Sapporo is remarkable for being, according to report, the cheapest ever built anywhere. It may also claim the distinction of being one of the slowest and most uncomfortable. We were foolish enough to buy first-class tickets, only to find that, except in being more roomy, the first-class car was less comfortable than the second-class, as its hard seats were arranged along the sides, while in the second-class you could at least sit and look forward. In itself the trip proved extremely interesting, full of novel sights. For half an hour or so the road is obliged, by overhanging rocks, to follow along the semicircular coast so close to the sea that there is hardly room for the numerous fishermen's huts between the rails and the waves. Wretched huts they are, with roofs made up of what looked like corn husks, and sides consisting of rude mats hanging down from the eaves.

affording about as much shelter as a bird's nest under a tuft of grass. Evidently the whole population lives on fishing and seaweeding. Several kinds of kelp and other seaweeds were spread out on the rocks everywhere to dry, like hay, scenting the air with a marine odor which I found rather more agreeable when thus mingled with the sea breezes than when emanating from a steaming soup bowl.

The ocean itself presented an animated scene. The whole population appeared to be amphibious, the shallows being full of boys and girls, who seemed to think that in such warm water no clothing was needed, not even swimming tights. Here was a boat full of naked boys, standing up and fishing; there, a group of women, wading in the water, holding each a bucket, into which she gathered some marine product or other. It was a unique panorama of oceanic village life.

At last, the train left the ocean, and made for the interior, through swamps covered with a dense, luxuriant vegetation, including a few flowers and plenty of lovely red berries. Near Sapporo we noticed some highly cultivated fields, and a military station was pointed out to us. We were now entering a town — the capital of Yezo — unique among Japanese cities for its origin. Hakodate and Otaru grew up into cities, because they had good harbors and formed convenient centres for the fishing trade, whereas Sapporo was created a city by order of the Imperial Government at Tōkyō. For this there were several reasons. Yezo is, at present, the northernmost of the large Japanese islands; but it was not always so. Up to 1875 the island of Saghalin also belonged to Japan; but in that year the big boy Russia bullied the little boy Japan into exchanging that island (which is valuable for its furs and fisheries) for the barren and useless Kurile Islands, so-called by the Russians because they could see the *kuril* (smoke) of their volcanoes from the Siberian Kamschatka. To prevent Yezo from being similarly gobbled up by the voracious Russian ogre (he made a serious mien to do so), the Japanese government decided that it would be advisable to colonize Yezo and multiply its scant population (then only six and a half persons to the square mile) as a bulwark against further Muscovite aggressions. Such colonization would, at the same time, serve as a convenient way of relieving Hondo of part of its surplus population.

But as the climate of Yezo, with its seven months of Siberian cold and its six feet of snow, did not tempt any considerable number of the Japanese to pull up their stakes and build again so far away from their old homes, the government offered inducements to samurai and others, in the shape of free homes and grants of land, and at the same time undertook to give them employment by establishing a number of agricultural and industrial enterprises, with Sapporo as a centre. Sapporo itself was laid out in the rectangular American fashion; and America also was the model for the various gigantic enterprises referred to, including grain fields, experimental farms for various vegetables, trees, flowers, and fruits, horse and cattle breeding farms, vineyards, mulberry and hop plantations, sawmills, a brewery, and so forth. An American, General Capron, was placed at the head of this department, called the *Kaitakushi*. It is said that $50,000,000 were thus expended in experiments, many of which proved failures. But Sapporo, at any rate, benefited by them.

and has become a unique city, in which, although only a few Americans reside there, the practical American spirit prevails to a striking degree, modifying the details of life more than in any other Japanese city. Hence the seemingly paradoxical heading which I have ventured to give to this chapter.

Conspicuous among the American buildings in Sapporo is the hotel, built originally for occupancy by the Mikado, when he was expected to visit the most northern of his cities. We were told that it was well managed, in the style of the foreign hotels at Yokohama, but as a matter of course we went to one of the Japanese inns, as did the other foreigners on our train; either because they knew it would be cheaper, or because, like ourselves, they wanted to see all they could of Japanese life. Shortly after our arrival, I sent my letter of introduction to the Governor-General, who sent back word by one of his attendants that he would be pleased to have me call the next day before eight in the morning or after three in the afternoon. It did not take me long, as the "gentle reader" may possibly guess, to make my choice, even though it would have been more novel and Japanesy to call on one of the highest officials in the Empire at seven in the morning.

An exploring expedition revealed the fact that Sapporo is indeed a curious mixture of America and Japan: America predominating in the surroundings, Japan in the city itself. The streets are laid out as regularly as an American chessboard, but the shops and the shoppers are Japanese, in many cases very much so. Certainly there was nothing American in the women who helped the men with scythes in cutting the barley in the suburban fields, nor in the girls of thirteen or fourteen who were cleaning the streets and roads with hoes, nor in the women with bared bosoms leading their perfectly naked children across the bridge or down the streets, nor in the blind shampooers with their everlasting whistles, nor in the low wooden houses and open shop fronts; but there were American fruits and vegetables in the provision stores, and foreign canned goods, and rows of beer and wine bottles, with many other evidences of our civilization. Then there were sights more difficult to classify, like the itinerant seller of sweetmeats, blowing a melancholy tune on what looked like a trumpet, and sounded a good deal like a Scotch bagpipe. Spain was again suggested by the numerous packhorses, with a basket on each side laden with vegetables; but the peasant women who perched on these ponies, sitting astride like men, appeared too Oriental even for Spain.

Leaving the city for the suburban fields and gardens, we came across some American cows seeking shelter from Japanese flies in a dense shady grove, Chinese pigs wallowing in Japanese mud; German geese happily navigating a Japanese pond. We passed along fields of American corn, acres of barley just ripening (two months later than in Tōkyō, so Mr. Yabi said), gardens with beans, carrots, and cabbages, and a vineyard, all of them in excellent condition, eloquent of the fertile, swampy soil of this region. Proceeding toward Kariki, about two miles distant, we were rewarded by a splendid view of dark and densely wooded mountains — a Japanese Black Forest suggesting the environs of Baden-Baden. We took a swim in the current of the Ebets River, which gave me occasion to note how the Japanese footgear hardens the feet. The river bed is covered with rocks and sharp rough pebbles which made wading disagreeable for me; but my friend, and some other Japanese who were in for a bath, walked over this stony bottom as if it had been a smooth marble floor. It is odd, also, to see how the foot of a Japanese, even when he wears foreign socks, looks as if it consisted simply of two big toes — the effect of constantly grasping and holding the clogs with their foot mittens; an art quite as difficult as eating with chopsticks, as I found on trial. I could not hold the getas, and the low slippers supplied in the hotels were almost equally difficult to keep on. What tourists should do, is to take along their own slippers.

Shortly after three o'clock on the following day we made our call on Nagayama, Governor-General of Yezo. His house, so far as we could see from the front, was entirely foreign in structure, and after passing through a foreign door we sent in our cards and were ushered into a parlor, with a carpet, comfortable chairs, a large table in the centre, and even American pictures on the walls. A moment later the Governor-General entered and welcomed us cordially to the Hokkaido. There was the usual exchange of international compliments, his Excellency remarking that all the improvements made in Yezo were due to Americans and American influence, upon which I replied, as usual, that America, too, had already learned much from the Japanese; and that if we could only import their universal courtesy, kindness to men and animals, passion for nature, taste in art, avoidance of vulgar display of wealth, and ability to enjoy life on a mere pittance, we should have received elements of civilization which would benefit us more than our factories, agricultural implements, fruits, vegetables, and clothes could ever benefit them. He offered to do everything in his power to make our stay in Sapporo and our trip into the interior as pleasant as possible, and promised to put us in charge, next day, of Mr. Hashiguchi, superintendent of the Agricultural College of Sapporo, who would show us all the important sights.

Although the Governor-General did not speak any European language, he wore European clothes, and shook hands with us in the European fashion. While we were conversing, he rang a bell, and gave an order to a servant, who presently returned with several bottles of beer and wine, which his Excellency said he wished us to taste, as they were all of them products of Yezo. The wine, he said, came from the vineyards I had seen, and the beer from the large German brewery in Sapporo. I gave my opinion that this beer was the best made in Japan, as indeed it was by far, being, indeed, equal to any American beer, and much superior to that made at Yokohama and Tōkyō. When we arose to go, the Governor-General accompanied us to show us his garden and orchard, where we found apple, nectarine, and peach trees, laden with choice, healthy fruit. Finally he took us behind the house, and enjoyed my surprise on finding myself suddenly in Japan again; for the back side of the house was Japanese in every detail. "I might have expected," I said, "that your house, like everything in Sapporo, would be half American and half Japanese." He smiled, and said, "If I had received you on this side of the house, you would have sat on a mat, drinking tea, instead of on a chair, drinking beer." He then asked us to call on him again in the morning, at his office in the City Hall; and we took our leave, with very pleasant impressions of this official, who is one of the handsomest, manliest Japanese I have seen — a man in whose bearing military dignity is very agreeably tempered by Oriental courtesy and affability.

We had hardly got up, the next morning, when a servant brought us a large basket of apples, with the Governor-General's compliments. We made a hole in it at once, and found them equal to the best Oregon apples, entirely free from blemish, and far superior to such fruit as Hondo produces. The trouble with most Japanese fruit is that it ripens in the rainy summer months, and gets wormy before it is — according to our notions — quite fit to eat, which seems to be one reason why the Japanese eat most of their fruit unripe. "We try to get ahead of the worms," as Mr. Yabi put it. But these Sapporo apples were not only sound, but unlike most foreign fruits and vegetables in Japan, had preserved their flavor.

At nine o'clock we found our way to the City Hall, — a fine large building, with a cupola, — just in time to see the Governor-General ride up on a spirited horse. He looked very handsome on his horse, and gave us a military salute in passing. We followed him up to his private room, where he introduced us to Superintendent Hashiguchi, who devoted the whole day to showing us the sights of Sapporo. I found him to be a travelled Japanese gentleman of the finest type, as intelligent as he was courteous, and speaking not only English, but French and German, — these accomplishments being, as he explained, absolutely needed in a man in his position in so cosmopolitan a place as Sapporo.

A carriage was waiting for us when we came down.

and we drove first to the Museum. It was not open on that day, but the keeper had been specially sent for, and the alcoholic atmosphere was soon dispelled by opening the windows. We saw here a fine collection of Yezo animals — fishes (including a swordfish which had sunk a junk), butterflies, bears, wolves, etc., besides minerals (fine sulphur specimens), and a valuable collection of Aino antiquities upstairs. What perhaps most attracted the attention was the enormous stuffed bears. I had seen one of these animals at the Ueno Museum in Tōkyō, which, without the slightest exaggeration, had a body as large as an ox, and I had supposed it to be an exceptional beast; but here was another just like it. Surely Russian Siberia cannot produce larger bears than Japanese Siberia. One of the bears in this museum had killed ten horses before he could be killed. He was ambushed by soldiers, who climbed on trees, and waited for a chance to shoot. The largest of the bears had been killed near the city, after gobbling up a child. The post-mortem showed that he must have been very hungry. The contents of his stomach are shown in a large glass jar. It is a ghastly sight. The bear had not taken time to munch the child's limbs, for the hands and feet, with their little fingers and toes, are preserved intact in alcohol. When the other bear, which had killed the ten horses, was dissected, it was found that he had been through more than one war, for the soldiers found in his flesh several old bullets and the point of an Aino arrow.

From the Museum we drove to the Agricultural College, where there was a fine assortment of ploughs, reapers, and other American field implements. There was also a large barn filled with fragrant hay, wild as well as cultivated. Yezo, with its thin population, has what Hondo lacks,— fine pasturage with excellent grasses, some local, others imported. Proof of this was afforded by the fifty cows belonging to the College: they looked sleek and happy, but were kept busy, as to their tails, by the troublesome flies. We were taken to the dairy cellar, where we had a few glasses of creamy milk, which is kept cool by a stream of ice-cold water, and which was all the more delicious as I had not tasted any since leaving San Francisco; for milk, cheese, and butter are things with which the Japanese have only recently become acquainted. Mr. Yabi said that to him milk was an acquired taste, and that few Japanese liked it at first. The man who handed us the glasses spoke English — indeed, I was surprised to find how many of the young men about the College and the factories spoke English, or some other European language, fluently. The superintendent kindly offered to send us a can of fresh butter in the morning, to take along on our trip into the interior — a most welcome gift.

In the afternoon Mr. Hashiguchi again called for us with his carriage to show us some of the "American" factories. We passed along peat fields with soil eighteen inches deep, and potato fields where this tuber was growing in rank luxuriance. We visited the large flax factory, the manager of which spoke French and explained to us the whole process of manufacture. In the beet-sugar factory, which we inspected next, the manager explained matters in German. Japan is usually considered a land of small things, but these factories were certainly as big in their way as the Yezo bears we had just seen. There are other big things in Japan, such as Mount Fuji, that would be a lion even in Switzerland; man-eating crabs measuring fourteen feet from claw to claw; the Kamakura Buddha, fifty feet high; pictures by Hokusai, thirty-six yards square; paper lanterns twenty feet high. There is also a legend that at one time rice grew as high as a tree and produced grains as big as an egg; and another legend of a devil eight feet high, strong as a hundred men, with a face black as lacquer, — all of which shows that the Japanese do appreciate big things on occasion. Nevertheless, these are only the exceptions which prove Japan to be the land of miniatures: a land where men average about the same in height as our women, and the women only four feet five inches; where houses are usually only one story high and large enough for one family; where chickens and their eggs are as small as our pigeons and pigeon eggs; where wine and tea cups and tobacco pipes seem to have been made for dolls; where carriages are kurumas, and horses men; where life in general is seen as through an inverted opera glass.

Once more we met Mr. Hashiguchi, in the evening, at the foreign hotel, where he had invited us to dine with him. He asked many questions about American methods of colonizing and booming, and about our abandoned farms, giving us much valuable information in turn. The dinner was so good that I almost regretted not having put up at this hotel. However, I had some novel experiences at the native inn we had stopped at. As usual, I had been asked there whether I would have a chair and a table, and whether I could use chopsticks. I flattered myself that I had made considerable progress in that art since that first dinner in Tōkyō, and was, therefore, quite disgusted when the black-eyed musumé kneeling opposite made the same

M

remark I had heard on that occasion, — that I plied my chopsticks "just like a baby." And I had been so anxious to make a good impression on her, for she was very pretty. However, I had, ere that, discovered a secret which I am willing to impart to the reader. If you wish to amuse and please a tea girl, do not sit and stare at her mutely, but if you don't know her language talk English at her as fast as you can. That will cause no end of merriment with peals of laughter, especially if you speak with dramatic sincerity and gestures, as if you expected her to understand you.

When I asked for my bath in the morning, the girl guided me to the room and left. Just as I was ready to get into the tub, she came back to ask if the water was not too hot for me. I put in my hand, and discovered that it was, — very much so, — so she ran away and sent a man who poured in a few buckets of cold water. But a glance at the bath showed me that I could not use it at all. It had evidently, *more Japanico*, done service for a number of bathers on the previous evening, and had not been renewed. I made the man dash a few buckets of cold water over me, and after donning my kimono, went back to my room, where Mr. Yabi explained the condition of the bath by saying that it was not customary at Japanese inns to bathe in the morning. Thereafter I took care to do as the Romans do, late in the afternoon.

As was to be expected, the sleeping arrangements were not much better than the bath. At Sendai I had two sheets, at Hakodate one, at Sapporo none, and I began to wonder what would happen next. It was not pleasant to lie thus between two quilts that had no washable covers, and had been used by Tom, Dick, and

Harry, but there was no help for it. These quilts, moreover, were stiffer and heavier than horse blankets, and altogether too warm for summer nights. In our beds we can use a sheet alone for a cover, or with one blanket, or with more, but in Japan it is either smother or freeze. Another absurd bedroom arrangement is the night light; formerly a candle or a wick in oil, now a petroleum light on a pedestal, looking like a metronome. These lamps are left burning all night, turned down low enough to make a stench, and give one a headache next morning. Mr. Yabi could give me no explanation of this custom, and, as a matter of course, after one or two experiences, I always put out the light after retiring. These lamps are not only very injurious to the health of the natives, but in case of earthquakes they are upturned, and cause many of the disastrous and fatal fires which always accompany those catastrophes.

For our toilet we usually had the water brought into our room, but Japanese inns are supplied with washstands and copper basins. You must, however, furnish your own towel, unless you are satisfied with one of the small and always damp washrags that are usually supplied. Of their teeth the Japanese appear to take good care, as they never neglect to clean them with small brushes with few bristles, but handles a foot in length, six of which, I was told, cost about a cent. Why the handles should be so long I do not know, unless it is to enable them to brush the throat too. At any rate, there is an amount of hemming and retching as if they were crossing the English Channel. Some brush their teeth dry, others use salt, which is provided in a saucer.

At this inn Mr. Yabi wrote another letter about our

trip for the *Mainichi Shimbun*, while I was writing mine for a syndicate of my own, including eight American Sunday papers. Nothing could have been more different than our methods. The New York journalist sent for a table and chair, took eight sheets of tissue paper at a time, with a sheet of duplicating carbon paper between every two of them, and by means of a hard pencil wrote the eight copies of his letter all at once. The Tōkyō journalist, *per contra*, wrote his letter on a little table about a foot high, before which he squatted on a mat, with one knee up in the air. His manuscript consisted of a continuous roll of paper (like a small imitation of the mile-long rolls which feed our newspaper presses), and he wrote, of course, downwards and from right to left, unrolling his paper as he needed it, and finally sending it off all in one piece, a yard or two long, for the copy-cutter to dish up to the compositors in as long or short clippings as he chose. Mr. Yabi's hand never touched the paper in writing, although, unlike most Japanese (who write with a small brush), he made use of pen and ink, — a trick, he said, which few of his countrymen had learned yet.

A Japanese written page is as different from a printed page as an English book is from a page of our manuscript. The printed Japanese resembles the Chinese, but of a Japanese manuscript you can get a fair idea by taking a page of your own writing, holding it up to the light, with the written side facing the light, and in such a way that the lines run down instead of horizontally. The first time I saw Mr. Yabi's handwriting I told him that it looked to my Occidental eyes as if a Buddhist rooster had got his feet in an inkstand and then tried to get at a worm under the paper, at which archaic joke he was polite enough to laugh good-naturedly; but after I had discovered the resemblance of my inverted manuscript to his, I came to the conclusion that it was, after all, only a question between horizontal and vertical. I must add, however, that Mr. Yabi admitted that he was using our pen and ink (*penu* and *inku*, in Japanese) because he could write faster with it than with a brush, and that he might save still more time by using English letters in place of the Japanese script.

INTO THE VIRGIN FOREST

A GREEK IDYL — IN A JAPANESE COAL MINE — CONVICTS — RIDE ON A COAL TRAIN — A POND AND A BATHING SCENE — CAUGHT IN THE RAIN — HORSES AND GUIDES — TREATING THE AINOS — BEAR FIGHTS AND POISONED ARROWS — AMERICAN CLEARINGS — JAPANESE PIONEERS — FOREST ENCHANTMENT — NIGHTINGALES AND FLOWERS — POLITE CONVICTS — A YEZO SONG — CENTRE OF THE ISLAND — MORE AINOS — BACK TO SAPPORO — NEWSPAPERS AND MAGAZINES

BOTH the Governor-General and Superintendent Hashiguchi agreed, that if we had to choose between making the circuit of Volcano Bay and seeing the interior of Yezo, the latter would be preferable for our purposes. The Volcano Bay route presents many fine views of mountains and coast, but it has been fully described by Miss Bird and others, whereas the road into the interior, as far as Kamikawa, — which is almost the exact centre of the island, — had been opened only a short time, and seen by only a few foreigners, so that it would be virgin soil. On the way there we would be able to utilize about twenty miles of the same railway that had brought us from Otaru, which would take us as far as Poronai, the coal mines of which would deserve a visit. From there the rest of the trip would be on horseback.

In the morning Mr. Hashiguchi met us once more at

the station, and brought us a letter recommending us to the special care of mayors, mine and prison officials, and innkeepers, besides a few books and circulars on Hokkaido, which I presented to Mr. Yabi, who subsequently gave me a verbal review of them. We also caught sight once more of the Governor-General, at the head of a band of soldiers; he returned our greeting with the foreign military salute. After the train had started, a man (foreigner) introduced himself to us as the builder of the road we were on. He had seen several notices about us in Yezo papers, and was anxious that we should have a good time. He was then, he said, busy building a new railroad northward, which was later on to be continued southward to Mororan, to form Yezo's trunk line. He told us of several places where we could find good fishing.

The scenery we passed through on the way to Poronai gave a foretaste of the forest that was to be our home for the rest of the week — a dense jungle, varied now and then by a swamp or an open stretch. In one of these open spaces a "living picture" suddenly burst upon the view, that made me rub my eyes, and wonder if I wasn't asleep, dreaming of Diana and the ancient Greeks. A short distance from the road, in the bend of a small stream, a dozen women and girls were bathing unabashed, in beauty unadorned. Fortunately I was not, like Actaeon, changed into a stag for beholding this idyllic spectacle.

It did not take us long to reach the coal region, which is the most important in Japan. Coal is the principal mineral product of the country, and, oddly enough, the chief deposits are near the extreme south, at Nagasaki, and near the extreme north, in Yezo, the latter being by far the largest. The American engineers who first surveyed the coal fields of Yezo for the government, estimated that they contained about 150,000,000,000 tons, or two-thirds as much as the coal fields of Great Britain; and these estimates, according to a recent English consular report, have been found rather under than above the truth. Nine-tenths of this coal is found in the Ishikari valley, in which is situated Poronai, where we now found ourselves.

Presenting our card from Mr. Hashiguchi to the superintendent of the mines, that gentleman, who spoke English fluently, kindly left his work to show us the coal veins personally. And what do you think was the first thing he told us? Any man in his senses would suppose that in order to get at coal, you must dig down into the bowels of the earth, even in Japan. Not so here. Japan remains consistently topsy-turvy. At the Poronai mines the veins of coal are followed upwards into the mountain. Belonging to a comparatively recent geological era, Japanese coal is nearer the surface than in other countries; and a lucky circumstance this is, for it does away with the necessity for costly timbering and complicated ventilating apparatus.

Our guide first took us to a room where coarse Aino suits were put over us to protect our coats. Then, instead of being lowered in buckets, we simply walked along a level tunnel, dug about half a mile into the mountain. Having reached the veins, we began to clamber upwards, holding on to the primitive timbering — exciting work, especially if you carry your own lamp in one hand, and have to look out not to soil your only pair of white flannel trousers. At last we reached the temporary end — a solid wall of black coal, almost five feet high, and containing, so we were told, only one-tenth of impure matter in the whole mass. The three local mines open at the time were worked by convicts — dangerous criminals from all parts of Japan, about 1100 in number, with some 50 soldiers and policemen to guard them. We met several detachments, under guard. They seemed less brutal in appearance than criminals of their class elsewhere. They get eleven cents a day, of which eight goes to the prison for their food, leaving three for clothing and luxuries.

When we were ready to return to Ichikichiri (*sit venia verbo*), where we were to pass the night, we found that there was to be no passenger train for several hours; but we were informed that we were welcome to avail ourselves of the next coal train. I supposed that a coal-train ticket would be third class, if not fourth, but the station agent, thinking, perhaps, that it would be an insult to offer such distinguished visitors anything but the best, made us pay for first-class tickets! *Noblesse oblige* — we took them. However, though we did have to sit on a load of coal, we were supplied with clean new mats by way of compensation. I must add that no American boys and girls ever enjoyed a hay ride more than we did that coal ride. I think that the ideal way to see such incomparable mountain scenery as that of the Canadian Pacific Railway would be on the top of coal cars — if there were any — with free access to every breeze, and nothing to obstruct the view.

I must not omit to note an amusing scene at the Poronai station, while we were waiting for the coal train. I watched a native boy who was busy catching the large flies that buzzed about the room. The bright fellow had discovered that foreign window panes are a good thing to corner flies on. We asked him what he intended to do with the flies, and he said he would take them home to feed to his chickens.

At Ichikichiri we found an excellent little tea house, with a fine view of a green mountain range. But alas! there was no smiling tea maiden to welcome us. Women must be scarce at this place. All our attendants were boys and men, — a very exceptional state of affairs. Nevertheless, we had two good meals here, our appetites being too good to be spoiled by two pictures on the wall intended to represent the Emperor and the Empress. They were "foreign" chromos of the most atrocious kind, framed in wood, and marked "Number 3." No doubt the Japanese think we like such pictures, and wonder why. We occupied a back room, of course, whence we could see the mountains, and, as I lay lazily on the mats, two *genre* pictures met my gaze. To the right, there was a pond occupied by some noisy frogs. Presently these were silenced by the arrival of several quacking ducks. But these, too, in turn, had to yield to superior size, for a large dog came along, and ousted them, to take his bath. More Japanesy was another bathing scene to the left. In the back yard of our neighbor's house there was a bath tub, into which a woman poured several buckets of steaming water. She then disappeared, and presently returned naked, with a ditto baby, which she proceeded to bathe. Then she took a dip herself; and, after she had returned into the house, her place was taken by a boy, followed by two grown girls, the last to go in being probably the servant girl, judging by her more muscular build.

When we had our first interview with the Governor-General, he promised, among other things, to see to it that we should be supplied with good horses, and especially with European saddles (which are difficult to obtain), for our ride into the forest. He kept his promise, for when we called on the mayor of Ichiki-chiri, in accordance with Mr. Hashiguchi's directions, we found that he knew of our coming, and had already provided for us. The horses, together with a mounted guide, appeared at our inn in time for an early start the next morning. Our baggage consisted of two valises, which the guide tied together with a rope, and slung over his horse's sides, whereupon he perched on top. The excellent road was wide enough for a carriage, and we congratulated ourselves on seeing a cloudy sky, which promised a cool ride; but, before long, the clouds opened their pores and gave us a copious, prolonged shower bath. We had foolishly left our oil-paper rain coats behind, as Mr. Yabi thought they would be an impediment, and our umbrellas were of little use on horseback in a violent, fickle storm that drove the rain in upon us from all sides. At the first wayside inn our guide stopped, and got us two red blankets. Some of the natives we passed were also wrapped in blankets, while some had native or foreign umbrellas. Others were wrapped in oiled paper, a few had on the regular rain coats made of grass, and, to cap the climax, and provide still further variety, there were some who had simply a mat or two suspended from the head or shoulders.

If our guide had asked us how we wished to be conducted, I should have replied as Archelaus did two thousand years ago, when his prating barber asked him how he would have his hair trimmed — "In silence." I have read somewhere that Ainos make better guides than the Japanese, because they are silent, while the Japanese are forever singing. Our guide was no exception; he sang without a pause for about five hours, and the expression of his song, amid all its Oriental disguises, was indubitably joyous, especially after he had secured those blankets for us. Subsequently we discovered the cause of his joy: he had paid only ten cents for the use of those blankets, and had charged us forty! I must not exaggerate, however, about the guide's continuous singing; it *was* interrupted, now and then, by an outburst of anger over his horse, who always " wanted to go home."

About noon we came across another wayside inn, at which we stopped for lunch; that is, we ordered some tea and rice, and supplemented them with our own corned beef, soda crackers, and delicious fresh butter from the Sapporo college creamery. The sole occupants of the inn seemed to be a man and his wife and a foreign dog. Our dogs, of various breeds, are now quite common among the Japanese, who call them, as my friend informed me, kami [komee], which they originally supposed to be their name, because they always heard the English and Americans at Yokohama call their dogs "come 'ere." I made an interesting experiment with this dog by offering him a slice of corned beef. He smelt of it long and suspiciously, then suddenly he pricked up his ears in a knowing way, swallowed the meat eagerly, and " wanted more." What made him prick up his ears and change his mind so suddenly? He could have never in his life tasted beef, for it is unknown in the Yezo wilds. Was it a

RAIN COATS

sudden Platonic reminiscence of a previous state of existence in a foreign dog's paradise where beef and mutton bones abound?

At this inn we changed horses and guides. Unfortunately our first guide took along the blankets, and there was a difficulty about getting others, for the innkeeper said he had none. Mr. Yabe thereupon asked me for the card which Mr. Hashiguchi had given us, which he requested the innkeeper to take to some soldiers who were encamped not far away, and ask if we could not borrow some blankets from them. At sight of the superintendent's card, our host's attitude changed immediately; hurrying into an adjoining room, he returned in a moment with two beautiful new blankets! Thus, in every detail of our Yezo tour, did we have occasion to bless the Chief Justice at Tōkyō for that letter to the Governor-General.

The road was beautifully lined with morning glories; it had been a morning for them to glory in, — they liked the rain better than we did. However, the ill wind blew us this good, that we were not molested by flies, which are said to be troublesome here to man and beast. In the dismal downpour, the luxuriant, green forest jungle made a dreary impression on the senses. My new pony was a good traveller, but shied at everything; especially if I opened my umbrella or leaned over to adjust my blanket. Raindrops suddenly falling on him from a wind-shaken tree, made him jump aside several feet; and when I kept my umbrella open, he fancied that the drippings from it on his haunches were flies, and tried to brush them away. His tail being covered with mud, and long enough to slap my clothes, this imaginary fly-brushing did not improve my appearance.

At an early hour in the afternoon we reached a river which we crossed on a primitive rope ferry, the boatman standing up and, after pushing us into the current, holding on to the rope and pulling us over. On the other side was the village of Takigawo, where I was surprised to find planted in the midst of a flower garden a really comfortable and tasteful tea house, one of the best kept I had yet found in Japan. The manager, G. Satomi, proved to be a very intelligent man, who most courteously showed us the sights of the village, and gave us much interesting information. Seeing that I was anxious to try fishing in Japanese water, he supplied us with tackle and bait, and told us where to go. We had no special luck, but brought back enough to help out our supper. Mr. Satomi said that the best fishermen were the Ainos, which led me to remark that I had been disappointed so far in my desire to come across those aboriginal inhabitants of Japan, the only ones I had seen having been a family on the steamer which brought us to Hakodate. Having seen many pictures of them, I recognized these at a glance by their color, foreheads, eyes, noses, and beards, all of which resemble those of Europeans much more than the corresponding Japanese features. At Hakodate and Sapporo I had kept a sharp lookout for Ainos, but had not seen a single one.

"Then you have come to the right place," said Mr. Satomi. "There is a small colony of them here, and three men are in a house near by at this moment. If you will follow me, I will show them to you."

He preceded me to a hut resembling the simple Indian habitations in Alaska, but apparently not a regular Aino hut. In the centre of the room there was a fireplace with a smoke hole above, around which a few rows of salmon were hanging to be cured. We found the three Ainos squatting in a corner around an enormous kettle full of rice, which they were transferring with chopsticks to three hungry mouths. Their coal-black hair and beards were long and thick, their limbs covered with long hairs almost like a fur, and their complexion several shades darker than that of the Japanese. Their remarkably high foreheads and dense long beards gave them an appearance of intelligence which was belied by their actions and their expression. They looked as gloomy as if they were to be hanged after finishing their rice. Knowing how fond they were of rice wine, I thought I would try to cheer them up a little by treating them to a bottle. Mr. Satomi explained my intentions to them, but they shook their heads sadly. This was indeed a surprise, for I had read in several books that the Ainos not only consider intoxication the highest of all enjoyments and spend all their gains on it, but even look on saké drinking as the most proper and devout way of worshipping the gods. A few questions put to them revealed the true inwardness of their unexpected abstinence. They had been hired to work on the road, and the contractor, familiar with Aino habits, had made them promise not to touch rice wine. After a while we succeeded in convincing them that our intentions were honorable, and they allowed Mr. Satomi to get a bottle. Being assured once more that it was "my treat," the three long-bearded men bowed their heads very low, waved their mustache lifters and smiled gratefully at me before they filled their cups and eagerly emptied them.

On the way back to the inn we stopped at a store,

wherein Mr. Satomi showed us some large round cakes which he said were made of a powdered root. From their hardness I judged that they would make good building material, but Mr. Satomi said that this was the "bread" of the Ainos. They have learned from the Japanese to eat rice, but it is said that they prefer the millet which their women raise in their gardens. Formerly, when deer and bear were more abundant, their two principal meals, morning and evening, consisted of venison or bear soup, seasoned with various vegetables, herbs, and roots, even the poetic but tough mistletoe being condemned to form an ingredient in this *pot-au-feu*. They eat the berries of the wild roses that abound along the coast, and in the autumn wild grapes are among their dainties. It is said that asparagus grows wild in Yezo, and I myself saw many acres of wild rhubarb. The most substantial part of the Ainos' meal consists of salmon or other fish, in the capture of which, with nets, spears, hook and line, and other ways, they show much ingenuity, as might be expected in a country where there is a river or mountain current every few miles. Herring, cod, mackerel, sardines, smelt, eels, flounders, halibut, and many other food fish abound in Ainoland. The octopus also is eaten, clams and crabs are not scarce, and oysters are so abundant that canneries have been established. One species of oysters reaches dimensions which make our Saddlerocks hide their diminished heads in shame. What would Thackeray have said to an oyster on the half shell measuring eighteen inches?

Mr. Satomi kindly made me a present of some Aino things, including specimens of the bark which they use for torches, and one of the arrowheads with which they kill bears. These arrowheads seemed rather small and frail for such tough beasts, but they are only intended to wound, the killing process being completed by an aconite poison into which they are dipped. Formerly bear hunting in the Yezo forests gained an added zest of danger from the custom of setting traps so arranged that a bear on entering was forthwith transfixed by a poisoned arrow. To warn hunters, large wooden signs were put up near the traps, in the shape of the letter T. Even then accidents occurred, and some years ago the traps were forbidden in many localities.

Mr. Blakiston tells us that,

"notwithstanding bears are so numerous in Yezo, the denseness of the underbrush and bamboo scrub is such that they are seldom seen, though their presence is not unfrequently made known by a rustling among the bushes, or the starting of horses as the less-frequented trails are followed. Japanese travellers usually keep up a song in such places, in order to scare the beasts away, for it is very awkward to come suddenly upon them, as they might, in such cases, prove dangerous."

Was that the reason why our guide had sung five hours that morning — as a musical charm to soothe the savage bear? At any rate, the hope of coming across a Siberian monster gave an added interest to our invasion of the primeval forest.

In the room which Mr. Satomi had assigned to us, there was spread over the mats the most superb bear-skin that I have ever seen. Its body was a brownish black, but the head was of the purest gold — almost like a lion's mane — a very rare color even in Yezo, and the fur was everywhere so thick that I decided to sleep on the skin, which, I found, made a softer bed than two or three Japanese wadded quilts. I made up my mind that I must have that skin. Ordinary pelts, I knew, could be bought at Hakodate for $10 and less, so I offered Mr. Satomi $20 for his. He said it was worth $22, but that he did not wish to part with it, as it was an heirloom. I have since ascertained that in New York such a skin would be cheap at $150. Had I offered my host $25 or $30, he would have probably succumbed. I have since come to the conclusion that ignorance is not always bliss.

At eight o'clock next morning we were again in the saddle. We had left Tōkyō on July 22, arrived at Hakodate on the 24th, at Sapporo on the 27th, and to-day was the 1st of August. Had we remained in Tōkyō, we should have been sweltering in the heat; here we were almost too cool — glad to warm our hands at the glowing charcoal brazier before eating our breakfast. More experiences with Yezo horses were in store for us. Our useless guide rode far ahead, and was out of sight and hearing on the only occasion when I needed his services. My pony suddenly refused to go on, and no persuasion, moral or physical, could make him budge for fully five minutes. Then he suddenly decided he would go on a little longer. His next caper was even more annoying. Discovering some dry mud on the flap of my coat, I struck it with my flat hand to brush it off. There must have been some electric connection between that coat-tail and the horse's bump of shyness, for the very instant that I struck it, I found myself sprawling in the middle of the road, fortunately with the bridle still in my hands. Then he behaved for a while, but every time we passed a tea house or a group of huts, he wanted to stop. Once he made up his mind he *would* stop anyhow. A stubborn "neigh" was his only answer to all requests to move on. I had no whip, but I had a beautiful new silk umbrella, with a fine natural-wood handle, which I had bought in Tōkyō. This I plied on his back and head till it broke in two, which made me so angry that I believe I should have been pleased to see that horse in a Spanish bull ring, doomed to have his belly ripped open. I might have remained before that tea house all day, had not a Japanese peasant taken pity on me. He seized a large stick and drummed on the pony's haunches till it set off at a trot. Thereafter we forbade the guide to go out of sight again. He, too, had his troubles, as his horse was forever trying to turn round, and it was all he could do to steer it ahead.

Soon after leaving the village where we had spent the night, I had a sensation of having been suddenly dropped into some Western American "backwoods" region with a frontier town. Lining the road on both sides, mile after mile, were shanties and "clearings," strikingly like our Western pioneer settlements. The houses, all in a row on either side of the street, were simply wooden boxes standing in the midst of clearings, in which the trees, recently felled, were still smoking, filling the air with the fragrant odor of burnt wood and leaves. As the same dense, monotonous forest frames in all these houses, which have no more individual differences than so many beans or peas, I do not see how the inhabitants can find their own homes unless they label them, or note the number and relative position of the ugly black stumps which still disfigure all the yards, — or did disfigure them at that time, — for I have no doubt that since then they have all been dug out to make room for vegetable and flower gardens.

The black, rich soil was being dug up, and, in some places, potatoes and other crops were already in full bloom. Such a luxuriant growth of potatoes I had never seen in my life as along this whole road, culminating at Kamikawa.

These Japanese pioneers will have a pleasanter time in summer than their relatives on the main island, but I do not envy them during the long Siberian winter, when their huts will be buried in six feet of snow for six or seven months. The trouble with these people is that, as these frail board shanties with paper windows prove, they do not know how to adapt their building to the needs of a cold climate. If they would only build their huts of heavier timber, with open fireplaces instead of their absurd charcoal pots, they might be tolerably comfortable in winter. Firewood for the most voracious of chimneys is more than abundant, and costs nothing but the trouble of cutting it in the forest, which extends illimitably into the howling wilderness from every back yard.

As an international curiosity, these American "clearings," pioneer shanties, and rows of foreign potatoes were interesting, but I was glad when we got away from them into the lonely grandeur and silence of the forest primeval. Japan is a paradise for trees, because two-thirds of its rain falls in the summer months when it is most needed. It has "as great a variety of trees as Eastern North America, and nearly twice as great a variety as Europe." The French Ministry of Agriculture has recently published a treatise of 172 pages on the forests of Japan,[1] in which attention is called to the great care the government takes to preserve these

[1] *À travers le Japon*, Paris, 1894.

treasures, a special college of agriculture and forestry having been established near Tōkyō, which has as many as three hundred students. It is obvious that some day, when fires and the lumberman's axe have destroyed our noble American forests, Japan will have a storehouse of great commercial value. "When will our nation," asks Mr. Griffis, "learn to have the same care for our forests that is seen even among these people, whom we consider far less civilized than ourselves?"

Of all the Japanese forests, that which covers the greater part of Yezo — an island about the size of Ireland — is the largest, the most varied, and the loneliest. Strange to say, for such a northern latitude, pines and other evergreens are scarce compared with the hard wood or deciduous trees. Many of these, including oak, maple, mountain ash, birch, magnolia, elder, chestnut, poplar, wild cherry, linden, etc., are familiar to us, yet they seem to differ from ours as English children born in America or Australia differ from the old stock; and there is a sufficient admixture of "exotic" creepers and bamboos to give the *ensemble* a distinctly Oriental effect. Usually these different kinds of trees are mixed up irregularly, but at intervals we came upon colonies where one or the other predominated. Some were straight as masts, others gnarled and bent crooked by wind and snow, while large regions received a tropical aspect from the monstrous trailing vines which wound themselves around the poor trees, like the tentacles of devilfish, crushing them in their unrelenting embrace, and putting forth their arms for fresh victims.

So densely are these trees usually crowded together, that our eyes could rarely penetrate more than a hundred feet from the road. How the bear-hunting Ainos can make their way through this tangle is a mystery, especially in view of the underbrush. I had expected that in this moist northern climate graceful, inoffensive ferns and mosses would chiefly clothe the ground, as in the damp forests of Oregon and Alaska. Ferns were, indeed, not rare, but there was no carpet of mosses. Along the road we found a good deal of wild rhubarb, with leaves as large as the bottom of a tub, but within the woods the undergrowth was chiefly a tough chaos of dwarf bamboo scrub, from a foot to three feet in height, with hastate leaves, of which we found the horses very fond, and which were also useful to brush away the flies from them and ourselves. Mr. Yabi looked quite picturesque with a bundle of them fastened around his head for a sunshade.

When Sir Rutherford Alcock wrote that Japan is a country in which flowers have no fragrance, fruits no flavor, and birds no song, he was ignorant of the charms of this Yezo forest. It is true that besides crows (which are not *very* musical) we heard or saw few birds or other animals, but in one place the air was suddenly musical with the song of several birds, one of which, my companion said, was the Japanese nightingale. It had a rich, full, sustained note almost as sweet as that of the German nightingale, and we heard it repeatedly on our lonely rides. As for the scent of flowers, has not the linden tree flowers, and did we not inhale their delicious fragrance by the hour as we rode along the wooded mountain sides — a fragrance rich and voluptuous as the atmosphere of an orange grove? Yet it must be admitted that the eye was better provided for than the ear or nose. Among the loveliest sights were the abundant morning glories, whose rank vines had climbed up and wound themselves around the stalks of plain roadside plants, about six feet high, adorning them with a beauty that seemed to be their own. There were other beautiful flowers in abundance, especially one of an exquisite blue color, whose name I tried in vain to discover. Though an habitual haunter of forests, I was amazed and delighted with the countless tints of green on the densely wooded hillsides, where forest fires never rage, because it rains so often; and I noticed again the peculiar softness and delicate feminine quality of Japanese landscape and atmosphere. For a long distance the rapids of the river along with which we rode were so wildly turbulent as to suggest the Merced in the Yosemite Valley.

Occasionally I dismounted and waited till the others were out of sight, in order to enjoy the ravishing silence of the afternoon forest, when not a breeze was stirring. The green mountain chain to the right looked unutterably desolate. Probably no human foot, not even that of an Aino, has ever trodden it, and the bears still roam its thickets undisturbed. Now and then a crackling stick, which caused the horse to prick up his ears, made me hope that a bear might come into the road, but no such luck was mine. We saw no trace of a bear except that superb fur at the inn. Yet, after all, what is the coarse excitement of seeing a bear compared with the esthetic delights of a virgin forest, with nothing but poetic sounds to break the golden silence?

In the chapter headed "Off for Japanese Siberia," I referred to the grounds that induced me to choose such a name as that for Yezo — its proximity to the real Siberia, the probability that it once formed a part of the Siberian continent, the presence on it of animals found also in Siberia but not on the Japanese mainland, the great cold and deep snows of winter, the monstrous bears, and, finally, by an odd coincidence, its choice by the government as a place of exile and punishment for dangerous criminals. We had already seen many of these convicts at the Poronai coal mines; on this road we met more of them, in numbers increasing as we neared Kamikawa. They wore brick-colored trousers and coats or blouses of the same color. A Japanese is nothing if not polite, though he be but a burglar or a cut-throat: these criminals, condemned to ten or twenty years' servitude, never neglected to bow low to us, or to lift their head-cover, if they had any, as did also their guards. Again I was surprised to see several dozens of convicts in charge of only one or two soldiers. Mr. Landor says he has heard of sixteen escaping in one month, but that must have been at or near Poronai, for in this wilderness escape would be difficult and recapture easy, as they wear a distinctive dress and there is but one road. This single road into the wilderness is like the thread in the Labyrinthian maze, or else it might be compared to a plank laid across the ocean. To leave this plank and get lost in the forest would be almost certain death; for, even if not eaten by bears, how is an escaped convict to find and make his way to the coast through this impenetrable, silent, illimitable jungle? Of course there are possibilities — he might reach a river and follow that, or he might be guided by the caws of crows to an isolated Aino settlement, or a stray Japanese fisherman's or hunter's cabin. But such settlements are extremely rare in Yezo, away from the coast. Even on this road, after leaving the clearings, there was no sign of human life except a semi-occasional straw hut or straw tent.

Early in the afternoon we reached Kamikawa, the terminus for the present of the forest road, which, however, we were told, was to be continued some day to the northeastern coast at Abashiri. Kamikawa lies, as I have said, almost in the exact centre of Yezo, and is intended to be its future capital; but when we saw it Sapporo had as yet no cause for jealousy, as there were only three or four buildings, surrounded by rows of potatoes growing in astounding luxuriance. The largest of the buildings was a commodious tea house, where we were welcomed and made comfortable. We intended to go fishing, but were told the water was too muddy after the rain. So we warmed ourselves with the aid of a few cups of hot tea and a hibachi, — it was so cold that I could see my breath, — and then the host took us a short distance to show us some of the convicts at work. These convicts, I should have said before, had made the road over which we had ridden, and built the cabins in the settlement, which, we were informed, was called Sorachi-Buto, and had already a thousand houses scattered along several miles of the road. We found quite a number of the criminals at work making and transporting logs; but their crimes did not seem to weigh heavily on their conscience, for they were all merrily and lustily singing a phrase which I jotted down in my note book as follows: —

That evening, as I lay on my quilts, this melody kept

haunting me, and I could not help thinking what would become of us if the convicts should overpower their few guards and pay us a nocturnal visit. Somehow the polite demeanor of these red-coated fellows had made such a soothing impression that this thought had no terror, as it would have had in a "Christian" country; it seemed as if these meek-looking men would be altogether too civil to do anything wrong unless they were drunk; and I fancy that this idea was not so very far out of the way. Confucianism and Buddhism (perhaps vegetarianism too) have worked together in making the Japanese wonderfully gentle, docile, and amiable. How different these religions are in their influence from the fanatical Mohammedanism! This thought led me to compare my present situation with my visit to Tetuan, Morocco. That place, too, I had reached after a lonely fifty-mile ride on horseback; and when I got there I felt as if I had been dropped back at least a thousand years into mediæval barbarism, dirt, and misery, and in the one night I spent there I had a slight attack of that feeling of utter isolation from the world which is said to drive European ambassadors and their companions who have to spend a few weeks in the city of Fez, almost to distraction and suicide. How different the feeling at Kamikawa! Here I was, in the centre of the Yezo wilds, perhaps the only foreigner in a two days' trip, among hundreds of the worst criminals, yet I had not the slightest feeling of isolation from the civilized world. Even that queer fancy, which so often overcomes one in Japanese cities, of having been transferred to another planet, was absent here, thanks to the cosmopolitanism of forest life and scenery. Indeed, the only exotic element in my feelings came from the wonder that criminals could be so urbane and gentlemanly, so cheerful and musical.

When, on our return trip, we rode up again to Mr. Satomi's neat little inn at Takigawa, we were barkingly received by a dog who had previously amused us by his odd conduct, and who had apparently not yet got over his surprise at sight of a genuine foreigner. He growled and barked whenever he caught a glimpse of me (to Yabi he paid no attention); yet his curiosity prompted him repeatedly to come and peep into my room.

A short siesta on the brown-and-gold bearskin was interrupted by a musical performance in front of the inn. A vocal quartet of four men was discoursing native music. One of them, who had a good baritone voice, sang a short solo, whereupon the others joined him in a few bars of chorus. The accompaniment was provided by four primitive instruments, — a few small bells attached to a handle, — which the men held in their hands and shook all the time, like sleighbells. I had on a new but pocketless kimono, which had been supplied when I took my bath, and therefore went back to my room for a few pennies; but when I returned the strolling musicians were gone, to my disappointment, as I wanted to hear more of their music, especially with a view to discovering whether the four voices would ever, accidentally or purposely, unite in genuine harmony.

Mr. Satomi showed us a pair of Aino snowshoes made of salmon skin, which he said would last several weeks. With these shoes on the Ainos pursue the bears and deer across the trackless forest in winter. We were also informed that if we wished to see some Aino women, we must go down to the river. We did so, and arrived just in time to see several Aino canoes, propelled by long poles, returning from the lower river with a fine catch of salmon. On the bank were a number of women awaiting the fishermen. The younger ones were rather pretty, with almost Caucasian features, and large, expressive black eyes. The older ones were hideous in their dirty clothes reaching up to the neck, and with their tattooed moustaches, which made them look like grenadiers in petticoats. Most Aino women have these moustaches tattooed on their upper lips. It is done before they are old enough to have a definite opinion as to whether their appearance is thereby improved or otherwise; but it is said that they like it, because it makes them look "very manly." Our "andromaniacs," as Dr. Parkhurst calls them, will doubtless be delighted to hear that their ideal — to be as much like men as possible — is shared by these Aino women, whom those who know them best place even below the black Australians in intelligence.

That evening we had for supper one of the salmon caught by the Ainos we had observed. It was juicy and well-flavored, though not equal to the best Columbia River Chinook. In the morning we were favored with the usual fog, lasting till after nine. No further incident worth recording occurred till we were back in our inn at American Sapporo. On examining my accounts I found that the travelling expenses for myself, Mr. Yabi, the guide, and our three horses, were under five dollars a day — and Yezo is considered the most expensive part of Japan. A horse costs three cents a mile, and the guide is thrown in free, but expects a fee of five cents!

That night I was kept awake a long time by a Japanese sinner reading to himself aloud, so Mr. Yabi said,

from a religious book, which he did with the singing
Chinese inflections, such as one hears on the stage. On
such occasions one realizes that brick is a better material
for building inns than paper screens, or thin wooden
walls extending only half-way up to the ceiling. To
while away time, I asked my friend some more questions
about Japanese journalism. He said he was anxious to
start a magazine, if he could raise the necessary capital
— about $3000. It would take four or five thousand
subscribers to pay expenses, and he added that there
were already several magazines with 10,000 to 15,000
subscribers. He knew that American magazines pay
their contributors from $15 to $25 and more a page,
whereas in Japan $5 a page is seldom exceeded. The
editors of the daily papers seldom receive more than $20
monthly salary, and many would be glad to get that.
But the publishers cannot afford to pay more, since,
according to Mr. Yabi, all but a very few lose money.
Some manage to keep on their feet by resorting to job
printing; others are owned by wealthy politicians who
support their "organ." Although editors receive such
small salaries, there is no lack of applicants, as journalism is considered an honorable employment. The low
price at which most of the papers are sold, — half a cent
to a cent or two per copy, — the small amount of advertising, and the insignificant number of subscribers, —
few having over 10,000, — combine to make journalism
a precarious venture. There are very few newsboys, as
the Japanese are not in the habit of buying their papers
in the street, and Mr. Yabi naturally looked on America,
where almost everybody buys at least one morning and
one evening paper, as the journalist's paradise. I was
surprised to hear that there are, in Tōkyō, weekly papers

specially appealing to ladies, with stories and pictures, and with large circulations — up to 50,000. But it will be a long time before Japan can afford illustrated weeklies or magazines like ours, though there is no lack of able authors and artists.

The growth of journalism is one of the marvels of Japan. In 1871 there were no newspapers in the country; in 1891 they numbered nearly 650. Mr. Black, who was the first to start a Japanese newspaper after foreign models, relates, in his *Young Japan*, some amusing stories of his experiences. An American newspaper office can print everything with less than 300 letters and marks. Mr. Black started out with 1200 separate characters, but gradually found that he needed over 12,000, which made the compositor's work anything but easy. He had considerable difficulty, too, in getting subscribers. One day he called on a merchant, asking him if he did not want to take his paper. The answer was, "Why, I've got it; what more do you want?" He thought that a newspaper was like a book, and that Mr. Black must be joking when he asked him to buy his paper every day. When, finally, the matter was explained, the merchant exclaimed, "What! as much as this changed and fresh every day? I cannot believe it possible!"

To-day Tōkyō is full of newspaper offices, for each political party, most of them rather primitive in appearance. On account of the strict censorship, every newspaper has its special "prison editor." In advertising, too, they are up to date. Netto relates how, on one occasion, a new liberal paper introduced itself by letting off some day fireworks, resulting in a shower of handkerchiefs, on which the name of the paper was printed.

Those who caught a handkerchief were not only allowed to keep it, but could receive the paper free for a month. The trouble with Japanese newspapers is that, even more than with us, politics takes up most of their space. One of the most interesting features of the *Japan Mail* is the summary of the contents of the leading Japanese papers, which shows that, in the matter of small happenings and crimes, Tōkyō is not so very unlike New York or London.

THE AINOS AND THE WHALE

YEZO APPLES — TIME NOT MONEY — STAGE RIDE TO MORO-RAN — A USEFUL LOTOS POND — ALONG THE WILD COAST — BEACH ROSES — FIRE-BOXES — A DESERTED AINO TOWN — EXCITEMENT ON THE BEACH — WHALE ASHORE — BLUBBER AND PRAYERS — AINO WOMEN — REVENGE ON THE KODAKER

WE had made our plans to start for Hakodate overland early in the morning. We had sent a letter of thanks to the Governor-General, and once more had called on Mr. Hashiguchi to tell him how much we had enjoyed our trip, in spite of rain, fog, and the rather un-Siberian temperature in the afternoon — drawbacks which were fully atoned for by what we had seen, and by the opportunity to sleep a few nights without musty mosquito nets over our heads. The superintendent was sorry we could not stay a few days longer and take a Japanese dinner with him. Shortly after we had returned to the inn he sent us some cream and another peck of apples as parting gifts. The apples were splendid big fellows, almost ripe, and Mr. Yabi said they would cost five cents apiece in Tōkyō. We ate all we dared to, packed some into the corners of our valises, and distributed the remainder among the tea-house girls, in addition to the regular chadai or tea money. Next morning, nevertheless, they made us wait a whole hour for our breakfast, which, however, did not make much difference, as our wagon also was an hour late. Haste is a mystery to all Asiatics, as I had found on the preceding afternoon, when I sent my horse-broken umbrella to several dealers to have a new handle put in. They all returned it with the message that it could not be done in so short a time as half a day!

To-day the trip from Sapporo to Mororan can be made in a few hours by rail. When we were there the railroad was not built — fortunately, for if it had been we might have been tempted to take it, and I should have lost the most interesting of all my experiences in Japan. After three hours' driving in our covered cart, we stopped at a wayside inn to feed the horses and sip some tea. The cakes served with the tea were in the shape of napkin rings, colored white, with a blue or red stripe around them. There were also round wafers with yellow leaves painted on them. Near the inn I was surprised to find, in this Siberian climate, two small lotos ponds full of large pink blossoms of delicious fragrance. So it was Lotos-Time even here. I took several kodak snapshots at them, to the great amazement of a small boy. No doubt the innkeeper and his family had sufficient taste to appreciate the beauty and fragrance of these flowers, for why, otherwise, should they have painted even their cakes and wafers? Nevertheless, I suspect that those lotos ponds were primarily intended as vegetable gardens for raising the toothsome lotos roots — ever-welcome ingredients in the soup bowl.

There were very few houses along this road. For hours it passed through a dense forest, which differed somewhat from that on the Kamikawa road, especially by the absence of ferns and scrub-bamboo in the undergrowth. Later on the road became very sandy. Presently there were no more trees ahead, and at the same time a stiff saline breeze indicated that we were nearing the ocean. We were, in fact, approaching the coast village of Tomakomai, thirty-four miles from Sapporo, where we were to spend the night, and as we drove up to the inn we heard the roar of the waves. Our room faced the beach, which we lost no time in visiting. The ocean is never so exhilarating to me as mountain and forest, but it is always a pleasant scenic and hygienic change. On this occasion it seemed as if we had been away for weeks, and the emotion on seeing the illimitable blue expanse once more was tinged by the thought that these waves, now dashing themselves against the Yezo beach, might have come in an unbroken series of swells from the Oregon coast, five thousand miles away. Why is it that we dislike a desolate town, but revel in the melancholy monotony of an ocean beach? It was an ecstatic pleasure to walk along this wild coast, with the foaming waves on the right, and high sand hills shutting out the rest of the world on the left. But on their tops these sand hills are anything but gloomy, for there they are green with the pretty bushes of the dwarf wild rose, only six inches high, but covered with thousands of large fragrant roses, and millions of large berries, green, yellow, and red, that once were roses too, and are no less beautiful as seeds than as blossoms. They are remarkably large, these berries are, reminding me of those lovely clusters of small yellow and red "cherry" tomatoes, which seem almost too pretty to eat, and which, in truth, are seldom eaten, although they are much better than the larger tomatoes. The Ainos eat these rose-berries. In Germany they make an excellent preserve of them. I hope the reader will pardon these frequent lapses from esthetics into gastronomy, but the Yezo air stimulates the appetite.

Like all the other houses in this village, our inn had only one story, and a dilapidated appearance. Our room, as I have said, faced the beach, and I made up my mind to leave everything open and let the sea breeze play over us all night long. But I had reckoned without the host, who came along, soon after dark, to do up all the shutters and seal us hermetically in our windowless rooms. This was more than I could submit to, and I protested firmly. The man said he must close the amado because there were many thieves about; but finally, after I had assured him that the burglar would have to pass over my body, and that I would make good any possible damages, he consented to leave them partly open. It seems almost incredible that so intelligent a nation as the Japanese should be willing to put themselves on a level with the mediæval Moors of Morocco, by sleeping all the year round in windowless, closed houses. Morse says that in some Japanese houses provision is made for ventilation, in the shape of long, narrow openings just above the amado. For my part, I never saw any such arrangement, but had to fight for fresh air almost every night. What makes this sealing up the more aggravating is the fact that the Japanese are not really afraid of night air or cold air. As one writer says, "Their indifference to cold is seen in the fact that in their winter parties the rooms will often be entirely open to the garden, which may be glistening with a fresh snowfall."

Were it not for the fact that Japanese houses are not quite air-tight, cases of asphyxiation would soon decimate the population. The amount of kerosene burnt at night may be inferred from the standing heading of "Floating Kerosene" in the newspapers, with lists of fifteen to twenty special vessels under way, at one time, from New York and Philadelphia. But the worst offender is the firebox, which, unless it is fed with charcoal well fired, gives out deadly carbonic acid gas, that seeks the level of the sleepers on the floor mats. These fireboxes are, however, interesting objects in themselves. The most poetic of them are those which simulate the crater of Fuji. These are portable; others are sunk in the floor, in the middle of the room. Often they consist of a section of a tree trunk, hollowed out and lined with metal to prevent combustion. Sometimes pebbles or ashes take the place of the metal lining.

The next morning we drove along the desolate sandy coast, mostly in sight of the ocean. The soil was poor, the road sandy, and many paths led off from it into the interior. We passed a few small, miserable villages, and as we were now in Ainoland we asked the driver where the largest settlement of the hairy men was on our road. "At Shiraoi," he replied, adding that we would have plenty of time to see them, as he always allowed his horses to rest there for an hour or two. We soon arrived at that village, which seemed to be a remarkably malodorous place, for we smelt it a long way off. Yezo is noted for its fishy odors, but this particular specimen was so ancient and offensive that I concluded it must come from some storehouse or manufactory of fish manure, a sort of guano made of the refuse of sardines and herrings, from which the oil has been extracted. But this theory, as we discovered ten minutes later, was incorrect.

"Ainotown" is usually separated some distance from

the Japanese portion of a village, as the Japanese look upon the Ainos as inferior beings, which, however, does not prevent them from marrying their pretty girls. Starting in the direction pointed out to us by our driver, we soon came across the Aino district. It consisted of a few irregular rows of straw houses, as primitive as gypsy hovels, with doors but no windows. There were no regular streets, but the huts were planted at random, in squatter fashion. We stopped at one of them and peeped in at the door, but saw nothing to reward our curiosity, except a mat placed on the bare ground, and a fireplace in the centre of the room. Nobody was at home, and the same was the case in the other huts we looked into. We met, however, several groups of women and children, hastening toward the beach, and talking so excitedly that they hardly noticed us, although a foreigner must be a strange apparition to them. Suspecting that something interesting was going on, we followed them to the beach, and as soon as we got on top of the sand dune which separates the village from the ocean we beheld a sight which made my heart leap for joy. A large whale had been cast ashore by the heaving waves, and around it, in the midst of the foaming breakers, were assembled all the Aino population of Shiraoi, about 200 men, women, and children. Here was the greatest bit of tourist luck that had ever befallen me. I might have lived right among these savages for weeks and months without getting such a fine opportunity to see them in their element. Indeed, the innkeeper afterwards told us that such an event occurred but once in five or six years.

The whale had been beached during the night, and now, at eight o'clock (we had left our inn very early),

the whole village had turned out to make the most of
the rare opportunity. The marine monster had been
fastened, by means of a strong rope, to a stake driven
in the ground, to prevent it from being washed out
again. It was a big fellow, sixty feet long, as we were
informed by one of the two Japanese policemen who had
appeared on the scene, presumably to prevent quarrels.
It had been considerably battered by the angry waves,
and it was no wonder that they had spewed it ashore,
for it was no longer fresh, and we now knew the source
of the horrible odor we had noticed on approaching the
village. We had to keep carefully on the wind side
of it, but the Ainos appeared to revel in the odor as
dogs do rolling on dry carrion. They crowded eagerly
around the carcass, brandishing long knives, with which
they deftly cut off big slices of flesh and blubber, re-
treating every other moment with wild shouts whenever a breaker dashed over the carcass. Their faces
were delightfully expressive and animated by the excitement of the sport.

Realizing the rare opportunity, I dashed recklessly
among them with my camera, holding my breath, and
firing away as fast as I could wind it up and "touch
the button." The savages "did the rest." Ainos,
Ainos, everywhere, — in all imaginable attitudes and
groupings! Did ever kodaker have such luck? I
took at least three dozen shots, and before long my
strange actions with the mysterious little black box,
which I kept aiming at them, distracted the attention
of the younger ones from the whale. The girls especially watched me with wondering eyes, and some of
them even followed me about. One young woman,
of perhaps seventeen, possibly suspecting what I was

doing, put up her hand before her face when I aimed at her,—but too late! She did not realize the rapidity of instantaneous photography. Several of the girls were rather attractive, and one of them was really very pretty, with regular Caucasian features, a light brunette complexion, and large, round, wondering black eyes that many an American belle might have envied her. She was about thirteen or fourteen, and, besides her, there were two or three older ones who would have been pretty, according to our standard, had they not been disfigured and masculinized by their tattooed moustaches, which are almost as bad as the blackened teeth and shaved eyebrows of Japanese married women under the old régime.

Some of the women were helping the men by carrying the big chunks of whale up the beach above the high-tide mark, where they made several piles of them, for future consumption. For, disgusting as it may seem, Aino epicures consider "high" whale as great a delicacy as our epicures do limburger and other decayed cheeses. These piles of blubber were indeed the signals for a grand picnic later on, when the tidbits were to be washed down in big chunks with copious draughts of rice wine. While the younger men were still engaged in cutting up the whale, the old men and some of the women and children were already squatting in groups on the sand, as if waiting for the good things to come. Going to windward for a moment, to rest my nostrils, I witnessed a comic family tragedy. A naked boy, who had evidently been up to some mischief (perhaps he had stuck his finger in the blubber and licked it off), was led by his father outside of the group, soundly scolded, and probably told that he shouldn't have any of the blubber to eat; at any rate, he tried to find consolation in standing there and blubbering all alone by himself. There he stood, in an ideal attitude of remorse, fit for a sculptor. Of course I bagged him in my kodak.

Of the groups that were squatting on the beach, the most interesting was at the extreme left. Here a dozen or more of the simple, quaint emblems of the Aino religion — peeled and whittled sticks, with the curled shavings hanging down from the top — had been placed in a row as a boundary, and within that line about twenty of the village elders were sitting — dignified-looking old men, with splendid long beards, and an intellectual cast of countenance, which was, of course, deceptive, as none of the Ainos are noted for their mental endowments, few being able even to count up to ten. They were squatting in a semicircle, facing the sea, with their hands uplifted, and waving what I took to be prayerful thanks for the godsend on which they were about to feast, — with perhaps a supplementary prayer that there might be wine enough to go round; for it is said that an Aino can drink five times as much as a Japanese before he feels tipsy; and, as previously stated, drinking is to him an act of worship.

Here was an opportunity which no true kodaker could possibly miss, — twenty superb specimens of the aboriginal population of Japan, sitting in a natural, photographic group, and needing no instructions as to pose and expression! I suppose it was a rude thing to do, but I could not resist the temptation to walk right up in front of the venerable group and take two shots at them, which I did as undemonstratively and "detectively" as possible, as I knew that they object violently

to being photographed, and that, although ordinarily
"savages in everything except in disposition," they
have been known to handle artists and photographers
roughly. Perhaps they did not know that a picture
can be taken without a tripod, and had never seen a
kodak. At any rate, they did not resent my actions.
At first they seemed a little surprised and interested,
but not at all indignant. But when I moved a few
more steps, close to the religious sticks, the chief got
up, and, with a pleasant smile and a gentle motion of
the hand, begged me to keep away from them. Kind
old fellow! I know I deserved a good kicking for my
impudence, — or perhaps an invitation to the picnic, —
but, at any rate, I had safely boxed my surreptitious
photographs, and once more chuckled over my rare
good luck. Indeed, this whole whale episode had been
a combination of lucky coincidences. In the first place,
— *mirabile dictu*, — that in all the miles and miles of
coast the whale should have been beached exactly in
front of the Aino village; secondly, that it was customary for the stage to stop there for an hour; thirdly,
that we came there not only on the right day, but at
the right hour to see the carving; fourthly, that we saw
some of the last parties hastening down to the beach,
but for which we might have missed everything and
seen nothing but a deserted village; and finally, that
the sun shone brightly enough to take good photographs,
while an hour later clouds spread over the coast and
remained for two days or longer.

This last bit of luck, however, was only apparent.
The Aino gods had their revenge for my irreverent act
in photographing the sacred sticks and the elders in the
act of worshipping. The chief Aino gods are the forces

of Nature, and it was Nature, in its manifestation as Climate, that came to their aid by almost spoiling all my pictures. When I left home I had been warned that if I wished to get any good out of my camera, I must keep my films in air-tight wrappers. I did so, but when the films were placed in the camera they were no longer protected from the extreme moisture of the Japanese summer air, the result being that most of my Yezo photographs were mere shadow-pictures.

What I especially regretted was the loss of that pretty girl's picture. She may have been a half-breed, — many of these Ainos of the southern coast are, — but there was nothing Japanesy in her features, and the very Oriental appearance of the Eurasians of the Main Island, — girls who are half Japanese, half European or American, — made it seem probable that Japanese physiognomy would not be entirely neutralized in case of a mixture with Aino blood. That the Aino women often have Personal Beauty is the opinion of several travellers. But it would obviously be hopeless to look for Romantic Love among these women; for they have not even yet learned to kiss, a gentle bite being the nearest approach to it. Naturally one would hardly expect folks who boil and eat the amorous mistletoe like cabbage, to know anything about the gentle art of osculation.

FROM MORORAN TO HAKODATE

ESCORTED TO THE MORORAN INN — CROSSING THE STORMY BAY — SUBURBS OF HAKODATE — EXPENSE OF THE YEZO TRIP — BATH IN THE SULPHUR SPRINGS — THE TYPHOON

AFTER leaving Shiraoi we saw only a few more Ainos, but the Japanese settlements became gradually more frequent. The scenery did not amount to much till we caught our first glimpse of the Bay of Mororan, studded with islands and looking like a lake, so completely is it land-locked. It is considered one of the finest scenes in Japan, and deserves its fame. A few miles from Mororan a young man on horseback came to meet and escort us to the principal inn, following the telegraphic instructions of the courteous Governor-General, whose kindness followed us even on our retreat. It was lucky that he had done so, for we would certainly not have secured the best room in the inn otherwise, as the town was full of native travellers waiting for a chance to cross the stormy bay. Half an hour after our arrival the Prefect called on us, and again he called at half-past six in the morning, before we embarked. It had been so stormy in this region that the little steamer which usually makes a daily trip to Mori had been detained in Mororan harbor for three days. This morning, however, the captain was going to risk it, although the sea was still quite rough. We were frankly told that there was a real risk of capsizing, but that the chances were in our favor, and the captain said he would return if he found it too rough outside where the bay is exposed to the Pacific swell. It did prove a very rough trip for such a small boat, but we got over safely, and after landing hired a covered cart for three dollars and a half to take us to Hakodate.

There were so many of the detained passengers that six wagons were filled beside our own. We paid our driver fifteen cents extra, which, we were told, would secure us first place — an advantage in case the road is dusty, which it did not happen to be. But it was rough and jolting, with pebbles and stones strewn broadcast, and we drove all the way at a furious rate of speed. Nevertheless, the drivers were very careful of their horses. Every two hours we stopped to feed or water them. The strange procedure was always the same. The driver took a bucket of water in one hand, seized the horse's tongue with the other, pulled it out and then dashed the water into the mouth to wash out the foam. Another bucket was then dashed on his belly, and after that the horse was allowed to drink and eat. In the meantime we were, of course, always supplied with tea and a *tabacobon*.

Villages now became more and more frequent, and they seemed to be inhabited mostly by young children carrying younger ones on their backs. One of the roadside curiosities was a man whose costume consisted of a loin cloth and a pair of high foreign boots reaching to his knees. All the house fronts were, of course, open, and the women engaged in cooking or other domestic employments were usually naked down to the waist. The number of dogs in the streets were legion, and almost always they lay right in the middle of the road, refusing to get out of the way till our horses were within a yard of them. If they had calculated that the hoofs and wheels would miss them by an inch or two, they refused to stir at all, lazily continuing their siesta. The driver, like the kuruma pullers, made allowance for this canine peculiarity, and tried to steer clear of them. Lucky dogs, to live in a Buddhist country! "Christian" drivers would either have lashed them with their whips or paid no more attention to them than to sticks and pebbles. But the Japanese are not all imbued with Buddhistic kindness to animals: we met peasants who were cruelly carrying large, fat, living ducks by the neck. However, what is that compared with the cruelty of Christian gourmets, for whom geese are tortured by overfeeding till their diseased livers swell to the size required for a first-class *paté de foie gras?*

Each of the seven drivers in our procession had a posthorn on which he sounded a loud, long tone on the slightest provocation, with the enthusiasm of a child who has just received his first penny trumpet. Not only whenever we entered a village, or neared a curve in the road, did the horn wake the echoes, but every time we saw a loaded peasant dray in the distance (to give it time to make room for us), or even when a man was seen coming up the road. Whether from a desire to emulate the dogs, or a wish to tease the drivers, these pedestrians never turned aside till the very last moment. It was well to have such things to amuse us, for, apart from a pretty lake with an island that had a building on it, there was nothing of interest to see on this part of the road, the forest itself being commonplace after the wilder scenes on the way to Kamikawa.

The scattering interminable suburbs of Hakodate made me impatient; for to get back to this place seemed almost like coming home. At any rate, I expected to get my first mail in three weeks, and did find it waiting for me at the office of Mr. H. V. Henson, who represents a branch of the Yokohama bank, on which I had a letter of credit. Mr. Henson contributed the articles on trade and shipping to Chamberlain's encyclopedic, and yet so entertaining *Things Japanese*. I found it unnecessary to draw much money; indeed, although I had taken only $150 with me on leaving Tōkyō, I discovered that I had almost enough left to take us back. However, I took a small extra sum to guard against accidents — luckily, as the sequel will show. I told Mr. Henson that our trip to Kamikawa and back had cost me only $65, or $8 a day for two men, including all expenses for horses, wagons, guides, beer, and the best available inn accommodations. He replied that he was not surprised: "It is almost impossible to spend much money in Yezo unless you drink poor champagne."

We had to spend another day in Hakodate, as our steamer was delayed. In the afternoon we took a ride to the Sulphur Springs, a few miles from the city. We met many foreigners, some on foot, some in kurumas, bearing out Mr. Henson's statement that, while Hakodate had only sixteen resident foreign families, there were many transient visitors in summer. The Japanese passion for bathing in water heated by volcanic forces of nature is shared by foreigners, and most of those we met were coming from these springs, where we found that things are done in mixed style, the semi-communism of our Turkish baths being modified by certain Japanese features. First you take a room, and a young girl serves tea, cakes, and a *tabacobon*. Then she brings a clean kimono, in which, after leaving your own clothes, you accompany her to the general room, where she abandons you to do as others do. There are two tanks of different temperature, into which hot sulphur water flows constantly. You drop your kimono and jump first into the tepid tank, then into the hot one, staying as long as you choose. There are no Japanese in this common room, but ever and anon one of the foreigners claps his hands, and in comes a pretty, smiling maiden to bring a towel, sponge, or whatever else is wanted, or to help in rubbing a bather down, utterly unconscious of the fact that her presence might embarrass any fastidious person in Adam's costume. For all these luxuries the charge is ten cents, which Mr. Yabi thought was very high, and so it was, perhaps, when you think that in Tōkyō a communal bath costs only a cent, not including, of course, kimono, towel, and tea.

Returning to the city, we asked our host for the latest Tōkyō papers (one of which, at least, appears to be on file at every tea house), and Mr. Yabi read the cholera news. We heard for the first time of the ill-fated Turkish man-of-war *Ertogroul*, on which there had been thirty or forty cases of cholera. It was said that the corpse of the first victim had been thrown overboard in the Bay of Tōkyō, in consequence of which the natives were afraid for some time to eat fish caught in the bay. The *Ertogroul* afterwards foundered in a typhoon, when all on board, including Osman Pasha, were drowned.

THROUGH MEDIÆVAL JAPAN

BEAR CUB — MELONS — ROOFS — FROM RAILWAY TO KURUMA — EARLY MORNING SCENES — RAVAGES OF THE STORM — CHANGEABLE RIVERS AND COOLIES — SILKWORMS — FOREIGNERS AS A CURIOSITY — A REMARKABLE RUNNER — TYPES OF FEMALE BEAUTY — DITCHES AND DEATHS — RAINY JAPAN — HOW COOLIES EAT — BABIES AND PICKLES — NAKED AND NOT ASHAMED — AN EXCITING FERRY

It is said that the island of Yezo is never visited by typhoons. When we had that cloudy sky and harmless rainstorm in the virgin forest, we did not dream that Yokohama was being visited by a genuine typhoon. It was this that had delayed our steamer a day. It happened to be the same *Wakanoura* that had brought us, and we greeted the officers as old friends. Poor Mr. Yabi was again seasick all the way to Oginokama, although the ocean was now like a placid lake. Some of the precipitous coast scenery again reminded me of Santa Catalina Island as approached from the California coast. I whiled away an hour on deck playing with a Yezo bear cub and feeding him apples. He was chained near a tub of cold water, and did not in the least share the aversion to bathing of his enemies, the Ainos. On an exploring tour of the steamer, in company with the first engineer, I came upon the Chinese cooks and waiters, taking their lunch. Strange to relate, they used knives and forks instead of chopsticks.

At Oginokama we were received by the same bevy of tea girls, who again seized our valises and escorted us to the inn, where we were to wait for the small boat to take us to the Sendai harbor. After we had had some tea, the girl brought in a dozen pealed slices of a kind of muskmelon. Mr. Yabi, still pale from seasickness, at once pitched into them, although I warned him that in view of our further trip on a small steamer he could not very well eat anything more inclined to make his stomach rebel. But he ate a few slices all the same. I tried a piece too. For a wonder, it was quite ripe, and as mealy as a good potato; but although it was slightly sweet, there was hardly a suspicion of the melon flavor. Yet the Japanese love their melons dearly — almost as much as their cucumbers. The first officer of the *Wakanoura* told me a story of a coolie whom he once saw sitting on the edge of a brook which ran through a village and received part of its sewage. He was eating a large cucumber, skin, bones, and all, without even salt, just as we eat an apple, and when he had finished he lay down and took a long drink from the brook. This was during a cholera epidemic. No wonder that in 1893, the deaths in Japan from cholera, typhoid, typhus, diphtheria, and dysentery numbered more than a quarter of a million. — 250,250.

Leaving my friend to enjoy his tasteless melons, I occupied myself studying the roofs below us. Our room was on the third story, a rarity in this country, where most houses have only one story, and very few as many as two. In describing the aspect of Hakodate as seen from the top of the hill, I referred to the monotonous aspect of Japanese towns. This monotony, as I now saw, disappears partly on a nearer view. Indeed, it seemed as if each roof had its individual peculiarities of material and form. One was made of tiles, another of shingles, a third of straw and mats. Some mat roofs were held down by large stones, others had soil on them covered with moss or other vegetation to prevent the rains from washing it away. The roof is the most picturesque and varied part of a Japanese house, architecture otherwise being an art in which this nation does not excel — a circumstance for which the frequent earthquakes and fires are doubtless responsible; for it seems hardly worth while to expend much money and artistic labor on a building which may be tumbled over or burned up in a few weeks.

The captain of the small steamer that took us to the harbor of Sendai gave us the startling information that the recent storm had destroyed almost a hundred miles of the railway track between Sendai and Tōkyō. This news was confirmed at the Sendai inn, where we were told that the only way to proceed would be to take kurumas for twenty-nine miles, then an uninjured portion of the railway for twenty-six miles, followed by another forty miles by kuruma. Here was a pleasant prospect of having the number of hours we expected to devote to the rest of our journey converted into as many days! At first I was annoyed, but after a moment's reflection it occurred to me that a luckier accident could not have happened to us. Our destination was not Tōkyō, but Nikko, which, with its temples, lakes, and waterfalls, is considered the scenic paradise of Japan. After seeing Nikko, my plan was to take kurumas, leave the beaten tourist tracks, and devote a few days to exploring regions where foreigners had, if possible, never been seen, and everything was still mediæval. The interruption of our railroad journey made it necessary to reverse these plans — to take the "mediæval" trip before seeing Nikko; that was all. Accordingly I accepted the typhoon and its consequences with true Asiatic composure.

In order to make connection with the train after our twenty-nine mile ride we had to start as early as 3.30, after a breakfast consisting of two kinds of soup and eggs, my companion taking his eggs raw on the hot rice. We each had two runners, and when we left the inn, it was still so dark that they had to use their paper lanterns. It took us about twenty minutes to get clear of the streets of Sendai, which were all neat and clean, and of course deserted at this hour, although we passed a few stragglers and some policemen with small lanterns. Just outside the city limits we had to cross a rapid river on a rope ferry. Half an hour later we came upon the first traces of the storm. There was a second, larger river, divided by sandbanks into several beds. A fine bridge stretched intact across the main current, but the approaches to it had been completely demolished and carried away by the raging current which a few days before had rushed down two of the channels which were now dry. We had to use a ladder to get down to the level of the river, across which we were then ferried, the charge for the whole crowd — six men and two kurumas — being twelve cents, which really included two ferriages, as the river's third channel also had to be crossed on a boat. There was no rope to hold on to; the ferryman simply pushed the boat into the strong current and steered it across with a long pole.

That we had plunged into the midst of Mediæval Japan was plainly manifest when twilight brightened into day. We passed through several villages the inhabitants of which had just pushed aside the wooden amado of their houses, before completing their toilet — which was perhaps not surprising since the full dress of the men consisted in most cases of a loin cloth, and that of the women of a short skirt reaching from the waist to the knees. Some made their toilet in the house, while others preferred to wash themselves in the river or the town ditch.

The ravages of the storm became more and more evident as we rode through a long alley of cryptomerias — stately pines, whose twisted red branches overarched the shaded road. To the left, for miles and miles, the fields were completely ruined, forming a large morass of mire, with the water still stagnant in the furrows it had ploughed. The gloomy effect of this devastation was heightened by contrast with the smiling fields to the right, which, having been protected by the elevated road and its double line of firmly rooted trees, were left standing in all their green beauty. Presently we came upon the cause of all this ruin — a wide river with very low banks, which had not been able to hold the waters precipitated by the storm clouds. Mr. Yabi remarked that these sudden inundations were the greatest curse of Japan, devastating large regions every summer and carrying off the laboriously prepared soil. If the reader has ever seen a large field green on one autumn day with potatoes, corn, or tomatoes, and again on the next day, after a blighting, withering frost had done its work, he will have some conception of this Japanese devastation, minus the mire.

Some of the streams we crossed were gentle and placid enough now, but a few days before none but the costliest stone railway bridges could have withstood the violence of their current. In some places the overflowing rivers had created a new sand bed a quarter of a mile wide, strewn with trees and shrubs rudely torn from the undermined soil and now piled pell mell in their own funeral pyres. To watch one of these inundations from the top of one of the green hills looking down upon these valleys, must be a saddening but sublime spectacle.

The mountains whose green sloping sides had poured these devastating waters into the overflowing river beds, became gradually higher and the air more bracing; yet it still breathed a certain Asiatic languor. Indeed, during my whole sojourn in mountainous Japan I did not once find the exhilarating air of the Swiss or Californian Alps, every inhalation of which is a conscious pleasure, like breathing the fragrance of a flower. I was told, however, that such bracing air may be breathed here on sunny October days. And I had discovered this morning that in Japan, as elsewhere, the most exhilarating air is that of the hour before sunrise —an hour which we, with our stupid late hours, always sacrifice to sleep.

In this region almost the whole population seemed to devote its time to the silkworm, its products, and its food. In some of the villages a basket of white cocoons was placed in front of nearly every house, and most of the fields were green with the luxuriant young mulberry shoots. In this case the Japanese do not try to "get ahead of the worm," but sacrifice the whole tree to him. Surely they must know how deliciously sour the unripe mulberry is, and how luscious the ripe black berry; but I believe they cultivate chiefly the white variety, which is insipid.

Nowhere in Japan had I been so much on exhibition as on this trip. To the children, especially, the apparition of a foreigner in a kuruma was as good as a circus. My runners had orders to pass very slowly through the villages, so as to give me time to see all the sights. The children seemed to have secret signals announcing my arrival; for no sooner had I entered a street, when from every house and side alley boys and girls swarmed out, most of them stark naked, and formed into two staring, smiling lines, through which I had to pass. Most of them probably had never seen a foreigner. Mr. Yabi was amused, and suggested that if I would let him put me in a cage and charge a few cents a peep, he would soon have money enough to start his magazine. The curiosity of both adults and children was so genuine and naïve that there was nothing rude in it; and although many of them doubtless considered me an absurd sort of an animal, there was never a word or look of ridicule. Once, as I sat on the verandah of a tea house, jotting down a few notes, a man stopped and stared at me fixedly fully five minutes. I must have looked appetizing; for suddenly he put his hand into his wide sleeve, brought out a raw egg, hit it against his teeth, and sucked it clean at one draught. At another place a young fellow who had just missed us, ran ahead about twenty feet, then turned and had a good look at me. I envied him his rare good luck.

At Shiraisi we had expected to take the train, but found that we must go on twelve miles farther. I was sorry not to be able to stop a few hours at this place, which is beautifully situated amid the mountains; we lingered for lunch in a cool and airy corner room. As we bowled down the street again, we passed two men with large bundles of papers on their backs, crying something for sale. I asked Mr. Yabi what it all meant, and he replied that they were newsmen, and that the bundles on their backs were newspapers, the contents of which (sketches of prominent politicians, etc.) they were proclaiming in loud, monotonous tones. We had again exchanged runners — all but one who actually came through with us all the way from Sendai to Kori, trotting before my kuruma from 3.30 A.M. till 4.15 P.M., — forty-two miles with less than two hours' rest! Much of our road had been up and down hill, and after noon the sun was so warm that I felt uncomfortable even on the kuruma and under my umbrella. The physical endurance of these fellows is certainly remarkable; nor do they ever complain, as long as they can have an occasional cup of tea and bowl of rice, a blue towel on the arm for wiping off the perspiration, and a bucket of cold well water to dash over their bodies on arriving at an inn. How they can do such hard work on such light fare is an Oriental mystery. It is an odd and interesting experience to ride twelve hours behind one of these finely built fellows, watching the play of the muscles in his naked thighs and the odd bobbing up and down of his bare shoulders and large white mushroom hat — a sight which continues to haunt one in dreams and awake for months afterwards.

At Kori we were at last able to board the train. The first thing I saw in the car was a notice in large Japanese writing. I asked my friend to translate it, and found that it was to the effect that if any passenger was suddenly seized with symptoms of cholera, he should at once notify the conductor. Obviously the dreaded microbes had made their way north beyond

Tōkyō during our trip in Yezo. Mr. Yabi had secured the last number of a newspaper published at Fukushima (where we were to spend the night), containing an account of the death of a prominent politician living there. He had gone to Tōkyō to attend a political meeting, was suddenly taken ill, got into a kuruma headed for a doctor's house, but died before he could reach it.

Near the station at Fukushima we passed several tea houses, whose pleasing exterior and brilliant illumination showed that they were the abode of frivolous geishas. As we had no desire to spend the night flirting with singing girls or being kept awake till dawn by samisen and drums played for the amusement of other guests, we gave these the cold shoulder and sought out a more humble but respectable and quiet inn. Its exterior was not inviting, but in Japan you must never judge a house by its exterior, as the plainest shanty often has a beautiful garden in the rear, with clean, airy rooms facing it. We chose our room on the second story, which is always preferable to the first. Here we were secure from all noises except the melancholy nocturnal whistling of the blind shampooers and the distant rumble of the geisha drums. For supper we had a dish of small eels raised in the irrigated rice fields. They are killed by being transferred from this rice water to rice wine, which gives them a delicate flavor and softens the bones; whereupon they are eaten entire, like our whitebait. Had it not been for the cholera, I would have tried some of the oysters, which Mr. Yabi said were abundant here, costing only five cents a bowl. He added that his countrymen did not care much for them, whereas eels were a great national delicacy, being favored by them very much as oysters are by us. A gastronomic surprise at this inn was fried chrysanthemum leaves, green on one side, with batter on the other.

The kuruma man who had helped to pull me forty-two miles on the preceding day had begged permission to follow us on the train and be one of our pullers on the second day. He was anxious to go to Tōkyō, and could not afford to go in any other way. He was a fine, healthy, courteous fellow, and we gladly accepted his offer, which was a convenience to both sides. He played the rôle of valet, taking care of our baggage, tying up our shoes, and doing errands.

As we proceeded, it seemed to me that the women were gradually becoming better looking and better formed. The monotonous national style of dressing the hair gives Japanese women an illusory resemblance; in reality there are as many types as in other countries. In the car which took us to Fukushima there was a well-dressed young lady whose beauty would have been almost perfect from *our* point of view, had not her lips been a little too thick. And now as we were riding along toward Nikko, I was pleasantly startled by meeting a young girl who had the loveliest Italian Madonna face, exquisitely refined. She had the complexion of a city belle. We also saw plenty of country girls with big arms and legs, large busts, full, rosy faces, like the most buxom rustic women of England or Germany. Japanese artists do not admire the plump rustic type of beauty, even in cases which would win our approval. Mr. Yabi spoke rather contemptuously of the mental endowments of these country women. Many of them, he said, are so stupid that they cannot give the simplest directions, and if you ask them a question, they always "don't know."

We had again started very early, and once more I received the impression that teeth brushing is the universal occupation of the Japanese from five to seven o'clock. Everywhere men and women were sitting by the gutters, dipping their brushes into the dubious communistic water, a habit which perhaps accounts for the length of the brush handles. One man walked calmly down a village street, vigorously cleaning his teeth with a brush that had a handle fifteen inches long. On being accosted by a friend, he replied without removing the brush from his mouth. In one case we followed a ditch into which we had seen a number of persons dip their brushes, and traced it to the rice fields, which are always manured by the village sewage. Thus a single case of typhoid, dysentery, or cholera may poison the water for a whole village and cause hundreds of deaths. In the years 1878 to 1891 six successive cholera epidemics killed 313,000 Japanese. Dr. Erismann of Moscow says that forty per cent of all human beings die prematurely of preventable infectious diseases. If that were generally known, the canvas-covered melon stands we passed along the road would probably not have quite such large piles of rinds heaped all about them during cholera time.

Effects of the rain storm were still visible on all sides. In some places the rivers had drawn their own high-water mark by depositing belts of leaves and mud-covered shrubs ten feet above their beds. The numerous lotos ponds had been filled to overflowing, to the obvious delight of their pink blossoms and large thirsty umbrella leaves. The mountain sides had all the dust washed off their tree mantles and looked bright green and happy. These mountains were all in the real Japanese style — small, pleasing, feminine. True, there are also mountains representing the martial, rough, masculine character of historic Japan; but these we did not see till later. A unique and picturesque feature of the scenery was the regular recurrence, about half a mile apart, of small villages, or groups of from three to a dozen houses, nestling at the base of the foothills, partly concealed by the trees and bamboos.

We got up among the clouds, or rather, the clouds came down to us, and gave us a few harmless sprinklings. August is supposed to be one of the fine months in Japan, and so it is except when it is rainy — an exception which seems to be chronic. Oregonians are called "web feet" by the sun-baked Californians, because Portland has fifty inches of rain a year. Japan has sixty. If all of this came down at once, the surface of these 4000 islands would be five feet under water. Sometimes it seems as if it did try to come down all at once.

Although there was water, water everywhere, and Yabi and the runners had their tea every hour or two, I had not a drop to drink till we came to the inn where we lunched. I made up for lost time by drinking two bottles of beer, with but slender assistance from my friend, who did not care much for that bitter beverage. I was sorry not to be able to get any more of the Sapporo beer, which I had found much better and more Germanic than the products of Tōkyō and Yokohama breweries; although I was glad enough to find that the latter are now to be found in every Japanese village, at a price varying from twenty-two to thirty cents per quart bottle. The charges for this lunch were ninety-one cents, of which sixty were for the beer and only thirty-one for the food for two persons, consisting of two soups, roast duck, rice, and five boiled eggs! I asked Mr. Yabi how much the five eggs alone would have cost, and he replied, after consulting the bill, "Eight cents!" Obviously, if these people are mediæval, their prices are mediæval too. As usual, the host gave us a letter commending us to the next inn, and after we had duly paid our bill and a trifle extra for "tea money" we were presented with the customary fans to take along as a souvenir. At one roadside inn we received, in place of fans, a plate of small apples, somewhat like Siberian crab apples in flavor.

While waiting for our more elaborate meals to be cooked, I often amused myself watching our runners disposing of their frugal lunches — usually rice and pickles, the pasty rice being moistened with water or tea if the pickles were not rasping enough to whet the salivary glands. They generally eat standing in front of the inn, and having no table, one could hardly expect them to have table manners. They use their chopsticks, not with the dainty grace of their superiors, but simply to shovel in the rice, in big lumps, the bowl being held close to the mouth. Nor do they monkey with microscopic teacups, but drink their tea, at the close of a meal, out of their large rice bowls. But the most remarkable gastronomic sight in Japan is seen when one of the coolies invites his children to eat with him. It is amusing to see a child of two or three years take up its chopsticks and boldly tackle a pickle as big as a banana.

Toward evening all the villages we passed through seemed to be on fire, for a dense smoke was pouring out of the open sides of the houses. But it was simply the smoke from the kitchen fires seeking an easy vent in the absence of stoves and chimneys. Kindling wood is much used here for cooking, but for warming the fingers the smokeless charcoal in the hibachi is preferred. The sight of all these gastronomic preparations sharpened my appetite, and I was glad when Mr. Yabi called to me from his kuruma that we were now entering Shirakawa, where we were to spend our second night. In one respect, the inn we put up at was the best I had seen in Japan. Our bedquilts were of silk — soft, light, and clean — a great improvement on the coarse, heavy *futon* that had hitherto crushed and smothered us. This one experience taught me that it is as foolish to generalize from one's experience in inns as to the bedding of the better-class Japanese, as it would be to infer the quality of the average American bed from the coarse horse blankets given to the occupants of the expensive rat-holes in our Pullman sleeping cars.

When supper was served, the waiting maid placed a mud-colored liquid before us, in a large cup, looking at me with a pleased smile, as if to say, "There, I am sure you will like that!" It had a faint odor of coffee, and the girl said it *was* coffee, but I could not persuade myself to drink it, even to please her. On inquiry, I found it had been made just like tea, by simply pouring tolerably hot water on the ground coffee and letting it stand a minute or two. The mistake was fatal, though not as distressing as that made by a Japanese host I have read about somewhere, who served up to a foreign friend, as a special treat, the remains of a bottle of beer that had been opened months before. Such little gastronomic solecisms do not disturb an experienced traveller.

Japan has been called the travellers' paradise, and after supper I beheld a scene which certainly suggested the garden of Eden, from one point of view. Two young ladies walked across the verandah opposite our room fresh from the hot bath. They were naked and not ashamed, their dusky skins suffused with a pink flush. It takes the Occidental mind some time to get over the surprise of seeing respectable women so indifferent to what we consider propriety. Yet these women would have been shocked to see an American girl in a décolleté dress dancing a waltz with a young man.

Next day we again made an early start, and soon found that we had not yet got beyond the ravages of the storm, which began to grow monotonous. Most of the streams were still bridgeless, and my men had to carry our vehicles over several of them on planks. Over the larger rivers we had to be ferried, and one of these ferries presented a wild scene which I shall never forget. The bridge had been destroyed, the stream was very rapid, though shallow, and the only way to get across was on a sort of raft, so frail that it took a dozen coolies to prevent it from swamping. As soon as the boat was loaded, the dozen men — strongly built fellows, stark naked — pushed it into the current, which seized and whirled it across in ten seconds to where the water was again shallow, whereupon they took hold and pushed it to the shore. Several dozen natives, many of them with horses, were there when we arrived, and I was afraid that if we had to wait for our turn we should lose our train. So I told my companion to bribe the boatman with a piece of silver and tell him that we were great dignitaries. The boatman took the silver hint, and spying me near the bridge, on his next return trip, he shouted, "Anata no kuruma"— "your kurumas." I hastened to call Mr. Yabi and our men, and we were set across without delay or accident. But I was sorry that my camera was not loaded, as I would have given a good deal for a picture of those naked, muscular coolies steering that crazy raft across the wild current.

We need not have bribed the ferryman; for when, after a few more hours of trotting, we reached the station (I forget its name) where we were to board the train, we found that it was almost an hour behind time. We paid our coolies, including the man who had accompanied us all the way from Sendai, and I could not help wondering at his cheerfulness and unsubdued energy, after helping to pull a one-hundred-and-eighty-pound man about a hundred miles in two days and a half under a broiling sun.

A PILGRIM'S PARADISE

A RAINY REGION — NIKKO'S LONG STREET — OUR SUMMER HOUSE — PILGRIM PROCESSIONS — NATURE AND RELIGION — IEYASU — THE TEMPLES — ART WORKS — A SACRED DANCE — FERNS, MOSSES, AND SUN JEWELS — LOTOS ROOTS

BEFORE we reached Nikko our train was washed clean by one of those rain storms which in a mountainous region convert a placid rivulet into a furious torrent in half an hour. This was doubtless to remind us that Nikko is the rainiest spot in Japan as well as the most beautiful. Indeed, much of its beauty is a consequence of this rain; for it takes many billion drops of water to keep the tumultuous river which runs through the town, and the thirty waterfalls and cascades which are to be found within a radius of fifteen miles, tuned up to "concert pitch." Nor would the picturesque mountain slopes be so deep green, or the lakes so brimful, were it not for these frequent rains. Waterfalls, cascades, lakes, trees, ferns, mosses, mountains, — these are the scenic charms of this region, which would attract thousands of esthetic pilgrims every summer, even if time or fire should destroy the famous temples built here centuries ago in honor of departed heroes, and considered the most beautiful and richly adorned monuments in the Empire.

Apart from the treaty ports, there is no town in Japan where so many foreigners are to be seen as in Nikko, many of them spending the summer here, where, two thousand feet above the level of the sea, it is comparatively cool. One gets the impression that all of these two thousand feet are gained on the way from the railway station to the hotel at the other end of town. It is almost two miles, all the way up hill, along a street which seems to consist chiefly of small curio and photograph stores. The harsh twang of the samisen in many of the houses indicates an abundance of trained music girls. We had been warned against the foreign hotel, and would have chosen a yadoya under all circumstances. But we were in the midst of the pilgrim season, and the long processions of these bipeds we passed made us fear that our inn would be crowded. This proved to be the case, but the landlord said he had a new little building up on the hillside, where we could dwell in peace and aristocratic seclusion, far from the noisy crowd. Needless to say that the offer was accepted. We were taken up to a plain, but delightfully situated little summer house, overlooking the city and the green mountains. It had never been used, and there were just two rooms and a kitchen, so that we had no fear that others would be sent up to mar our isolation. An old woman was there to prepare our meals, and a man and boy to take care of us otherwise. We had new bedding and our own bath tub — a typical outfit consisting of a wooden box with its own heating attachment, so that a hot bath could be prepared in a few minutes by simply putting in some burning charcoal. Unlike our hot baths, these become hotter the longer you stay in them, as I found out to my cost.

More delightful still than the private bath was our private spring. Right behind the cabin a thin stream of cold water came trickling out of the mountain side. Here, for the first time in Japan, I actually drank water, because I saw its source with my own eyes. I frankly admit that I see no harm in drinking water, provided it is pure. Only a fanatical anti-hydromaniac would have refused to drink that water.

In this cottage we ate and slept several days, which proved very restful and cosy after our fatiguing journeys. Though situated several hundred yards above the main street, it was not far from it, so that we could see whatever was going on below. Every morning from seven to nine o'clock there was an unbroken procession of pilgrims, the middle of August being the height of the pilgrim season. Most of them seemed to be young men, and some were mere boys. They were all dressed in a white upper garment and white cotton drawers. On the head they wore large mushroom hats, and a fringed mat was generally thrown over the shoulders, to serve as rain cloak or sunshade in the day time, and as mattress at night. Most of them were on foot, while the few who rode on horseback wore rain cloaks made of yellow oiled paper. They looked clean and expectant as they passed, but on their return, two days later, there was a lamentable change in their appearance, their white drawers being now mud-colored, and the most respectable looking being, indeed, those who had taken theirs off entirely, and were returning "barefooted to the hips." They were dirty, bedraggled, and tired; they had walked many miles in the mud, and made the ascent of the sacred mountain. Nantiazan,

8140 feet in height, with the aid of the pilgrim staff which each of them carried.

Nikko is the paradise of Japanese pilgrims. Here they can enjoy some of the finest scenery in the whole Empire, and at the same time satisfy their sense of religious duty. In Europe and America it is only the men of genius and a few other refined souls who really *love* nature; but with the Japanese the love of nature has the intensity of a passion. The poorest and most ignorant inherit this passion from generations of esthetic ancestors; if their purse is too slender to permit them to leave home, they contribute a few cents to a special pilgrimage "pool," which gives them at least a lottery chance to travel. It is said by those who know them well that their love of scenery and travel-picnics is much stronger than their religious ardor. But the astute priests have here as elsewhere contrived to blend the esthetic and religious feelings, making the one subserve the other. In the time of their strength they usurped all the finest scenic points, built temples and monasteries on them, and invited the people to come and worship.

That such a choice site for combined esthetic and religious devotion as Nikko could not long escape the attention of the priests is obvious. For more than a thousand years, as far back indeed as historic records go, Nikko has had temples, at first Shintoist, then Buddhist, and again, by Imperial decree, Shintoist. But it was not till 1616, when the body of Ieyasu was transferred to Nikko, that it became the goal of the most patriotic pilgrimages; for what Pericles is among the Greek statesmen, Cæsar among Roman generals, Ieyasu is among the military rulers of Japan. It was he and

Iemitsu (whose body also lies here), the first and third Shoguns of the powerful Tokugawa dynasty, that founded Yeddo (Tōkyō) and inaugurated the policy of isolating Japan from the rest of the world, which lasted more than two centuries. Apart from the mountains, lakes, and waterfalls, it is the tombs of Ieyasu and Iemitsu, and the wonderful temples erected in their honor, that attract visitors to Nikko. I have no intention or desire to describe these sacred edifices. No one has ever succeeded in describing them; the best pen-pictures make but a confused impression on the mind; and warned by the failure of others, I shall mercifully abstain, mentioning only a few striking objects.

Following the procession of pilgrims to the upper end of the street, we come to the river Daiyagawa, which rushes noisily down hill. It is spanned by two bridges not far apart, on the lower of which we were allowed to cross, the upper, the Red Bridge of legendary fame, being reserved for royalty. This bridge was built in 1638 on the spot rendered famous by an old Buddhist legend of Shōdō Shōnin. This saint, according to a fantastic old memoir summarized by Mr. Satow, being in pursuit of four miraculous clouds of different colors rising straight up into the sky, found his advance barred by a broad river which poured its torrent over huge rocks and looked utterly impassable; but he fell on his knees and prayed, whereupon there appeared on the other bank a divine being of colossal size, who flung across the river two green and blue snakes, and in an instant a long bridge was seen to span the waters, like a rainbow floating among the hills; but when the saint had crossed it, both the god and the snake bridge vanished.

Stone steps, stone lanterns, rows of cryptomerias, granite torii, pebbled floors, carved ceilings, red pagodas, gilded bells, shrines and tombs, ferns and mosses, hideous idols, gates adorned with beautiful carvings of plants and animals, — elephants, tigers, lions, monkeys, dragons, unicorns, birds, — who could describe all these and a hundred other temple scenes and details without the aid of dozens of photographs which would make description superfluous? Especially odd are the monkeys calling attention by their gestures to their various sense organs. These animals are carved true to life, for Japan produces monkeys, whence we may perhaps infer that the various lions, *per contra*, are so indescribably grotesque for the reason that no Japanese sculptor has ever seen the king of beasts, except perhaps in a menagerie. Even more grotesque are the green god of wind with his wind bag on his back, and the red god of thunder with his bolts; apparently these, too, were not copied from life. The general ensemble struck me as being Hindoo rather than Japanese, possibly because I have never been in India. The eight-storied pagoda was of course after the Chinese model, but it had red Japanese lacquer over it, which is rather expensive to keep in repair, requiring renewal every fifty years. It was worn off in some places, and in others a red powder had been put on to conceal bald spots. Our guide remarked that at present the priests were too poor to keep things in thorough repair, though the government lends a helping hand. True, before the different shrines the floor was covered with money offerings; but these were mostly the perforated *rin* of which it takes ten to make a cent. The Japanese manage to live very economically, and they seem to think that their gods and priests can live more cheaply still — a notion which is becoming rather prevalent in other parts of the world.

In Japan religion and dancing still go hand in hand as among the ancient Hebrews. In one of the temple courts we passed a small building in which two women were kneeling, one young, one old, both dressed in white. You "drop a nickel in the slot" to see a dance; that is, you wrap a small coin in a piece of paper and throw it at their feet, whereupon the girl bows, gets up, makes a few slow steps forward and backward, turns around, does it over again, all the while swinging a fan gracefully in her left hand while her right rings the tiny bells attached to a sistrum. This continues about a minute, when her feet become rooted, the fan and sistrum move more and more slowly, till they too cease, whereupon the girl sinks down on her knees, bows, and the performance is over. It was amusingly like the movements of a wound-up doll, though not without a certain dignified grace. Beside this dancing booth there were others with more material attractions — tea, saké, cakes, photographs, carved idols, and various trinkets.

Unique among the objects in the temple courts is a holy-water cistern cut out of a solid block of granite. "It is so carefully adjusted on its bed, that the water conducted through a long series of pipes from the cascade called *Sō-men-daki* behind the hill, bubbles up and pours over each edge in exactly equal volumes, so that it seems to be a solid block of water rather than a piece of stone." I am always interested in noting the effect of a scene or object on different observers. Miss Bird cites part of the sentence just quoted from Mr. Satow's guidebook, with approval. When I saw that cistern, I wrote in my note-book: "Satow's comparison to a block of water is exaggerated, but gives a conception of the really wonderful regularity with which the water overflows the edges." Messrs. Chamberlain and Mason, in editing the new edition of Satow's guide, omitted the above passage entirely; wrongly, I think, because, though hyperbolical, it appeals to the imagination. The holy water in this cistern, by the way, is not used for dipping in the fingers and touching the forehead, as in our Catholic churches, but for drinking. Cups are supplied for that purpose.

In the Ieyasu museum we saw the beautiful silk kimonos worn by that hero, beside many other relics, including a row of swords presented by various Shoguns; also the kago in which Ieyasu sat when he was shot at, the hole made by the bullet being pointed out near the top. To see his tomb, we were obliged to ascend a steep hill, where it stands, shaped like a small bronze pagoda, surrounded by a stone wall. Had I been a patriotic native, I would have been seized here, doubtless, by a thrill of historic emotions; but being merely a foreigner, fond of art, and fonder still of nature, I was less interested in the tomb than in the approach to it up the stone gallery of more than two hundred steps ascending between two high walls, which are covered with rare ferns, mosses, and liverworts, fed by daily rains and shaded by stately, gloomy trees — an ideal camping place for such amphibious plants. Here it is always cool, moist, silent, and rarely does a ray of sunlight get a chance to peep in between the moving branches of the dark-green trees. One of these trees was a twin — half hard, half soft wood, the former probably grafted on the latter. The priestly guide, evidently an amateur botanist himself, helped me to find some of the rarer ferns and mosses. Say what you will, the carving of these ferns is more exquisite even than the famous miniature sculptures of the greatest Japanese artists, while the natural polish and color of ferns and mosses surpasses in beauty the finest and costliest Japanese lacquer.

We are apt to pity the poor because the beautiful things — diamonds, gold, works of art — are expensive. But are not too many of us blind to the beauty of cheap things simply because they are so cheap and common? So I thought as I sat in the shady silence of that solemn, moss-grown staircase. I recalled the first scene which had greeted my eyes when I looked down on the town from our cottage that morning. Nikko itself is not beautiful; its houses are old and decayed, its roofs covered with moss and pebbles. But when I looked down on these roofs, a rainstorm had just strewn diamonds, rubies, and emeralds all over them; at least, if all the royal jewels in the world had been cast on those roofs, and all the electric lights poured on them, the colors could not have been more brilliant and varied than those of the little drops of water left on the pebbles by the shower and irised by the rays of the morning sun.

When our supper was served that evening, I was interested in a dish of lotos roots which our cook had prepared for us. It was tempting to the eye, the roots having been sliced, perforated, and colored so as to look like pink seed pods; but I could not find much flavor in them, and I believe that one reason why they eat them is because they crackle under the teeth like a cucumber or pickle. For this crackling sound they seem to have a special liking, the tea-house girls often having a sort of quill in the mouth with which they produce it.

After our beds had been made up, I had great difficulty in persuading the old woman to leave the outside shutters partly open. She said it was against police regulations, and that there was danger from burglars; but I pacified her with my usual promise to make good any loss by theft, and to ransom her if she was carried off herself; with which promise and a bunch of grapes she smilingly contented herself. I suspect that this old woman was a geisha in her youthful days: at least, she evidently sympathized with the geishas, several of whom were indulging in noisy music in a neighboring tea-house. She had an animated conversation with my friend, in which the word *geisha* frequently recurred. She was offering her services to provide a couple of geishas to be our companions while we remained in Nikko.

NIKKO LAKES AND WATERFALLS

BACK VIEW CASCADE — TEA OR LIES — KEGON-NO-TAKI — LAKE CHŪZENJI — A LAKESIDE INN — DRAGON'S HEAD CASCADE — MOOR OF THE RED SWAMP — LAKE YUMOTO — PUBLIC BATHS — THE HOT SPRINGS — FOAM CASCADE — NEARLY A WATERFALL — SNAKE STORIES — A CHOLERA SCARE — A NIGHT HALF WAY UP FUJI — SLEEPING UNDER AN UMBRELLA

IN the morning it was still raining, and we had to spend two more days in Nikko. I began to wonder what our bill would be, and was surprised to find that the charges for the cottage, three nights, with meals for two, three servants, and four bottles of beer, was only $10.90. At last the rain ceased, and we started, without any baggage except tooth brushes, leaving our valises in charge of the old woman. We had decided to walk, as the road is all the way up hill, difficult for kurumas (three runners being required for each), and in some places even for horses. Desirous of seeing as many of the famous waterfalls and cascades as possible, we did not always keep to the main road, but made an occasional detour. In this we merely followed the example of many of the pilgrims, who thus served as free guides. The first of the cataracts was the Urami-ga-taki, the first view of which, from the bridge over the stream below it, resembles that of the Multnomah Falls made by one of the small tributaries of the Columbia River. The Japanese name means Back View Cascade, the falls resembling the Multnomah also in this, that you can go behind and under them to the other side. This should be done by all means, the best view being on the other side. There is a spacious grotto under the falls, cool, sprayful, and fern-clad, also a stone image of a god, with strips of paper stuck all over it and a number of coins lying around it, of so small a denomination that no thief would be petty enough to steal them, though he be a disbeliever in idols. Two ice-cold springs are also below the falls, tempting to the thirsty. Emerging on the other side, we get a fine view of the water as it flows from a large cleft in the rock overhead, and falls in a wide, green curve into the pool fifty feet below, the beauty of the scene being increased by the green arch formed by overhanging shade trees.

At these falls I had an odd experience in rural tea-house etiquette. On arriving, I had asked Mr. Yabi if he was thirsty. He replied that he was not, so I said we had better not waste any time on the tea house which was perched near the foot of the falls. When we were ready to proceed, I noticed that a group of pilgrims climbed the hill instead of taking the path. I suggested that we follow their example, but he thought they might be going in another direction. "Why not ask at the tea house?" I said; and he replied: "Because we did not stop to take tea. They might not tell us the truth!" So it seems that even a Jap's obliging civility may be affected by the money question. We soon had reason to regret that we had not paid tribute to the tea house, or followed the pilgrims, for we got into a muddy ditch, and found, on meeting a peasant, that we were making a big detour. He set us right, and after a few miles of arduous climbing we reached a second waterfall, the Kegon-no-taki.

I am surprised that the excellent Murray guide, the joint work of Satow and Hawes, Chamberlain, and Mason, should give only a dozen dry lines to this superb fall, which I found next to Fuji the grandest of all Japanese scenes. I can account for this only by supposing that it was "sized up" for the guide book at a time when a week's cessation of rain (if such a thing is possible here) had reduced the volume of the fall. If that was the case, we were particularly lucky in having been delayed two days by the torrents of rain which now swelled the torrent that makes the great fall. We had followed this river all the way from Nikko; it was almost always in sight, a series of foaming, headlong rapids as far as eye could reach. In the seven miles to the lake it seemed as if there were hardly a stretch of a hundred yards in which a boat could have lived half a minute. Were the waters trying to see how quickly they could get from the sacred green slopes of Nantaizan to the sacred Red Bridge at Nikko? At the falls they make a reckless tumble of 350 feet into a huge cauldron. A tea house is situated near the precipitous bank whence you look down on this grand spectacle. But to realize its true grandeur, you must leave the edge and climb down into the cauldron by a path behind the tea house. You cannot get down far, — only a hundred feet or so, — but it is enough to bring the fall opposite and partly above us, and to help us realize its depth and the stupendous dimensions of the mountain cauldron into which it tumbles as into a subterranean prison. There is one narrow outlet for the water; the rest, all around, is precipitous wall, the more impressive for being bare rock, except in a few green spots, to one of which we are clinging, holding on to a young tree which may or may not be firmly rooted. An earthslide would carry us to perdition in ten seconds. But the scene would be worth much greater risks. One would like to spend days here, watching the effect of the changing light and shade. An odd freak is a small stream of water running from the rock about half down the fall, on the left. One wonders how it ever found an aperture there. Stranger still is the fact that in the river below the falls salmon have been caught which must have come from Lake Chūzenji down the big fall, for they could not have come up from below.[1]

Like Niagara, this fall is the outflow of a lake — Chūzenji — which, in this case, is less than a mile beyond it. It lies at an elevation of 4375 feet above the ocean — only about 1500 feet lower than the most romantic of our mountain lakes, the Yellowstone and Tahoe; we were, therefore, about half a mile higher than we had been at Nikko, and only 3765 feet below the summit of Nantaizan, which can be reached from here by a two hours' climb. The lake lies at the foot of this mountain, being framed in on the other side by low, green mountains prettily serrated and densely forested, continuous except for one break. The first building seen on entering the village named after the lake is the fish commissioner's house, situated on an isolated, breezy site, looking inviting to a warm pedestrian, with its spacious rooms and foreign rocking chairs. Thousands

---

[1] The authority for this fish story is the *Japan Weekly Mail* of July 11, 1891. It is pretty well established that Norwegian salmon can jump *up* sixteen perpendicular feet.

of young salmon, salmon trout, and white trout are officially turned loose in the lake every year, and those that are not gobbled up at once by the older inhabitants (who insist on this income tax) grow up to make fine sport for fishermen.

Chūsenji is simply a pilgrims' village, being deserted except in Lotos-Time. Most of the pilgrims go no farther, but make the ascent of Nantaizan and then return to Nikko and their homes. To judge by the number of long, barrack-like, empty houses on both sides of the street, there must have been a time when pilgrims were more numerous than they are now; for we were in the midst of the season. We put up at a clean-looking inn on the edge of the lake, intending to spend the night there and proceed leisurely next day to Yumoto. We found an unengaged room facing the lake, but were told that the charge for it, not including meals, would be no less than three dollars a night; the reason given for this being that they could put up ten pilgrims in it at thirty cents each, and would be sure to get them. The landlord told us, also, that we would not find good accommodations at Yumoto, if we should decide to go on. Having some knowledge of human nature, we paid no heed to this probable lie and decided to push on after consuming the meal we had already ordered. Mr. Yabi's lunch, I was surprised to find, did not come with mine, but was served much later and was of inferior quality. I suspected that the innkeeper was perhaps trying to get even with him for not urging me to stay, but he said that it was simply a consequence of his being taken for a professional guide. "The pilgrims and others who pass us," he said, "frequently refer to me as a professional 'interpreter,' in a sneering sort of way. The extortions of the Yokohama guides, who make a regular business of fleecing foreigners, have brought them into contempt among their countrymen."

There was no time to lose if we were to make the six more miles of ascent to Yumoto before dark. Owing to our detours to see the falls, and our mistake in one place, we had walked twelve miles instead of seven. There were two more fine cascades between Chūsenji and Yumoto, one of which I intended to see now, leaving the second for our return trip. We reached the first of them, which bears the name of Dragon's Head Cascade, shortly after we had left the lake behind us. It reminded me somewhat of a section of the mammoth Hot Springs in the Yellowstone Park. The water swishes down over half a dozen narrow rock terraces, which, however, are not white, but dark, in some spots almost black, contrasting strikingly with the white foam which, geyser-like, seethes up from the hollows into which the water has tumbled. To the left are two pretty trout pools, without trout, however, I fancy. At the foot of the cascade the water is divided into two small streams by a rock from which the finest view is obtained, not only of the cascades above, but of the deep, tortuous cleft into which the main stream tumbles below, where it is soon lost to sight in the gloom.

After traversing a desolate forest section which, according to the guide book, was ravaged by fire some years ago, we presently came out into the Moor of the Red Swamp, "probably so named from the color of the dying grass in autumn." It is a genuine mountain valley, reminding one in its atmosphere of melancholy Andermatt in Switzerland. Had it been earlier in the day, we should now have devoted an hour to the Yu-no-taki Cascade to the left; but three waterfalls in one day seemed quite enough, and I felt sure that we should appreciate the fourth one more in the morning, after a night's sleep in the mountain air. So we just cast a glance at it in passing and proceeded on our way to Lake Yumoto, which was not far off. A prettier mountain lake it would be difficult to find anywhere. Densely wooded, fragrant, dark green mountain slopes form its shores with a few very picturesque promontories or projections. But the distinctive peculiarity of this lake lies in the way in which the trees and the water are blended. It looks almost as if some giant power had pushed the wooded slopes right into the lake. As a matter of fact, I fancy the water must have risen till it almost touched the lowest branches of the overhanging pines, which consequently seem at a distance to actually grow out of the water.

Lakes should be seen, not smelled. The waters of Yumoto have the one fault that they can be smelled even before they are seen, if the wind happens to come from the village of the same name at the other end, where the famous hot sulphur springs, that attract so many health seekers, run into the lake. The clear, greenish tint of the lower lake is changed by this sulphurous invasion into a light blue, hardly less pleasing to the eye, provided it can forget its nasal neighbor.

Yumoto village consists chiefly of bath houses conducted in the old-fashioned Japanese way. The first building, to the left, was one of these bath houses — or rather a large pool with a roof over it, the sides being open to the view. Here about a dozen men, women, and girls were enjoying the hot water, some immersed up to the neck, others reclining on the edge and gossiping, all in the original costume of Adam and Eve, and as unconscious of impropriety as so many babies. The other bath houses usually had two tanks, one filled with men, the other with women, but not separated by any partition. There were always a few men on the women's side, and a few women on the men's side. The fashionable costume for bathers on the way to or from the baths seemed to be a blue towel hung over the arm or shoulder. It is so much more convenient, you know, to leave the kimono at home and let the sun complete the drying process on the way back to one's room.

Of course we were bound to have a hot sulphur bath too, and I began to wonder whether our inn would provide one, or whether we should have to do as the Romans do. We found that the inn did have a private bath, not on the premises, but a few hundred yards away, in a separate little building to which the hot sulphur water was conveyed in a pipe direct from the springs. We donned the kimonos and slippers supplied by our waiting maid, and taking a couple of blue towels, followed our guide to the bath house. I was amused to notice that my companion, in spite of his foreign experience, used his towel in the Japanese way; that is, he dipped it in the water, washed himself with it, and then, wringing it out, tried to dry himself with it,—a process requiring considerable faith or imagination. The water was of a supportable temperature, and the bath a refreshing luxury after our eighteen miles' walk. Somehow water warmed by volcanic forces seems to have a more soothing, voluptuous effect on the nerves than artificially heated water. 'Tis an ill wind, etc.; the Japanese suffer terrible calamities from earth-

R

quakes, but the same volcanic forces that cause them constantly heat for them thousands of these springs in which they can luxuriate by the hour and chuckle at the great saving in charcoal.

Our conjecture that the innkeeper at Chūsenji lied when he said we would find Yumoto crowded, proved correct. There were no pilgrims here at all, and we had our choice of rooms in the inn, which was clean and well kept, our maid being as extravagantly attentive as she was ugly. She was one of the type of peasant women we had met on the way, with limbs as massive and well rounded as those of Swiss-Italian dairy maids.

On our way back we stopped at the Yu-no-taki Cascade. To see it at its best, it is necessary to descend to its foot. I do not know what its Japanese name means; but the thought that flashed into my mind, after the first almost bewildering impression, was: "This ought to be called the Foam Cascade." In the last cascade described by me the foam was mingled with the darker water; but here it was all one white sheet of foam swishing down over the sloping rock like a perpetual avalanche of snow dust. The slightest increase in the angle would have entirely altered the scene; I have never seen another cascade which so narrowly escaped being a waterfall. I was glad it had escaped; no fall could have taken its place in my admiration; no fall could have thus spread out like a white fan from a narrow top to a broad base; no fall could have conveyed the same "arrow-water" effect of swiftness. A fall would have dropped into an agitated pool, whereas at the base of this cascade the foam suddenly resumes the form of water, and flows away in an almost placid brook. It is about thirty or forty feet wide, and several hundred in height. The sides are lined with ferns and mosses, the top and the left edge all the way up fringed by overhanging trees; as in the Bridal Veil in the Yosemite Valley, the water seems to flow right out of the blue sky above. When the overhanging maples are touched with autumn colors, the effect must be finer still.

Returning to the desolate Moor of the Red Swamp, we were favored with a fine view of the sacred Nantaizan, once a volcano, but so long at rest that all traces of its crater have disappeared. As we looked, the clouds were rent in twain, leaving the summit in mists, while the lower slopes were bathed in warm, yellow sunlight. To the right a perpendicular rainbow added the finishing touches to the sublime spectacle. We would have ascended this mountain, but as our next expedition was to be to Fuji, it seemed scarcely worth while to attempt a peak almost a mile lower. The prospect of going up Fuji helped to console me for having to leave this elevated region, where I had felt more braced up than in any other part of Japan. Everything was in our favor on the return trip,— a cool wind in the face, fleecy clouds above to serve as sunshades, and every step down hill. Nevertheless, when we reached the edge of Lake Chūsenji again, we could not resist the temptation to take a cooling bath in its clear waters, to the delight of the small fry of fish which swarmed about us and nibbled at our toes and legs. We had of course taken a hot sulphur bath before leaving Yumoto, and on getting back to Nikko we had another hot bath. Three baths in one day! I began to feel quite Japanese.

Both in going and returning we saw a number of

snakes along the roadside, some of them being two or three feet in length. Mr. Yabi said they were harmless, and that although poisonous snakes do exist in Japan, they are rare, and their bite not fatal if the limb is cut off at once. The peasants boil these snakes (a species of adder) and eat them as a medicine. Mr. Yabi also maintained that in the southern part of the island there exists a kind of boa, large enough to swallow children, and that formerly some of these monsters led an amphibious existence at Lake Chūsenji. They play a great rôle in Japanese legends, but the geologists have not yet officially certified to their existence, although only a few years ago, as Professor Chamberlain tells us, the vernacular press printed a circumstantial account of the swallowing alive of a woman by one of these serpents.

On the following morning we took the train for Tōkyō, where we remained a day to make preparations for an ascent of Fuji. Had we succeeded in reaching the summit, it would have been worth while to devote a chapter to this excursion; but as the incessant rain made us turn back before we had got half way up, I will mention only two picturesque incidents of the trip. Knowing that nothing is so refreshing and strengthening to climbers as tea, I took along half a pound of the English breakfast variety, of which I prepared a strong infusion at a wayside inn. We had several miles more to ride before reaching Uma-gaeshi, or " horse-send-back." Now, on the day before we left Tōkyō, there had been about thirty local deaths from cholera, and about as many at Yokohama. My companion had spent the night at home, and knowing his carelessness in regard to eating and drinking, I had felt some little

FUJI FROM HAKONE LAKE

anxiety about him. He seemed to be all right, however, till suddenly, shortly after we had left the inn where we had made the tea, he stopped his horse, got off, and lay down on the ground, looking pale as a ghost. Here was a predicament! I felt sure he had caught the cholera, and expected to see him a corpse in an hour; for Asiatic cholera often makes short work of its victims. I offered him a spoonful of tea mixed with a few drops of acid phosphate (which I carried in my pocket as a germicide, in case I should have to drink suspicious water or tea), and he took it. Five minutes later, to my surprise and joy, the color returned to his face, and presently he sat up, smiled, and said: "I guess that Chinese tea was too strong for me!"

So our tragedy luckily ended in comedy, and we proceeded up the mountain, clad in oil-paper cloaks, leaving our horses at the next station. The rain drenched us in torrents all the way up, and I wondered more and more what became of all the water, which sank into the black ground as fast as it fell, and nowhere came to the surface again in the form of brooks or springs. We passed a few pilgrims with tinkling bells attached to their belts, — the only thing to break the Alpine silence about us. Luckily, the pilgrim season was over; else we might have found the station where we had to spend the night overcrowded. There are six of these stations, ours being, I believe, the third. It was a sort of cave dwelling — a wretched hovel, dug partly into the lava, partly built up of big stones, heavy enough to resist the winter winds. We had two porters, and our party of four, with the host and his wife and child, just about filled up the one small room, the little space available being diminished by a large pile of wood and a tank full of rainwater. In the middle of the room there was a fire hole in the ground, with a tripod, but no chimney, or even a hole in the roof; consequently, when the preparations for supper began, the cabin was soon filled with smoke so dense that I had to close my eyes. This prevented me from seeing what the innkeeper's wife put into our soup. However, I boldly drank some of the liquid and, with my chopsticks, fished out the pieces of hard-boiled egg floating in it; but I could not persuade myself to tackle the other solid ingredients, which had a mysterious appearance and taste. Mine host, seeing me push the bowl away, asked if I had finished; when I said I had, he seized the chopsticks and the bowl and eagerly gobbled up the remains. They cannot afford to waste wood or food at such an altitude. I found solace in a can of cold chicken, with jam and crackers for dessert. We must have formed a picturesque group — Yabi and I on one side, demolishing our foreign canned viands, picnic style, and on the other side our porters and the innkeeper's family, with a huge bucket of rice between them, from which they helped themselves to four or five large bowls each, shovelling in the unflavored mush with an appetite bred of mountain air.

Our beds were made up soon after supper, each of us receiving one quilt to lie on and one to use as a cover, besides a square block of wood for a pillow. By keeping on all my clothes and putting over them my overcoat, which one of the porters had brought up, I managed to keep tolerably warm. But the night was a burlesque on sleep which I shall never forget, though I should live a century longer. The storm was increasing when we lay down. After about an hour's nap, I awoke to find the rain dripping fast and furious on my unprotected nose. I moved my "pillow" a few inches, but the rain followed. I opened my umbrella, and Mr. Yabi, whose experience was a duplicate of mine, did the same with his. This was the first time I ever slept under an umbrella, — and I have no desire to repeat the experiment.

When we woke up in the morning, the rain was coming down more violently than ever, and our host agreed with the porters that it would be unwise to proceed. It had been raining that way for several days, and all the signs indicated that it would continue several days longer. We were told that a few pilgrims, who had persevered on the preceding day, had seen nothing whatever, and had been so cold in the lava huts on the summit that they could not hold the tea cups in their hands. Under the circumstances, it would have been foolish to proceed, so I named our station jin-gaeshi, — man-turn-back, — and we retraced our steps, the sympathetic clouds drenching us all the way down with big tears over our disappointment.

RAILWAY GENRE PICTURES

THE LEGEND OF FUJI AND BIWA — A POPULAR RAILWAY — HOW JAPANESE WOMEN SMOKE — A MARRIED BEAUTY — THE DRESS PROBLEM — FAT WRESTLERS — LUNCH BOXES — CHEAP TEA SETS

IN Portland, Oregon, they tell a story of an old resident, who took a "tenderfoot" from the East up the heights, and with great pride pointed out the snowy cone of Mount Hood. "You see that mountain? It is now about 11,000 feet high. When I came to Oregon, it was a mere hole in the ground!"

In Japan they have a legend which beats even that story. It is related that one night Fuji suddenly shot up from the ground, and what is more, that on the same night Lake Biwa, near Kyōto, 140 miles away, was formed by the simultaneous subsiding of a corresponding area of land. These stories, after all, are not quite so ridiculous as they seem, for it is known that volcanoes *have* thus risen suddenly from land or sea, and that they really *do* grow from the overflow and hardening of the lava, to which they owe their regular conical shape, which always distinguishes volcanic peaks from others. It is only fair to add, too, that not all the Japanese believe in the Lake Biwa part of that legend. Thus, one old writer says, with some force, "On consideration, I think that the vulgar reports which say that the earth from Hako [Lake Biwa] became Fuji-san are falsehoods; for how could the earth be well transported thither when Suruga and Omi are separated by more than 100 ri?"

While it may not be true that the mud of Biwa was carried 140 miles north, it is undeniable that such mud of Fuji as clung to our boots was carried 140 miles south to Biwa, as we took the morning train from Gotemba to Kyōto. This railway was not completed till 1889. Before its construction the trip from the new capital to the old took ten days by kuruma, or nearly two days by steamer. To-day it can be made in sixteen to twenty hours by rail, the distance being 329 miles. Such a saving in time makes an impression even on the leisurely Oriental minds, and as the cost is proportionately reduced (only one cent a mile, third class), the cars are usually as crowded as in America and northern Europe, wherefore the Kyōto railway affords excellent opportunities for studying manners and customs *en route*.

Some of the second-class cars have notices forbidding smoking. To these the natives do not always pay attention, unless specially requested, for the simple reason that it does not occur to them that any one could possibly object to a habit in which they all indulge, women as well as men. A smoking woman is to me an unpleasant sight, but I could not help getting considerable amusement from watching the process. A Japanese pipe, as used by both women and men, is not as large as a thimble, — about the size of a Chinese opium pipe, — and holds perhaps as much tobacco as would make a pinch of snuff. There was a pretty girl of about eighteen sitting opposite us, who took a smoke several times an hour. She filled her little bowl from a dainty little pouch, lighted a match, took three or four whiffs, then knocked the bowl against her wooden shoe, so that the glowing pellet fell on the floor. In a moment she refilled her pipe, but instead of relighting it with a match, she tried to pick up the fiery lump with the bowl, which, after a few failures, she dextrously succeeded in doing. Matches are extremely cheap in Japan, but one gets the impression that they have not been long in use. Most of the men, after striking one, perversely hold it head upwards, with the result that it usually goes out before it has been of any use.

The offensiveness and injuriousness of the smoking habit are greatly lessened by the smallness of Japanese pipes. Every smoker knows that in a pipe or cigar the first whiffs are the best. In Japanese smoking all whiffs are first whiffs; there are no offensive cigar ends or big bowls saturated with sickening nicotine. Smokers do not perpetually smell of the weed as elsewhere, and altogether the indulgence is more esthetic. The ideal process of smoking, however, would be to simply ignite the tobacco and smell of it, as of incense sticks, without taking the smoke in the mouth; for in this way the fragrance of good tobacco would be much more agreeable, and the offensiveness of bad tobacco much less disagreeable.

There was a certain historic fitness in making smoke studies on the way to Kyōto, for it was in that ancient capital that *tabako* was first made fashionable in Japan, about half a century after its introduction into Europe. Mr. Satow quotes from a native chronicle of 1605 that "the inhabitants of Kyōto contended with one another in smoking, and the habit is rapidly spreading over the country." In the same year a native physician wrote of tobacco as having lately come into use. He describes it as leaves " of which one drinks the smoke," and alludes to a current belief that it was "a cure for all diseases."

When the young woman opposite us was not smoking, she was chewing — not tobacco — that filthy habit is unknown here — nor the flavored gum beloved of our young ladies, but something which looked (but probably did not taste) like a small red-pepper fruit. My comrade said it was called *hodsuké*, and was for sale in fruit stores. At one of the stations our girl got off, and her place was taken by a married woman of about thirty accompanied by two children of about five and seven. She was still remarkably beautiful, showing that not all Japanese women lose their physical charms soon after marriage. Of course her teeth were not blackened nor her eyebrows shaved, these mediæval mutilations being no longer indulged in by women who are " in the swim." On the other hand, I was pleased to see that she had had the courage and good sense to retain her Japanese costume, although both her husband and son were dressed in foreign clothes, from the hat down to the shoes. The Japanese female costume undoubtedly has its disadvantages in practical life (it hampers the gait), but it is infinitely more picturesque and becoming than a Parisian costume on a Parisian woman ; and when the Parisian costume is transferred to a Japanese woman, the effect is usually deplorable — an utter absence of fit, style, ease, and naturalness.

Among all the women who entered and left our car from station to station there was only one who wore a foreign dress, and she was a warning example of self-conscious awkwardness, the direct negation of the artless grace which constitutes one of the inherited charms of Japanese women. Her dowdiness was emphasized by the appearance of a young girl sitting next her, a maiden with pretty features and a finely moulded figure, whose picturesque dress indicated that she was a geisha. She was accompanied by an old man, her guardian, and was doubtless on her way to enliven some banquet with her song, samisen, or dance. But no rose without thorns — her complexion was so utterly marred by paint and powder on lips and cheeks that even the merry twinkle of her coquettish black eyes could not repair the damage.

Japan is proverbially a land of miniatures; everything is planned on a small scale. But there are some astounding exceptions, to which reference was made in a preceding chapter. With one of these, Fujisan, we had just wrestled in vain, and I am sure we should have fared worse yet had we attempted to wrestle with one of the human Fujis who came into our car at Nagoya — four professional wrestlers, who would have been regarded as giants even in America, while here, among the small Japanese, they appeared like actual Brobdingnagians. Their loose dress could hardly cover the huge masses of fat and muscle on their arms, abdomen, and legs. They looked absurdly like disgustingly fat old women, the illusion being heightened by their old-fashioned feminine way of dressing the hair. Some of these fellows astonished the members of our Perry expedition when it opened up Japan. One man carried a sack of rice weighing 125 pounds suspended by his teeth; another took a sack in his arms and turned a series of somersaults with it, as if it had been a feather.

But I believe it is by their weight rather than their muscle that these monsters win, hence eating is the principal part of their training. I had no chance to see a match, but in Kyōto, one evening, I found a crowd of Japanese children and adults in front of an eating house, gaping with open mouths at the gluttonous feats of a group of wrestlers. I fancied that these brutes must belong to a special branch of the Japanese race, or at least come from a special province; but Mr. Yabi said that this was not the case. They come from various parts of the country; they are great popular heroes, like the bull fighters in Spain; hence, whenever a man of the lower classes grows up abnormally big, he becomes a wrestler for profit and glory, which is sometimes gory. A native writer says that his countrymen become so excited over wrestling matches that "they throw their clothes and valuables into the ring, to be redeemed afterwards in money; nay, in his excitement, a man will even tear off his neighbor's jacket and throw it in."

There are no eating stations along Japanese railways, and as the dining-car stage of evolution has not yet been reached, we had taken our lunch along. But we would not have starved if we had neglected this precaution, for at meal time the station platforms were crowded by boys and men carrying trays full of lunch boxes, besides cakes, eggs, unripe fruit, bottled beer, lemonade, etc. The lunch boxes usually contain rice with fish, or pickles, the more expensive ones including sandwiches or cold meat. But the most remarkable things — real "bargains" — are the pots of tea that are offered to the passengers — small earthen pots, neatly decorated, filled with a pint of hot tea and costing, with a thin, pretty porcelain cup, only three or four cents!

Some of the passengers bought several of these tea sets, and before we reached the end of our journey they had a regular pantry under their seats. A party of American missionary women at the other end of our car, though supplied with knives and forks, ate their lunch with chopsticks, perhaps in order to conciliate the natives. They distributed tracts from the car windows.

FASCINATIONS OF KYŌTO

WATERMELONS AND CHOLERA — THE JAPANESE ROME — A CITY OF TEMPLES — COREAN EAR MOUND — BUDDHIST CHANTING — RASCALLY PRIESTS — SILK FACTORIES — SOUTHERN FEMALE BEAUTY — THE SPANISH TYPE — A BLIND MUSICIAN — KOTO CONCERT — CHEAP ART TREASURES — AN ORIENTAL NOCTURNE

From Tōkyō to Kyōto is almost as far as from Boston to Baltimore. It was, therefore, not surprising that the fields and mountains gradually assumed a more southern aspect as we neared Kyōto. The broom cane in the fields reminded one of Missouri; the wells scattered through the rice fields indicated that rivers are less abundant than farther north. There had been much less summer rain here than in Tōkyō; the air was drier; the hillsides were not so luxuriantly green, but scarred with many rocky patches entirely bare of vegetation.

It was dark when we reached Kyōto. As we rode through the streets in our kurumas, it seemed as if the houses were even more open to view than at Tōkyō, hardly a detail of domestic life being concealed. And what a careless people they are, taking their pleasure to-day, regardless of to-morrow! On that very day there had been a hundred cases of cholera in the city of Osaka, only thirty miles away, and a number of cases in Kyōto itself; yet it seemed as if half the population had turned out to spend the evening eating watermelons. Kyōto would be a real "nigger's heaven." Every other house appeared to be turned into a melon stand, and behind each huge pile of green watermelons stood a man with a large knife cutting them into juicy slices, and distributing them for a trifle to his customers, who stood or sat around on benches demolishing them *con gusto*. There was so much to see that I wished our long ride to the hotel were much longer. Our men dragged us up a steep hillside, and finally landed us at the Yaami hotel, noted for its fine view of the city below, and the semi-bare mountains beyond. It is a site that any Buddhist temple might be proud of, and I found it cooler at night than I had expected. The hotel is more than half foreign, and we were excellently taken care of, the rooms being airy, the beds soft, the meals well cooked; and while we were eating, small boys armed with huge fans kept us cool. Yet the guests here were all foreigners; the charges are three dollars a day, which seems very high to natives of a country where the average earnings are twenty cents a day, and where one can live on about seven dollars a month.[1]

Kyōto suggests Rome in some respects. For more than a thousand years — 794 to 1868 — it was the capital of Japan, the seat of culture, licentiousness, etiquette, religion, and learning, with a population of over a million pleasure-loving people, devoted to religious fes-

---

[1] A Tōkyō paper, the *Jiji Shimpo*, says that in that city a man can get board and lodging for six or seven yen (dollars) a month. It adds that "one summer and one winter suit of clothes should suffice a man for three years," and that "to ride to and from one's office in a kuruma is simply thriftless self-indulgence."

tivals and secular picnics. Here dwelt the Mikado, revered as sacred, inaccessible, infallible ; here were the headquarters of the religious orders. To-day Kyōto, like Rome, has dwindled to a quarter of its former size ; but whereas Rome, with a population of 270,000, has what is considered the remarkable number of 354 churches, Kyōto, with exactly the same population, had, as late as 1875, as many as 3500 temples, with 8000 priests. Since the disestablishment of Buddhism, twenty years ago, their number has rapidly diminished, and of those that remain, many have been left isolated in the suburbs by the shrinking of the city, like anchored vessels stranded by a receding ocean. In addition to these city temples there used to be countless others on the picturesque sites of neighboring mountains. Thus the "chilly mountain"—Hiei-zan—was, according to the historians, covered during mediaeval times with as many as three thousand Buddhist buildings ; and we read that "the monks, who were often ignorant, truculent, and of disorderly habits, became the terror of Kyōto, on which peaceful city they would swoop down after the manner of banditti," until the great warrior Nobunaga arose in just wrath, burnt the temples, and dispersed the monks.

But if the Buddhist monks did not always behave themselves, they were great patrons of the fine arts, and many are the marvellous sights still to be seen in their principal temples in Kyōto. The reader will, I am sure, pardon me for dismissing those sights with a reference to the red guide book in which they are minutely and admirably described by experts. But a few running comments at random may not be out of place. The kurumayas who took us from temple to temple were practical fellows. They brought along covers of blue muslin to put over our shoes, so that we did not have to waste time by continually taking them off and putting them on again. We saw many priceless works of art, in looking at which it made one shudder to think that they were constantly exposed to the danger of fire in such inflammable wooden buildings. We saw old pictures showing that even in conservative Japan, costume and the style of wearing the hair have often changed. We saw the famous temple with the thousand quaint images of Kwannon standing in rows like soldiers, and we saw the gigantic bell and the giant Daibutsu or Great Buddha, fifty-eight feet in height, whose nose is nine feet long and his ears twelve (no disrespect intended). Near by, we saw also the Ear Mound, in which the ears and noses of slain Corean warriors were buried, three centuries ago — a mound which may without frivolity be said to mark a new *era*, since it had been previously the custom to bring to the victorious generals the whole heads of the fallen enemies. We saw the special room in which Hideyoshi used to inspect these heads. Ear and nose cutting, however, seems to have had no more effect on the Coreans than decapitation, for did not they send the following insulting and taunting message to Japan as late as 1872?

"We Coreans are a very small country, but yet we have the courage to put in writing to you that Western barbarians are beasts. The above we intend as a direct insult to you and your allies, the barbarians. We desire that you should join them and bring your great ships and your army here. Fusankai is the nearest port of Corea to Japan."

In some of the temples the evidences of rapid decay were mournfully apparent. But in one respect these were the most interesting of all: their dim religious silence harmonized with their dim religious light; the carps in the lotos ponds, unused to the sound of footsteps, splashed to the surface to be fed whenever we approached. In one of the more frequented temples we stopped to hear the "musical" service. It made me long for more of the dim religious silence. A few dozen priests were chanting in the inner enclosure. If Schopenhauer called the Catholic cathedral service *Pfaffengeplärr*, I wonder what he would have said of this performance; I am afraid it would have severely tested his Buddhist predilections. Each priest raised his voice independently, and after exercising his lungs for a while he seemed to make a faint attempt to get somewhere near the notes sung by others; but these efforts rarely resulted in exact unison, and the general effect, especially at a slight distance, was surprisingly like the bleating of a flock of sheep. The congregation listened to the service, kneeling, some counting off their beads. Near the door stood a group of men, smoking and talking, as if in a tavern. But the priests themselves sometimes hire temples for political meetings, dramatic dances, and other geisha entertainments.

From the Kiyomizu temple we went down a gulch into which tumble three miniature streams of water. Here a girl had a stand with selected sweets, and a number of bottles filled with sacred water, to the use of which the priests ascribe beneficial effects. Another of their pious frauds (how the human race does love to be bamboozled by priests!) is that you please the gods by letting the first of those cascades tickle and chill your back. The girl lends bathing tights for the purpose. We saw a poor old woman, between seventy and eighty, all shrivelled up and naked, standing under the stream, her hands clasped in prayer, shivering in the cold water. I felt sorry for the decrepit, foolish victim of priestly mendacity.

They are a rascally lot, these Buddhist priests, quite as bad as were the mediaeval monks of Europe. The Japanese themselves cheerfully admit this. A Buddhist paper, the *Bukkyo*, points out that the three failings of the priesthood are idleness, immorality, and disloyalty to the faith; while another paper not unfavorable to Buddhism, the *Ajiya*, says that the great evil to-day is that "now the priesthood is composed, for the most part, of the lowest dregs of society, bankrupt spendthrifts, knaves who have no other place of refuge left, and good-for-nothing fellows incapable of earning a livelihood in any sterner line of life."

Theoretically, the Buddhist priests are so averse to taking the life of even the humblest living thing, that they have invented legends about the punishment inflicted in hell on those who spend their life scalding silkworms. In practice, however, they are not at all averse to wearing silk gowns whenever they can afford to do so. Nor do I wonder at their inconsistency; Japanese silks would have tempted a ragged mediaeval anchorite to dress up and change his asceticism to estheticism. Kyōto has for ages been a famous silk centre, and as a matter of course we spent an afternoon visiting some of the places where it is woven. In a country where silk is made in such enormous quantities, both for home wear and for export, one would expect to find enormous factories with complicated machinery. But Japan has not yet reached that stage of "civilization" where thousands work for one capitalist. The largest place we could find here had only about twenty looms. Men, women, and girls were employed, the women for the reeling, the men for the weaving. It is slow work. Of some of the finer kinds we saw, an expert can weave only five feet a day. It was fascinating to note the skill and taste with which they wove in the patterns of flowers and other ornaments. I asked the price of some superb velvet just finished, and was told it was fourteen feet for ten dollars. We visited three factories and were in each case courteously escorted by the proprietor. It is very warm in these places, consequently the men wear only a loin cloth, and the women too are unclothed to the waist. Most of them would have been more attractive if they had concealed their physical charms; the silk weavers evidently do not, like the innkeepers, choose their assistants for their beauty of form and face.

Kyōto has been famed many centuries for the beauty and grace of its women; and with justice. In Japan, as in America, in Spain, in Italy, in Germany, the women become more beautiful, the farther we go south. This seems to be a law of nature which can only be accounted for by the beautifying effect of abundant sunshine and open-air life all the year round. Tōkyō is not exactly a northern city, yet Kyōto lies three hundred miles south of it, and to a trained eye there is a perceptible difference in the average physiognomy. In all probability Japan was originally peopled by Malayans coming from the south and by Tartars and other Mongolians coming from the north and west. Of the Tartar type, which is perhaps the ugliest in the world, one sees many specimens in northern Japan, while the Malayan type, physically one of the most beautiful in the world, prevails largely in the south, with its more regular features and straight, large black eyes. True, the ordinary pictures on fans, screens, and vases would lead one to think that all these women have absurdly oblique, almond-shaped eyes; but these pictures do not correspond to reality, Japanese artists being realists only in their paintings of plants and animals, whereas in human drawings they are idealists, or rather conventionalists.

In Kyōto even more than in Tōkyō, I was struck by the fact that, when Japanese girls are very pretty they greatly resemble Spanish beauties in their sparkling black eyes, dark tresses, olive complexion, petite stature, and exquisite grace, at least from the waist up. The resemblance would be greatly heightened if they would copy Spanish ways of arranging the hair and give up their stereotyped style of combing it back from the forehead — the most trying and least becoming of all modes of coiffure. It is to be hoped, too, that Japanese women will before long realize the vulgarity of smearing their hair into a dead, greasy mess with their bad-smelling pomade — a custom which puts them on a level with our "perfumed" masculine barbers' pets, and makes one sometimes dread to be near them.

The Kyōto beauty uses her fan a good deal as a cooler, but less frequently in the Andalusian way, holding it up as a sunshade. She is more apt to use it to keep her lord and master cool and comfortable. Imagine an Andalusian beauty doing such a thing — or an American! We have spoiled our women, gentlemen! I assure you there is nothing more cosy and delightful in the world than to recline on soft white mats on a sultry summer afternoon, with one bright-eyed music girl to entertain you, a nimble second maiden to bring you dainties to eat and drink, and a patient third beauty to cool your brow with her gayly ornamented large fan. Why have we voluntarily given up man's aboriginal and inalienable right to such luxuries? And yet our spoiled and petted women are clamoring for their "rights"! *O tempora, O mores!*

I asked Mr. Yabi what he thought of Kyōto girls. He said the general impression among his countrymen was that the Tōkyō girls are more lively, the Kyōto girls more gentle and pretty. But with the modern decline of Kyōto, he added, many of the famous beauties had emigrated to richer cities, especially to the neighboring Osaka, the commercial metropolis of the country. We visited some of the leading photographers in Kyōto to add to my collection of Japanese beauties. In each place they put before us a number of black lacquer trays, each containing a dozen photographs of popular geishas. You can buy not only the pictures, but the girls too — that is, you can secure their address and get them to assist at a banquet with their song, samisen, or dance. Private pictures are not sold by these photographers — a fact which some that I saw made me regret exceedingly, for they were faces of the most refined and fascinating beauty.

The charming geishas of Kyōto are also specially famed for their skill as musicians; but when I told Mr. Yabi that I would like to hear some of their music, he asked: "Would you not rather hear one of the blind musicians? They play even better than the girls." After a brief struggle with my conscience, I decided that I would in this case sacrifice the love of beauty to art for art's sake. So a messenger was sent to a famous blind musician, and in the afternoon he arrived punctually at the hour designated. He had a koto and a samisen, — the latter in five pieces, so that it could be carried in a little box. But it was his koto that I specially wanted to hear. He was reputed the best player in town; and when he began to tune up in the hotel parlor, all the guests, as well as the native attendants, came in, or crowded around the door. The player squatted on the floor and had his instrument lying flat before him.

The koto is the Japanese harp. In national estimation and artistic value it is related to the samisen as a piano is to a banjo. As it lies on the mats it looks somewhat like a large zither. Under each of its thirteen strings is a movable bridge, by means of which the pitch can be raised or lowered. However widely the music of the Japanese may differ from our own, their sense of pitch is as keen as ours; the slightest deviation was at once detected by the ear of our player and corrected by moving the bridge without interrupting the playing. To my ears there seemed to be more rhythm than melody in his music, and the rhythm had the irregularity or lack of symmetry characteristic of all Japanese art. Still, there was an occasional melodic strain which seemed quite definite, and, what was more interesting still, there were suggestions of harmony here and there, — fifths, sixths, and minor sevenths. His glissando effects were as dainty as Paderewski's in a Liszt rhapsody. He was indeed a great virtuoso, and there was to me a genuine, though somewhat bewildering, pleasure in listening to him. Toward the end of

his last piece he worked himself up to a climax that was really admirable, and was more like our own music than anything I had heard in Japan.

I came to the conclusion that the koto is really a charming instrument, which could not fail to find favor in our own musical circles. Of course there are kotos and kotos, as there are pianos and pianos; there are four principal kinds, with seven minor varieties, the cost varying from $5 to $500. Our player's instrument was probably one of the best; it had a rich, sonorous tone very agreeable to the ear after the twang of the samisens that filled the ear every night like the chirping of multitudinous insects. After every piece or two our blind virtuoso drank a glass of sweetened water. A boy kneeling beside him kept him cool with a huge fan, while another boy in picturesque attire provided similarly for my comfort.

Other artists called on me at the hotel, uninvited, but none the less welcome. One of them brought some exquisite cloisonné vases, at prices about one-tenth of what they would be in New York. Another unrolled for me a superb collection of silk kakemonos painted with cherry blossoms, lotos, autumnal maple twigs, and so on. The silk itself cost him a dollar apiece, but he asked only $2.50 and $3.50 for them. These poor artists had evidently seen better days, when Kyōto was still the capital.

Our evenings were devoted to sight-seeing along the principal streets, especially one which seemed to be the fashionable promenade for all classes. Here we found the same clean, well-behaved crowds as in Tōkyō, the same gentle curiosity in our doings, the same rows of booths in the street, with toys and toilet articles, the same dime museums and theatres, the same ice, tea, and fruit stands — green persimmons being the seasonable novelty on the latter — and, of course, watermelons everywhere. Here, too, the crowds were so dense that we had to leave our kurumas and walk. The whole street was brilliant with flaming torches and paper lanterns, and when we came back to the hotel on the hillside, late at night, this street could be distinctly traced, from end to end, by the string of brilliant lights, threading its way through the comparative darkness of the rest of the city. Kyōto, in the dark, is a dreamy Oriental nocturne. It is pleasant to sit on the hotel piazza and think of all the romances, comedies, and tragedies, that are being enacted in the thousands of humble houses that lie between the hill from which we gaze and the low mountains, faintly visible beyond in the rising mist; pleasant to review the kaleidoscopic scenes of the day, amid which only one is disquieting — the rather frequent funeral processions we had passed in the streets — two men, in each case, carrying on their shoulders a kago-like box in which the corpse sits upright (invisible, of course), followed by a number of mourners. Although we had been told at the hotel that the cholera had not yet reached the city, these funerals aroused suspicions which afterwards proved to be well founded.

LAKE AND LOTOS POND

OTSU — PUNS AND POETRY — JAPAN'S LARGEST LAKE — ACRES OF LOTOS FLOWERS — DIFFICULT TO PAINT — THE LOTOS IN JAPAN, INDIA, AND AMERICA

In order to complete the round of famous places in Japan, we had intended to extend our trip to Osaka, "the Venice of Japan"; Nagasaki, where for more than two centuries the small Dutch colony formed the only connecting link between Japan and Europe; and the picturesque Inland Sea. But as the ravages of cholera were increasing in all this region at an alarming rate, we reluctantly gave up this part of the projected journey, and decided to cross Lake Biwa, and then return to Yokohama and seek a safe retreat at Miyanoshita, or some other mountain resort. In pursuance of this plan, we took the evening train to Otsu, the largest city on Lake Biwa. I do not know what "Otsu" means, but it ought to mean "city of smells" or "poverty city"; for smells and poverty seem to be its most striking features, unless it be the dangerous-looking wells in the back yards — ideal bacterial breeding places. In this stifling atmosphere of bad odors, I was glad to hear that the *Bon-odori* festival was to be celebrated at Otsu that very evening. I shall not apologize for that Eurasian pun, for in perverse Japan, the pun, as a matter of course, is a respectable and highly esteemed literary condiment.

Indeed, scholars tell us that Japanese wit consists almost entirely of punning: that the different kinds of pun are classified and explained in a special treatise called "The Philosophy of Wit": and that as early as the eighth century dexterity in punning was the most important element in verse making. It was probably this antiquity and respectability of the habit, combined with the national amiability, that caused my Japanese companion to laugh at my *bon-odori* pun, just as he had laughed on previous occasions when I told him that it was impossible to buy furniture in Japan without being bamboozled, and that the oddest thing about a Japanese fire is that the go-downs are the only buildings that do not go down. Mr. Yabi was kind enough to say that if I had been born in Japan I would probably have been a poet. *Quien sabe?*

On account of threatening rain the Bon-odori festival — an annual dance and musical carnival of villagers and peasants — did not take place, after all. In the morning we found ourselves steaming northward on the largest body of fresh water in Japan, its dimensions being thirty-six miles by twelve, or about the size of the Lake of Geneva. In beauty and grandeur, however, it cannot be compared with the Swiss lakes of Geneva, Thun, or Lucerne, not to speak of our Californian Lake Tahoe. Yet it is not strange that the Japanese, who have never seen a grander lake, admire Biwa. Its water is perfectly sweet, yet its peculiar green color makes it look like a bay of the ocean. This verdant hue partly compensates for the absence of luxurious green vegetation on the sides of the mountains which frame it in. There is considerable variety of form in these mountains, but on the whole they are rather commonplace, and I do not wonder that the Japanese poets, in celebrating the "eight beauties" of Biwa, should have laid stress on adventitious features of the *mise-en-scène*, such as the autumn moon, mountain snow, sunsets, evening bells, rain, summer breezes, wild geese, and boats sailing on its surface. We saw many of these boats, especially at the widening upper part of the lake. If they can catch fish enough to feed the innumerable villages along the shore, the lake must indeed be inexhaustible.

When we arrived at Hikone, near the upper end of the lake, we left the boat and took kurumas to a famous tea house about a mile away, noted for its landscape garden with lakes and bridges, and for its fine lotos pond covering several acres, the largest and loveliest I had seen in Japan. It had once been a Daimyo's palace. Its compartments were as numerous as the rooms of an American seaside hotel, and we would have lost our way hopelessly in its labyrinths had not a young musumé served as our guide. Leaving us finally in a room commanding a fine view of the lotos pond, she went back to fetch tea and tobacco for us. She had so much beauty that I easily persuaded her that she would not suffer if she allowed me to carry off some of it in my camera.

The beauty of that lotos pond in full bloom I shall never forget; unluckily my camera was quite as unable to register it as its faint but exquisite perfume. The reader has perhaps wondered why, after naming my book *Lotos-Time in Japan*, I should not have attempted to describe the lotos more fully. But how can any one be expected to sketch this marvellous flower in words, when even a great painter can give but a vague idea of its beauty? No one has painted Japanese scenes more realistically and picturesquely than Mr. Alfred Parsons, yet read his confession: —

"The lotos is one of the most difficult plants which it has ever been my lot to try and paint; the flowers are at their best only in the early morning, and each blossom after it has opened closes again before noon the first day, and on the second day its petals drop. The leaves are so large and so full of modelling that it is impossible to generalize them as a mass; each one has to be carefully studied, and every breath of wind disturbs their delicate balance and completely alters their forms. Besides this their glaucous surface, like that of a cabbage leaf, reflects every passing phase of the sky, and is constantly changing in color as clouds pass over."

It is difficult to imagine what the Japanese would do without the lotos. In their art it is almost as frequent a subject as Fuji. The children use the big leaves for sunshades, the seeds for marbles, or to eat, while the adults would answer the conundrum, "when is a pond not a pond?" with "when it has no lotos in it." The one blemish in Professor Chamberlain's delightful *Things Japanese* is the omission of all reference to the lotos; for is not the lotos of all things the most Japanese? True, it is an importation from India, and does not grow wild in Japan; but like other foreign things which the Japanese adopted centuries ago, they have made it peculiarly their own; and since the Japanization of our art and furniture began we have gradually learned to take the Japanese *esthetic* view of the lotos, dropping the sensual *gastronomic* suggestiveness given to it by the older poets, who relied on the tales of Herodotus and Homer about the lotos-eaters who ate the fruit, and drank the wine made of a special variety of the plant. In India, too (and in China), the lotos has an esthetic significance, being the emblem of female beauty. In

Southern India it is believed that the color of the red lotos comes from the blood of Siva when he was wounded by Cupid's arrows. One of the loveliest bequests of Buddhism to Japan is the symbolical idea that as this exquisitely pure and fragrant flower grows out of the mud of a pond, so the human mind should rise above earthly conditions into the pure regions of spiritual life. The images of Buddha are usually seated on a lotos, and with the worship of Buddha the adoration of the lotos flower has impressed itself on the whole nation.

America is not likely to be converted to Buddhism, but I predict that early in the twentieth century lotos ponds will be as frequent in America as they are now in Japan. It is perhaps not generally known that there is a species of the lotos which grows wild in America, but it is shy and rare, and does not flourish so well as the imported lotos. Eight years ago an attempt was made to acclimatize the Japanese lotos in the ponds of Central Park in New York. Ignorant, apparently, of the fact that it is a very hardy plant which flourishes even in the Siberian climate of Yezo, the gardeners for a few years carefully housed the roots in winter. Now they allow them to remain undisturbed, the result being that there are already over five thousand plants in the Park. Indeed, they grow so luxuriantly that some of the plants have to be weeded out every year. The Homeric lotos made the companions of Ulysses forget their home, but these lotos plants give to parts of Central Park an exotic local color that must remind our Japanese visitors of home. I believe that these plants have a hygienic value, too, for the roots must destroy the foulness in which they live, and it seems to me that these ponds are less offensive than they used to be. I hope, too, that American epicures will ere long ask for the lotos root, because that would help to multiply the number of fragrant lotos ponds.

The lotos is only one of the many desirable gifts Japan can send us. The remaining pages of this volume will be devoted to a consideration of some of the other flowers of civilization which we might advantageously transplant to our own gardens.

ARE THE JAPANESE TOPSY-TURVY?

TWO COMIC INCIDENTS — SOCIAL ANTIPODISMS — A PERVERSE LANGUAGE — A JAPANESE LETTER — LACQUER AND WIND — WHEN WE ARE TOPSY-TURVY — HOW TO STABLE HORSES — THE PROPER WAY TO ADDRESS LETTERS

CONGREVE probably knew little or nothing about the Japanese, yet he neatly summed up a notion still prevalent about them when he wrote: " Your Antipodes are a good rascally sort of topsie-turvy Fellows — If I had a Bumper I'd stand upon my Head and drink a Health to 'em." This notion was naturally confirmed by the "Mikado" of W. S. Gilbert, whose specialty is topsy-turviness; and many of the incidents related in the present volume bear it out. But the funniest tale remains to be told. It was related to me by a Yokohama friend. One evening he arrived at a mountain inn with an educated Japanese companion. They had been caught in the rain, and their trousers were wet half through. It was too early to go to bed, and no change of clothes was at hand; so what does the Japanese student do? He takes off his trousers, turns them inside out and puts them on again, explaining this strange proceeding by saying that he was afraid he might catch cold! This is almost as perverse as an incident related by the Rev. W. E. Griffis. When he first arrived in Japan, a number of foreigners had been killed by chauvinistic fanatics, wherefore the government took special measures to protect the imported teachers: and this is the way it was done: "One betté (armed man) accompanied one foreigner, four of them went with two, and eight with three. One would suppose that a single foreigner was in greater danger than when with a companion."

Japan is a land without bakers and butchers. Rice takes the place of bread, fish, and meat. No meat, no hides; hence shoes are made by the carpenters. If you are ill and call on the doctor, you pay for the medicine only; if he calls on you, he charges no fee, but expects a present, as it is considered more honorable to take a present than a fee. There are no special drug stores. The merchant comes to the customer. Tradespeople are lower in the social scale than artisans or farmers. Our society people pride themselves on their fast horses; the Japanese consider it vulgar to ride fast. Theatrical performances begin in the morning. Very long calls are in good form. A woman indicates her exact age in dress and coiffure. Dancing is done by hired girls, courtship carried on by proxy. There is no harm in being seen naked, but a kiss is always improper. Man is heavenly, woman earthly. Filial love is above conjugal love; a bride wears mourning, because she leaves her parents. A widower mourns his wife three months, a widow must mourn her husband thirteen months. Infants under three months are not mourned for at all.

Japanese religions dwell together in peace. Christian missionaries aver that "no sermon can be prolix enough to stay the insatiable appetite of their converts." Ghosts are not feared, but welcomed. Theatres and temples are good neighbors. In literature plagiarism is considered a merit, because it proves a good memory. A poet's productions are not as a rule published separately, but as part of an anthology of all the poets of his time. The pun is the most esteemed form of wit. In school, dissatisfied pupils dismiss their teacher.

Heine wrote that if the Romans had been obliged to learn Latin they could not have found time to conquer the world. But Latin is child's play compared with Japanese, which the early missionaries were convinced had been invented by the devil to prevent them from converting the natives. One variety of American newspaper humor consists in translating jokes verbatim from German or French papers; for instance: "Bachelor (in restaurant) — 'I know at all not, wherefore a man marry should! One can certainly also quite well alone two portions eat.'" This, at any rate, is intelligible, but what the logical process of the Japanese mind is, may be gathered from this letter from Japan which a New York merchant has kindly allowed me to copy: —

"We shall present to your company the bamboo fishing rod, a net basket and a reel, as we have just convenience; all those were very rough and simply to your laughing for your kind reply which you sent us the catalogue of fishing tackles last, etc.

"Wishing we that now at Japan there it was not in prevailing fish gaming, but fishermen. In scarcely therefore but we do not measure how the progression of the germ of the fishing game beforehand. Therefore, we may yield of feeling to restock in my store your countries fishing tackles, etc.

"Should you have the kindness to send a such farther country, even in a few partake when we send the money in ordering of them should you."

As the reader may *possibly* suspect, this is an order for fishing tackle. The merchant informs me that he filled the order and got his money! But this mixing of words, like dice in a box, is only one phase of the total depravity of the Japanese language. In this language *arimas* means pretty much anything you please, — "I am," "you are," "she is," etc., while *arimasen* means the opposite. In English "I" is "I" for short and good, but in Tōkyō a man says *watakushi* in speaking to a friend, *ore* in addressing an inferior, *temage* if he wants to be humble, *boku* if he is a student among students, *wattchi* among rustics, *watashi* or *oira* to be familiar, and so on. Japanese grammar, in short, reminds one a good deal of the joke played on a French emigrant by an American wag who told him on the steamer, by way of illustrating the difficulties of the English language, that the verb "to go" was conjugated as follows: "I go, you leave, he departs, we clear out, you skedaddle, they absquatulate." The Frenchman took the next steamer back to Havre.

Nature herself occasionally assumes a rascally sort of topsy-turviness. Lacquer is the most Japanese of all products — to japan means to lacquer. And what does lacquer do? It flies in the face of all the laws of nature; it refuses to dry in the sun, but amiably submits to any amount of desiccation if you humor its whim by supplying a *damp* atmosphere. Again, the prevailing wind is south in summer, north in winter. For this, indeed, the most fanatic admirer of Japan could offer no excuse.

But the oddity is not always on the side of the Japanese. Often their way is as wise as ours, sometimes wiser. Circumstances alter cases. We eat rice with sugar and cream, the Japanese eat it with pickles. Pickles are cheaper, and in a hot climate more agreeable and digestible than cloying sweets. Japanese kitchen girls wash their dishes in cold water; it is cheaper than hot water, which is not needed, as no butter or grease is used in their cooking. We build our houses of the solidest materials we can find — iron and stone, they build theirs of wood, paper, and bamboo; our walls are fixed, theirs movable. Our houses are more sensible in solid America, theirs in earthquake-shaken Japan. In entering a house we take off the hat, they the shoes; their way is cleaner, and we admit it practically by now wearing rubbers on muddy days and removing them at the door. Japanese women make the mistake of preferring straight hair to curls; but they atone for that by preferring a natural waist to a wasp waist. Courtship by proxy is an absurdity which is largely responsible for the fact that there is one divorce to every three Japanese marriages; but I can see some sense, in a hot climate, in hiring dancers instead of dancing yourself. It is absurd to begin meals with wine and sweets; but I think it is more sensible to drink soup out of a lacquer bowl than to sip it from the side of a spoon instead of from the end as intended by the spoonmakers. It is foolish for the Japanese to make the abdomen the seat of the mental faculties, but do we not locate the soul in the heart? We prefer sitting to kneeling; but the Japanese attitude keeps the feet warm in cold weather.

The Japanese begin the year in spring, we in midwinter. Which is topsy-turvy? We think it strange that they should cultivate plum and cherry trees for their flowers, not their fruits: but their cherries are like choke cherries, and even if they were good to eat, is not "cherry blossom viewing" more refined and refining than munching cherries and spitting out the stones?

Consider the Japanese way of carrying babies on the back. Is it not much more sensible than our way, since it leaves the carrier the free use of her arms and hands? Take another case. Everybody has heard of the showman who fooled the rustics by advertising a horse that had "the tail where the head ought to be, and the head where the tail ought to be." He had simply turned the horse round in the stable. That is the Japanese way of placing a horse, and it is more rational than our way. He can be fed from a suspended sack or bucket, the hostler runs no risk of being kicked, and the horse is in proper position to be taken out and hitched to the wagon. Our fire companies have admitted our topsy-turviness by adopting the Japanese way.

I would even go so far as to approve of the Japanese way of beginning a book or newspaper at what we call the end. I speak from practical experience. For a number of years part of my work in a large newspaper office consisted in reading all the English, French, and German exchanges. After a while I found that I had unconsciously got into the habit of beginning at the last page, in spite of obvious obstacles. Finally, — for I must stop, not for lack of material, but of space, — I think we are unpardonably topsy-turvy in the way we address letters. When you mail a letter, who gets it first? The postal clerk. What does he want to know first? Whether it is for America or Europe. What does the next distributor want to know? What country in Europe, and what city it is for. And the next? The street, of course; and finally the number, the family and the individual. Now that is the way the Japanese address a letter. They write "America, New York,

Broadway 210, Brown John Mr.," while we say, "Mr. John Brown, 210 Broadway, New York," thus compelling everybody who handles the letter to read it from below up, contrary to all our literary usages.

THE MOTE AND THE BEAM

SIX HUNDRED MISSIONARIES — DENOMINATIONALISM — AN AGNOSTIC'S OPINION — CREEDS AND DEEDS — OCCIDENTAL BUNKUM — SLAVERY AND INDIAN WARS — GETTING CIVILIZED — COMMERCIAL AND SEXUAL MORALITY

There are at present more than six hundred foreign missionaries in Japan. Nevertheless, the reports do not show a rapid rate of conversion; the whole number of native Christians in 1894 was only 105,000 in a population of more than 40,000,000 — one Christian to every 400 Buddhists, Shintoists, and agnostics. The converts are, indeed, largely recruited from the educated classes, but it is from these same classes that the strongest opposition to the new religion comes. They read the books of Spencer, Darwin, Huxley, and other leaders of European thought, and declare bluntly that they do not care to take up dogmas which such thinkers are discarding. The masses, devoted to ancestor worship, shudder at the idea that their beloved ancestors are damned forever, because they were not of the true faith : if converted at all, they prefer the more liberal creeds. They will never adopt a Puritan Sunday, or believe in hanging a cat on Monday for catching mice on Sunday. Strict Buddhists consider attacks on their beliefs as blasphemous as Christians do attacks on theirs. On the thoughtful Japanese the missionaries are apt to create a bad impression by their sectarianism, of which Mr. Gordon, in his candid volume entitled *An American Missionary in Japan*, says : —

> "It is doubtful whether the world has ever seen or ever will see a more striking exhibition of the absurdities of Christian denominationalism : more than thirty different societies, all bearing the name of Christ, but each with something peculiar in its character, its history, or its methods, working in one small country, the majority of them in a single city."

A Japanese agnostic said to me one day : "We have just discarded Buddhism, with its numerous sects and factions, and we are not going to take up a new religion with the same ecclesiastic shortcomings. If the missionaries want to convert us to Christianity, would it not be well for them first to come to some agreement as to what Christianity is? Another question. I read the other day that Berlin has only eighty-eight churches for a population of nearly two millions! I am told that other Christian cities are not much better supplied. And in a New York newspaper I have read the serious assertion that the majority of the people, and more especially the educated people, are as much pagans as the inhabitants of Tōkyō. Why don't the missionaries Christianize America and Europe before they come to Asia?"

Three centuries ago, when Xavier first attempted to introduce Christianity, the Japanese told him that they would hear what they had to say and then wait and see whether their conduct agreed with their words. Is the reason of the slow progress of Christianity to be sought in the fact that foreigners have been judged, not by their creeds, but by their deeds? Does not the Rev.

W. E. Griffis bear witness to the fact that "in their financial and warlike operations in Japan, the foreign ministers seem to have acted as though there was no day of judgment"? To take only one instance, as summed up by Professor Wigmore: "The murder of Richardson, and the British retaliatory expedition to Kagoshima, which bombarded and destroyed an innocent city of 100,000 people, in revenge for the well-provoked killing of a single insolent brute, and then demanded and obtained $3,000,000 from a poor nation, in payment (grossly excessive) of the expenses of the raid." Like other Eastern nations the Japanese have long ago found out that, as Professor Chamberlain remarks, "Our Christian and humanitarian professions are really nothing but bunkum. The history of India, of Egypt, of Turkey, is no secret to them. More familiar still is the sweet reasonableness of California's treatment of the Chinese."

And what can the Japanese say of our "Christian" treatment of the Indians when they read Mrs. Jackson's 514 page volume, *A Century of Dishonor*, which tells a tale "too monstrous to believe" — a tale which Bishop Whipple of Minnesota characterizes as a "sad revelation of broken faith, of violated treaties, and of inhuman deeds of violence" which "will bring a blush of shame to the cheeks of those who love their country"; a tale based on official documents — the commission appointed in 1869 by President Grant having reported that "in our Indian wars, almost without exception, the first aggressions have been made by the white man" — a verdict true of nineteen out of twenty cases of murder of foreigners in Japan. What can the Japanese say when they read that American slavery, which John

Wesley called "the vilest that ever saw the sun," with its cruel separation of families and abrogation of the marriage institution, was not abolished till 1865, or thirteen years after our "civilization" was supposed to have been introduced in Japan by Perry's gunboats? Buddhist Japan never had any slavery, while Christian America has only just abolished hers, yet we are always throwing stones at Japan.

There are two charges, in particular, that are constantly flung in the face of the Japanese by foreign merchants and missionaries — the imputation of commercial and sexual immorality. Yokohama merchants love to contrast the honesty of the Chinese with the rascality of the Japanese. *Apropos*, I have just read an account of a lecture given in London by Mr. A. G. Stanton, of the condition of the Chinese tea trade. Thirty years ago China had practically the monopoly of the British market, and to-day it supplies only 12 per cent of the imports, mainly because of the commercial dishonesty of the Chinese, their growing habit of selling "lie tea." No doubt, Japanese merchants are not always models of honesty and reliability; but are *our* merchants? Foreigners at Yokohama tell you that the native traders are apt not to keep their promises "if the market goes against them"; but can you blame a guileless native for trying to get out of a trap which may have been laid for him by sharp "Wall-Street" practices by foreigners who expect to buy in Japan for ten cents and sell in New York or London for a dollar?

Adulteration of food is another form of commercial dishonesty for which the Japanese have been censured. But I doubt very, very much if Japan could match the report of Special Agent A. J. Wedderburn of the United

States Agricultural Department, which reveals the horrible fact that the amount of food adulteration "reaches the immense sum of $1,014,000,000 annually. As at least 2 per cent of the whole is deleterious to health, $135,200,000 constitutes the annual amount paid by the American people for sacrifice of their lives or injury of their health."

Sexual immorality is no doubt a most prevalent vice in Japan — as it is in all other countries. It cannot be denied that the foulest stain on Japan's fair name is the historic habit of selling pure, innocent young girls into a life of shame to get their parents out of debt. But it is wrong to judge this barbarous custom entirely from a Western point of view. It is simply a corollary of the Confucian idea that filial love and obedience are the highest virtues, to which all others, even chastity, must be sacrificed. Thus it happens that a certain ethical glamour is thrown around the sacrifice of such girls, who are frequently the heroines of Japanese novels. But it is extremely absurd to infer from this state of affairs that chastity is not esteemed a virtue at all. The fate of such girls is deplored, the *joro* is abhorred, and the average of chastity is as high as in Europe or America; Professor Ono's comparative statistics show that crimes of personal violence and sexual crimes are far fewer than in the West. By the old laws of Japan, adultery was punished by crucifixion; later by decapitation and exposure of the head. Concubinage, though allowed by law, is considered a degradation.

There is nothing in Japan to compare with the horrible prevalence of incest in the London slums; nothing to compare with the rate of illegitimacy in Vienna, and the *Japan Mail* of May 21, 1892, says: "The unfortunate truth is that the most flagrantly immoral parts of Japan at present are the slums and neighborhood of the open ports." "Before they opened any port to foreign trade," says the Rev. Mr. Griffis, "the Japanese built two places for the foreigner — a custom-house and a brothel. . . . They believed the foreigners to be far worse than themselves. How far were they wrong?"

How far, indeed! The New York *Medical Journal* of June 9, 1894, contains an article showing on the concurrent testimony of the Hon. Elbridge T. Gerry and Superintendent Byrnes, of the police department, that the number of prostitutes in New York is "at least 40,000," and that "the yearly expenditure of dissolute men in New York upon prostitutes would aggregate over $40,000,000."

Is it not about time to protest against the constant references to Japanese immorality in missionary reports? "Why beholdest thou the mote that is in thy brother's eye, but not the beam in thy own?"

NUDITY AND BATHING

PUBLIC BATHS — MODEST EXPOSURE — A FOOLISH LAW — NUDITY, CLIMATE, AND CONVENTION — CUSTOMS OF VARIOUS COUNTRIES — SHOCKED BY OUR HABITS — NO "GREAT UNWASHED" — A SENSUOUS LUXURY — BATHING TO GET WARM — SCENES IN BATH HOUSES — AN ESTHETIC QUESTION — NEGLECT OF THE NUDE IN ART

WE are so accustomed to regarding Oriental races as barbarous or half-civilized, that it is a wholesome check to our vanity to dwell occasionally on those things in which we are barbarians and the Asiatics civilized. In their attitude toward nudity, and in their bathing habits, the Japanese are far superior to ourselves as a nation; yet their indifference to nudity and some of their bathing customs were largely responsible for the moral misrepresentations to which foreign visitors have given vogue. Explorers and students of anthropology have pointed out that tribes which go naked are not a bit less moral than those which wear clothing. Yet these visitors fancied that because Japanese men and women were seen together naked in the public baths, therefore they must be as degraded as Americans or Europeans who would do such a thing must necessarily be with our ideas of propriety. Even so intelligent a man as Commodore Perry made this mistake. Writing of Simoda, he says, " A scene at one of the public baths, where the sexes mingled indiscriminately, unconscious of their nudity, was not calculated to impress Americans with a favorable opinion of the morals of the inhabitants." Laurence Oliphant notes, without comment, that when his party passed along the streets of Yeddo, " bathers of both sexes, regardless of the fact that they had nothing on but soap, or the Japanese substitute for it, crowded the doors" to get a glimpse of the foreigners. Sir Rutherford Alcock refers to " the bathing houses, which, strongly lighted, show through their lattice bars and open doors a crowd of both sexes on opposite sides, with a mathematical line of separation"; but he is broad-minded enough to explain that " where there is no *sense* of immodesty, no consciousness of wrong-doing, there is, or may be, a like absence of depraved feeling."

It is characteristic of the Japanese that when Commodore Perry expressed his surprise at the promiscuous bathing at Simoda, they told him that it was not a universal practice throughout Japan! They would rather tell a lie than have a visitor think ill of them, though they doubtless wondered why he should be so absurdly fussy. It was this sensitiveness to foreign opinion that led the Governor of Kanagawa in 1867 to post this notice : —

"Those who come from diverse places to Yokohama, and make their living as porters, carters, laborers, coolies, and boatmen, are in the habit, especially in the summer, of plying their calling in a state bordering on nudity. This is very reprehensible; and in future no one who does not wear a shirt or tunic, properly closed by a girdle, will be allowed to remain in Yokohama. The coolie masters are to give liberal assistance for the suppression of such people."

The historian Black, from whose work the above edict is quoted, thus comments on the then prevalent habit of going about with only a loin cloth: "No Japanese ever saw any impropriety in it until we pointed it out to them. And they altered it to please us." I am sure it was a foolish thing on the part of the amiable Japanese to make this concession to the false modesty of foreigners. Instead of passing the general law of 1872 against nudity, they should have replied to their censors somewhat in this fashion: "In a climate where even those who remain idle in the shade are covered with a profuse perspiration which, on account of the damp air, evaporates very slowly, or not at all, clothing of any sort is a torture to those who have to toil in the sun ten or more hours a day. The well-to-do are more or less dressed anyway, but the coolies must be allowed to go naked, for the sake of their health as well as their comfort; and if any foreigners see harm in this, they are at liberty to leave by the next steamer. Nudity is essential to the health of the coolies, on account of their profuse perspiration. Your physiological science tells us that we breathe through the pores of the skin quite as much as through the lungs; but if the skin is swathed in wet clothing, how can its pores breathe? A coolie cannot be clean unless he is naked; and do you not say that cleanliness is next to godliness? It is from this point of view that we can understand why in some parts of India there is, according to an English writer, 'a profound suspicion of the *irreligiousness* of clothing.' Anthropology proves that it was not modesty, but the necessity of protection against cold, that led to the adoption of clothing. It has been found in Java that the children of foreigners do not live unless they are allowed to go naked. If the English in India would allow their children to go naked, they would not have to send them to the mountains or to Europe to save their lives. Only those who submit to the laws of nature are found fit to survive.

"Furthermore, the attitude of various nations toward nudity is purely a matter of convention. Mohammedan women think it sinful to show their faces, but uncover their legs without hesitation. Chinese women consider it shockingly immodest to let any one see their crippled feet. Hindoo women hide their faces, while their figures are clearly revealed through their transparent gauze dress. Plato, whom Christians honor as one of the greatest of philosophers, said that young men and women should see each other naked in order to be able to see what sort of a person they are to marry. The Greeks in general, whom you honor as the most civilized nation of all times, would have been as much surprised as we are at your prudish horror of nudity.

"Remember the mote and the beam. One of your own writers says that 'to a Japanese the sight of our dazzling ballrooms, with girls in décolleté dresses, clasped in the arms of their partners, and whirling to the sound of excited music, must seem the wildest debauch imaginable; for in Japan the sexes, except among the lower classes, never intermingle.' Another of your writers, a woman, has summed up the matter admirably in these words: 'According to the Japanese standard, any exposure of the person that is merely incidental to health, cleanliness, or convenience in doing necessary work, is perfectly modest and allowable; but an exposure, no matter how slight, that is simply for show, is in the highest degree indelicate.

... To the Japanese mind it is immodest to want to show off a pretty figure.' Your 'living pictures' would be strongly condemned by us. You will be able to appreciate all these points more easily when you bear in mind your own variable standards. If your women should reveal their bosoms on the beach as they do in a ballroom, they would be denounced as immodest; if they should expose their legs in a ballroom as they do on the beach, they would be handed over to the police."

As a matter of fact, neither the American ball dress nor the bathing costume is immodest, whatever Japanese may think of it; and, conversely, Japanese exposure is perfectly proper, whatever we may think of it. To a pure mind there is much more modesty in the unconscious nudity of rural women than in the conscious gesture with which a Tōkyō girl covers her bosom whenever she sees a foreigner. It is surprising how quickly foreigners usually adopt the naïve Japanese point of view: in a few weeks one looks on nakedness with the same indifference as the Japanese, except when a beautiful figure arrests the esthetic attention. Our artists go into raptures over the fine opportunities for the study of muscles in action afforded in Japan. The reader will find in Miss Bird's *Unbeaten Tracks* (I. 305) an amusing illustration of how even such a model of propriety as that distinguished tourist found herself taking the part of her runners against the police trying to enforce the cruel law against nudity.

Not only are the Japanese in their indifference to nudity more sensible and pure-minded than their censors, but in the matter of bathing and cleanliness they are as a nation infinitely more civilized than Europeans and Americans. That *Japan has no " Great Unwashed,"* is a statement of such wide bearing that the Occidental mind can scarce grasp its significance at first hearing. You may be hemmed in by the densest crowd in Tōkyō on a sultry summer day, or stand among busy workmen whose scant clothing is wet, and never will your nostrils be offended by that disagreeable summer odor of humanity, which would be noticeable in other countries under similar circumstances.

Being a nation of agnostics, the Japanese could hardly be expected to sympathize with the old Hebrew doctrine which places cleanliness next to godliness. They make cleanliness the first of all virtues, and the daily bath the first of all duties. While New York had to wait until the year 1891, before a project was started for supplying the Great Unwashed with baths at a reasonable rate, the metropolis of Japan has offered such opportunities as far back as the records go. Tōkyō has to-day about 800 public baths, in which 300,000 persons, or almost a fourth of the population, bathe every day, at a cost of one cent for each hot bath; and besides this every family, except some of the very poorest, has its own private bath room in the house, or at least a tub and plenty of hot water. If you stop at the humblest village inn for lunch, a basin of water is brought, in which to wash the feet; and if you stay for the night, hardly has a room been assigned to you, when a girl appears to conduct you to the bath, for the use of which no charge is made. Nothing surprises them more than a foreigner who refuses to take at least one hot bath a day. They themselves are more likely to take two or three; and the consequence is that they are the cleanest people in the world.

It has been said that they value the bath not so much

for its cleansing effect as for the enjoyment of a sensuous luxury. Suppose we were to grant this, what difference does it make, so long as it leaves them the cleanest people in the world? But it is not true. The aspect of their streets and houses shows that they value cleanliness for its own sake. They have, besides, a use for the hot bath which may be considered unique. Their houses affording but poor protection against chilling winds, and having no fireplaces, the hot bath is frequently used as a last resort for getting warm. Professor Chamberlain relates that one day some of the inhabitants of a certain village, famed for its hot springs, excused themselves to him for their dirtiness during the busy summer months. "For," said they, "we have only time to bathe twice a day." "How often, then, do you bathe in winter?" "Oh! about four or five times daily. The children get into the bath whenever they feel cold."

Farsari's guide book attributes the premature aging of Japanese women in part to their too frequent indulgence in the hot bath, but Dr. Baelz, the best authority on Japanese physique, declares that these baths have many advantages, but not a single disadvantage, so far as he could ascertain. It is commonly supposed that hot baths unbrace the nerves and invite colds, but this is true only of *warm*, and not of *hot* baths, such as the Japanese indulge in, at a temperature of 110° to 115°, which, in some cases, is increased to 120°, and occasionally even to 130° Fahrenheit. Foreigners cannot endure such temperatures, but the natives revel in them, and the effect on them is so bracing and strengthening that they can, and often do, emerge from the tub and walk some distance in the coldest winter weather without a stitch of clothing on, and without catching a cold. When foreign physicians were first imported and looked up to in Japan, about twenty years ago, they actually succeeded, in their ignorance, in making the Government pass a law forbidding a higher temperature than blood heat; but the mistake was soon discovered, and the law repealed. To-day those of the foreign residents who are wisest, have given up their cold baths, and try to approximate the Japanese temperature as closely as possible.

The Japanese bath tub is usually a square wooden tank, sometimes large enough to admit several persons at a time. The water can be heated in a short time by means of a copper tube standing in one corner of the tub, and having a grating for charcoal at the bottom. For economical reasons the Japanese never have bath tubs to lie in, but usually make them only wide enough so that one can sit or kneel, which requires less water, and therefore less coal.

So far all seems well; but there is (apart from the indifference to nudity) one thing about Japanese baths which is apt to stagger foreign visitors — the use of the same water by a number of persons. When the family bath is ready, the father, mother, children, and servants all enter it in the order here given. In crowded inns, a score or two of guests, entire strangers to each other, are expected to use the same water (to economize fuel). This may seem better than no bath at all, and as the natives wash themselves all over before entering the tub, the objection may be largely imaginary; but we cannot overcome our predilection for a fresh tub for each individual, and communism in bathing does not seem an inviting form of hygienic diversion. We have similar forms of aqueous communism at Baden-Baden, the hot baths in Switzerland, and the large tanks in our Turkish baths; but there, at least, the water flows incessantly. Many of the Japanese are fastidious enough to have a bucket of fresh water poured over themselves after the communal tubbing.

It is not only the poorest families — those who cannot afford a tub at home — that frequent the public baths; many go there to gossip with friends; wherefore, as previously intimated, more than a quarter of a million of the natives of Tōkyō scrub and boil themselves together every afternoon. In obedience to law, the bath rooms are no longer fully exposed to the street, but they are only closed below, and any one who chooses can look in through the latticed bars above; nor do the bathers object to such a proceeding. There is always a separate tank for women and one for men, but the partition between them is only a few feet in height, and what is stranger still, a man may be seen waiting on a score or more of women on their side, while on the men's side a girl stands to receive the admission fee. There may be twenty or thirty men or boys on one side, and as many women and girls on the other, chatting, scrubbing, tubbing, some standing, others kneeling before a small tub or bucket, using their bran bags, which make the skin soft and smooth. Soap is not favored, for there is a superstition that it makes the hair turn red, and red is the color of the Japanese devil. Every minute one or two leave the room, their skins glowing with health, while the newcomers disappear behind a screen and in a moment emerge stark naked and join the chatting crowd.

When Taro took us for the first time on a tour of

inspection of the public baths, he opened the door on the women's side and seemed surprised at the Occidental diffidence which prevented us from accepting his invitation to walk right in. It would have been, not improper, but impolite to do so. For purposes of esthetic study and comparison it was sufficient to take a peep through the grating. Thus we saw in Tōkyō, and especially in Kyōto, many "living pictures" that would have delighted the most fastidious Occidental sculptor of Psyches. It is true that the majority of the women, in Japan as elsewhere, have ugly or imperfect figures; but the proportion of well-rounded, symmetrical shapes to be seen at these baths is larger than one might expect. While the faces of the aristocratic women (who bathe at home) are as a rule more refined and beautiful, there can be no doubt that sculptors would find more available models in the communistic bath tubs than in the private ones, because in all countries the most shapely figures are habitually found among the classes who are obliged by poverty to exercise their limbs into muscular rotundity.

A very interesting but perplexing question occurred to me in gazing at these Oriental beauties. It is one of the commonplaces of art historians that the main reason why the Greeks were such great sculptors and lovers of human beauty was, that they could feast their eyes daily on beautiful nude models at their games and elsewhere. If this view be accepted, why is it that the Japanese artists, who have had even more abundant opportunity to study the nude, have sculptured and painted no Oriental Venus, Psyche, and Apollo?

It cannot be that the neglect of the nude is due to the want of good models, for such models are as abundant here as anywhere else except perhaps in Spanish countries; and it is, moreover, a function of artists to assist nature by judicious selection and imaginative combination of perfect parts occurring in different individuals. Some writers have attributed the neglect of the human figure by Japanese artists to a religious prejudice — that is, to the Buddhist tradition which, like the asceticism of mediaeval European churchmen, inculcated contempt of the human body as being a mere prison for the immortal soul, whose chief desire is to get away from this living carcass. If this be true, — and there is doubtless some truth in it, — we owe to Buddhism a tremendous grudge; for these Japanese painters who have drawn flowers, fishes, birds, and other living things, with an art nowhere equalled — think what visions of loveliness and grace they might have copied and perpetuated during the centuries when they had so many thousand of living human models before their eyes daily!

I believe, however, that the deeper explanation lies in the traditional eagerness of these artists to paint the kaleidoscopic patterns and colors of the kimonos, — the gorgeous dresses of their women, — which afforded them an endless variety of patterns and tints. In looking at the conventional classical pictures of women it is easy to see that in most cases "the kimono's the thing." Some of these garments are dreams of beauty, and they lend themselves to many graceful folds, curves, and attitudes. Not only the nude figure, but even the face, is sacrificed to this love of bright kimonos. Of the whole body nothing is usually visible in these pictures, except the hands and face, with perhaps a glimpse of the neck; the face being a stereotyped doll physiognomy —

always the same straight nose, the same exaggeratedly oblique eyes, barely open enough to admit a ray of light, the same impossible distance between eyes and eyebrows, and the same tiny and absolutely characterless mouth, painted apparently with a single stroke of the brush. These pictures no more resemble the faces of actual Japanese maidens than an Italian soprano's florid aria resembles her every-day speech.

THE ESTHETIC NATION

MUSIC AND NATIONALITY — LAUGHING AT OUR MUSIC — A SUGGESTIVE EXCEPTION — SCULPTURE AND ARCHITECTURE — GREAT IN SMALL THINGS — DECORATIVE ART — IMPRESSIONISM — IRREGULARITY — LOVE OF NATURE — FLOWERS VERSUS BOUQUETS — FLOWER SEASONS — POETIC FLOWER NAMES — MOTTOES ON SCREENS — JAPANESE POETRY — LOVE LETTERS ON TREES

ONE of the strangest of Japanese paradoxes is this: that, although in the principal arts — music, sculpture, architecture, painting, and poetry — the nations of Europe have surpassed all the Orientals, nevertheless, the Japanese are the only truly artistic *nation* in the world — the Esthetic Nation *par excellence*.

Music. — It is in the "divine art" that the Orientals are most distinctly our inferiors. That Japanese music does not, as a rule, please resident foreigners and tourists, is amusingly obvious from the words in which they usually allude to it: "horrible beyond description," "an agonizing mystery," and so on. This, however, would not prove much in itself, since musical history shows that from the time of Monteverde to Wagner, Europeans have quite as fiercely and savagely abused the music of the men of genius who dared to make innovations within the sphere of their own music; wherefore one could hardly expect them to take kindly to such an utterly novel tone-art as the Japanese. It must be borne in mind, also, that there are two sides to the shield: to the Japanese *our* music seems quite as funny and excruciating as theirs does to us. Netto has an amusing page on his experiences in this line, and Chamberlain tells of a memorable performance in Tōkyō, by Italian opera singers. The native hearers " were seized with a wild fit of hilarity at the high notes of the *prima donna*, who really was not at all bad. The people laughed at the absurdities of European singing till their sides shook and the tears rolled down their cheeks; and they stuffed their sleeves into their mouths, as we might our pocket handkerchiefs, in the vain endeavor to contain themselves."

Some foreign residents have found Japanese music an acquired taste which gradually became a fascination. Thus Mr. Lafcadio Hearn speaks of "the strange music called Ōjō and Batto, — music which at first no Western ear can feel pleasure in, but which, when often heard, becomes comprehensible, and is found to possess a weird charm of its own." As for my own experiences, they are related in the preceding pages of this volume. I frankly confess that I found the koto musical, and even enjoyed an occasional tune on the samisen.

The Japanese have shown a gift for assimilating our music, and I believe they will ere long learn that the martial drum is more appropriate in a military band than in a tea house or temple; that the flute is decidedly *not* a sacred instrument, especially when it deliberately indulges in quarter-tones; and that there are physiological and esthetic objections to their way of making young girls "cultivate" their voices by sitting on a roof on cold nights, singing until hoarseness passes into dumbness. I believe that Japanese music has no future except such as will approximate it to European music. It appears to be just learning the first harmonic steps, which our music took several centuries ago; but it is likely that herein, as in so many things, Japan will jump from the sixteenth century to the nineteenth, disdaining to pass through the stages of the parallel fifths and fourths of the organum, the parallel thirds and sixths of the faux bourdon, and the counterpoint of the Netherlanders, but plunging at once into Wagnerian harmonies.

In looking over the bound volumes of the *Japan Weekly Mail*, that wonderful storehouse of valuable information, I came across a description (printed June 13, 1891) of a musical performance heard by a correspondent at Matsue. It lasted an hour, and consisted of ballads sung by girls and women of the outcast class known as the Yama-no-Mono. Three of them began with a "clear sweet burst of soprano song totally differing from anything I had ever heard in Japan before." Presently, the voices of three more women, "deeper but equally sweet, joined in producing a delicious harmony; and a kind of burthen was chanted by all in unison. . . . Certainly no singing I have heard from the geishas could compare in charm with this simple ballad singing of a despised outcast class." This interesting letter suggested to me the thought: Is not perhaps the nasal, shrill voice, and artificial song of the geishas a phenomenon similar to the absurd pictures spoken of in the last chapter — a result of conventionalism and the following of traditional unnatural models; and is it not likely that a lively war on this conventionalism would give Japanese music a tremendous impulse in the right direction; rubbing off the paint and powder, and restoring the clear beauty of the natural complexion?

Sculpture and Architecture. — A few summers ago I had the pleasure of spending a few days in the mountains of British Columbia with Mr. Alfred East, who was on his way back to London, where he soon thereafter had a special exhibition of his 106 oil and water-color sketches on Japanese subjects. Before leaving Japan he delivered a lecture on its art, one sentence in which has been often quoted since as a compact expression of its essence. Japanese art, he said, "is great in small things, but small in great things." Of course, this generalization is too sweeping; for while the neglect of the nude has, as we saw in the last chapter, prevented the Japanese from giving us Aphrodites and Apollos, they have, nevertheless, created many beautiful figures, some of them not only large, but gigantic, notably the famous Daibutsu of Kamakura. Mr. Wores describes some figures he saw which for their action and anatomically correct modelling rank, in his estimation, "as high as anything in the sculptor's art of modern times." In the "small things" of wood and ivory carving and metal work, the Japanese are unrivalled. Their netsukés have been compared to "the Tanagra figures of Greek origin, and to the finest sculptures of the Gothic age."

As regards architecture, it is obvious that monumental structures are impossible in a land where three earthquakes occur every two days. The high pagodas are kept from tumbling by means of an ingenious pendulum arrangement which would be impracticable in other buildings. To the remarkable variety and individuality of Japanese roofs, reference was made in an earlier chapter. This subject is elaborately treated by Mr. Morse in his *Japanese Homes*, wherein it may be seen that in many details of house-building and furnishing the Japanese show a taste far superior to ours. To note a sample or two, a Japanese would never be guilty of "the absurdity of covering a good grained woodsurface with paint, and then with brush and comb trying to imitate nature by scratching in a series of lines." In building a house, great care is taken to secure wood that matches in grain and color; and in order to avoid mixing up of woods, the boards into which a log has been sawed are replaced and tied together. For pillars, twisted trunks are often preferred to straight ones. Not infrequently the bark is left on tree trunks which are used as pillars, and even when it is removed, the holes bored by insects remain, so fond are these people of naturalness.

Painting. — In Japan, painting is not a separate art, but simply the highest form of the decorative art. The painter works, not for galleries, public or private, but for the adornment of temples and homes. As Schubert could not see a sheet of paper without scribbling a song on it, so a Japanese artist cannot see a surface without feeling tempted to adorn it with flowers, birds, maidens, and mountains. Screens, sliding or folding, fans, vases, trays, tea and flower pots — nothing escapes his pencil, and *Nihil tetigit quod non ornavit* acquires a double meaning when applied to him. To the average Japanese, art is not a recreation, to be indulged in semi-occasionally, but it is, like oxygen, a constituent of the atmosphere he breathes every moment; and the humblest coolie wants his share of art as much as his oxygen. The shops contain thousands of objects for use and entertainment, and each of these objects, though it cost but a tenth of a cent, is artistically shaped or decorated.

"It is the fault of foreign pictures," says a Japanese writer, "that they dive too deeply into realities, and preserve many details that were better suppressed. Such works are but as groups of words. The Japanese picture should aspire to be a poem of form and color."

The Japanese artist is usually an impressionist; that is, he avoids superfluous details, seizing only on what is essential to his purpose, but presenting that with such virtuosity that the mood he desires to suggest is transferred to the spectator as instantaneously as the current of our emotions is changed by a dramatic modulation in a Wagner music-drama. Professor Fenollosa believes, no doubt justly, that the impetus to French impressionism was given partly by a thorough study of Japanese art.[1]

Nor is impressionism the only lesson taught Western artists by their Japanese colleagues. The principle which underlies it — the suppression of redundant and distracting details — is applied by them not only to a picture in itself, but also to the surroundings of a picture. As we crowd too much furniture into our parlors, so we hang too many pictures on our walls, and our wall papers usually consist of the same figure repeated a thousand times in monotonous geometrical patterns.

---

[1] While thus indifferent to details, it is a striking fact that the Japanese artist has a keener eye than his Western colleague. Herr Ottomar Anschütz of Lissa, Prussia, has shown that certain Japanese pictures of birds and other animals which seemed unnatural were really correct, as proved by instantaneous photography.

Not so the Japanese. In painting a screen or kakemono, they leave most of the space bare, being contented with a simple spray of cherry blossoms or maple leaves, or a few cranes in a pond among the lily leaves, or a flight of birds, or a tree on shore with a glimpse of the sea, or a group of deer under a tree, or a miniature bridge over an iris pond — thus preventing the spectator's attention from being distracted by "a rabble of inartistic patterns and ornaments."

An artistic innovation of still greater charm and value is the Japanese passion for irregularity. Western art, like Western thought, is utterly distorted by our vain habit of making man the centre of the universe. Because *we* are symmetrical, having a right hand and a left, a right eye and a left, a right ear and a left, our misguided painters have made symmetry a pervading principle of all art, with the result that if, for example, "on the right hand there was a Cupid looking to the left, then on the left hand there must be a Cupid of exactly the same size looking to the right." "The Japanese artisan-artists," says Chamberlain, "have shown us that this mechanical symmetry does not make for beauty. They have taught us the charm of irregularity: and if the world owe them but this one lesson, Japan may yet be proud of what she has accomplished."

Nature and Flowers. — It is rather odd that in this passion for irregularity versus symmetry, the Japanese should again be on the side of Nature versus Man, as in their habit of neglecting the human figure for birds and flowers. But the comparison is suggestive; it emphasizes the fact that nature is a passion, a cult, an ecstasy, to this Esthetic Nation. Wherever there is a site commanding a fine view of lake and mountain, there will you find a temple or a tea house, where poor and rich alike can enjoy the prospect. Millions of pilgrims make long or short journeys every summer, ostensibly to visit some shrine, but really to enjoy the scenery and outing. Nor is there a lack of enjoyment for those who stay at home. "On moonlight nights, in mild weather," says Mr. Griffis, "thousands of people throng the bridges, walk the streets, or lounge in boats on the river, enjoying themselves in looking skyward. The houses have moon-viewing chambers." "In August and September both young folks and middle-aged will sit up all night until well into the morning to see the moon rise over the sea, meanwhile drinking rice wine and composing poetry."

There is a sermon in stones as treated by this esthetic nation. You find them everywhere, in hills, in parks, in cemeteries, in gardens, and they are not stones chiselled into artificial shapes of Occidental symmetry, but worn into smooth irregularity by rain and frost, and other forces of nature. Japanese gardens, again, are not aggregations of geometrical flower beds, but miniature landscapes, imitations of famous bits of scenery, with lakes and bridges, trees and mountains, lilies and lotos, frogs and fishes. Here you may see pine trees hundreds of years old, only a foot or two in height, embedded in small pots, the prime object of this dwarfing having been obviously a desire to give verisimilitude to the miniature garden landscape.[1]

If, with their usual "rascally topsic-turvyness," the

[1] The poetic charms of a Japanese garden are admirably mirrored in Chap. XVI. of Mr. Lafcadio Hearn's *Glimpses of Unfamiliar Japan*, and in Mr. J. Conder's two superb volumes on *The Flowers of Japan* and *Landscape Gardening in Japan*.

x

Japanese do not make flowers the principal feature of their gardens, and often, indeed, omit them entirely, their attitude toward flowers is nevertheless what most unmistakably marks them as *the* esthetic nation. In profusion and variety of wild flowers Japan is not nearly so well supplied as Southern California, for example, but as cultivators and lovers of flowers the Japanese stand in the very front rank. A Boston gardener once wrote to the *Transcript*: —

"The Yokohama Gardeners' Association grounds cover 200 acres of land; they include greenhouses and stores too numerous to mention, and the floral and nursery business is carried on in the most perfect manner. Palms, pæonies, plums, cherries, evergreens, magnolias, and all classes of shrubs are in cultivation; also 600 to 800 varieties of chrysanthemums, including about seventy altogether new ones which I obtained. . . . I never saw a chrysanthemum flower until I went to Japan, where everybody loves it. I visited five hundred places where it is cultivated. But these were only the principal gardens in a few large cities. Go to Japan!"

Go to Japan, indeed, if you want to see not only 800 varieties of chrysanthemum, but 269 different shades of color in them! Go there if you wish to see a number of kinds on one stem or the energies of a whole plant concentrated on one giant flower; go there to see "living pictures" in flowers — historic scenes and landscapes made up somewhat like woven tapestry of potted chrysanthemums, — the pots being of course "behind the scenes." Go there to see other favorite flowers treated with similar care and love; to see even forest leaves classed and adored as flowers when they have taken on their autumn tints, in which Japan rivals America. No coolie is too poor to have his flowers daily; none too coarse to scorn them; for a small frac-

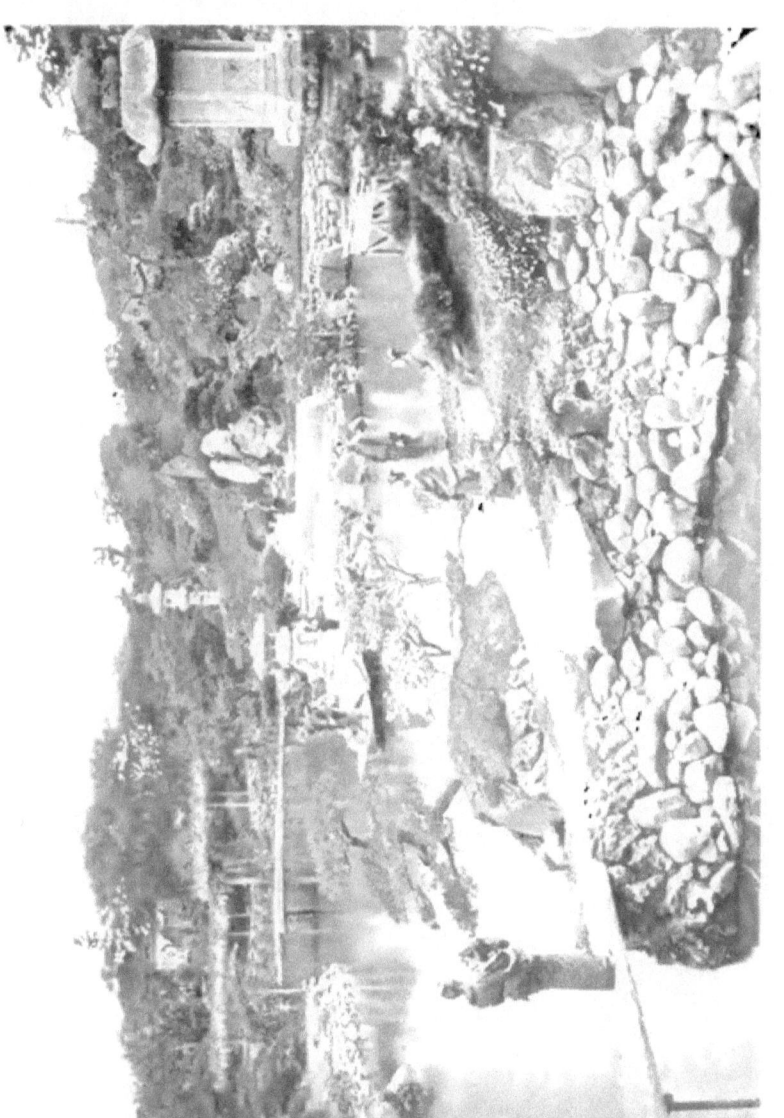

ARTIFICAL LANDSCAPE GARDEN

tion of a cent he can select what he wants from one of the "hanging baskets" which the itinerant flower sellers carry down the street attached to a pole on their shoulders. On your travels, if you stop more than a day at an inn, the girls will bring in every day a fresh potted plant to spice your life with variety; and the same thing is done in the humblest home. Indeed, the passion for flowers may become as absorbing as the passion of love. Look on this charming genre picture drawn by a correspondent of the *Japan Mail*, after the terrible earthquake at Ogaki in October, 1891, while the shocks were still continuing every few minutes: —

"In wandering through the desolate waste I saw a girl, not even in one of these temporary huts, but simply amongst the heaps of broken tiles and the like, tending a few chrysanthemum blossoms that she had in a vase of water — from whence she had procured them heaven only knows."

We, too, are fond of flowers, and some of us love them as tenderly and treat them as tastefully as the Japanese. But as a rule, in our arrangement of them, we are utter barbarians compared with them. What could be more monstrous and misshapen than the masses of inharmonious buds and flowers crowded together in a large bouquet, tied with a string, all life and individuality squeezed out of them, and perhaps even — *horribile dictu* — a rim of perforated white paper around them? Small wonder that people who are willing to hold such horrors in their hands should value them in proportion to their size and expense. The only redeeming thing in such a bouquet is its fragrance, and possibly an accidental or designed harmony or contrast of colors. Here again the Japanese teach us the charm of simplicity, the ugliness of crowding. To them a flower in the house is the same as a flower in the garden or forest — the efflorescence of an individual plant whose stem, branches, and leaves, though less beautiful than the flower, are quite as important in the ensemble. Their list of fine arts accordingly includes an art of flower-arrangement which teaches the proper training of potted plants so as to make them look true to nature. This art is a regular feature in the education of girls, and it certainly seems a thousand times better suited to bring out those exquisite feminine qualities of tenderness and taste which make men fall in love with women, than the algebra, anatomy, and political aspirations which are turning our charming women into "andromaniacs" — neuter beings who have ceased to be women without having become men.

Flower festivals are a specialty of Japan. Almost every month has its favorite flowers which millions turn out to see and worship; the schools have flower holidays, and even prisoners are not so cruelly treated as to be kept indoors when plums are in blossom. The plum comes in January, the cherry blossoms in April, May is pæony-time, August lotos-time; in November comes the chrysanthemum, with the colored maple leaves, and so on, these being only a few in the long list. The plum blossom, coming immediately after the snow (like our crocus), is a special favorite, but it is in beauty surpassed by the cherry blossom, which all who have seen it acclaim as the loveliest floral sight in the world. "When, in spring, the trees flower, it is as though fleeciest masses of cloud faintly tinged by sunset had floated down from the highest sky to fold themselves about the branches." Mr. Lafcadio Hearn gives this as an ancient Japanese description of

the cherry trees in full bloom. I wonder if James Russell Lowell had ever read that old simile when he thus depicted a New England landscape: "The fresh-pond meadows made all oriels cheap with hues that showed as if a sunset cloud had been wrecked among their maples."

Poetry.—Sometimes a mere statement of Japanese customs reads like a prose poem, as when Mr. Conder says that "Flower-viewing excursions, together with such pastimes as shell-gathering, mushroom-picking, and moon-viewing, form the favorite occupation of the holiday seeker throughout the year. By a pretty fancy, the snowclad landscape is regarded as Winter's floral display, and snow-viewing is included as one of the flower festivals of the year." How much more poetic, too, than our "Mrs. Tom Brown" and "Mrs. James Smith," and the like, are the Japanese names of chrysanthemums, —"silver world," "thin mist," "terrestrial globe," "companion of the moon," "basket of flowers," "shadows of the evening sun," "sky at dawn," "moon's halo," "leaves in the frost," "golden dew," "moonlit waves."

In poetry, as in painting, the Japanese are impressionists, a few words being considered sufficient to paint a picture in the reader's mind. I used to ask Mr. Yabi to translate for me the mottoes on screens at the inns. Here is one that I remember; it was appropriate for a summer resort: "Green fields in summer, people sitting under shade trees." Only this and nothing more: the rest was left to the trained imagination. "How pleasant," exclaims a poet, "is the sound of the ship rising on the waves, when it wakes us from deep slumber during a long night!" A very different mood gave rise to this sentiment: "It is only with the aid of wine that one can tolerate this melancholy existence." The pun will intrude itself even in a lover's lament, as in this: "Like to the pine trees I must stand and pine. . . . Till my long sleeve of purest snowy white, with showers of tears is steeped in bitter brine." Says an old Japanese song: "When the roaring waterfall is shivered by the night storm, the moonlight is reflected in each scattered drop."

The love of poetry seems to be almost as universal as the passion for flowers. This is quaintly illustrated in the *Log of a Japanese Journey* by Tsurayuka (tenth century), a little book describing a journey of nearly two months' duration, from Tosa to Kyōto, a trip which a steamer might make in a day or two. There was plenty of time to while away during the numerous stoppages, and most of it seems to have been devoted to the composing of stanzas on anything that happened to turn up. Everybody, from the passengers to the crew, is accused of perpetrating some of these poems. Most of them are rather weak, but they show a great emotional susceptibility and sensitiveness to the charms of nature. "In Japan," writes Tsurayuka, "and China as well, humanity, when moved by sorrow, tells its bitter grief in verse."[1]

This universal love of poetry, like the national taste for art, is an inheritance from the Middle Ages. In those days poets were honored above all other mortals; a poet could by means of a successful stanza attain the rank of a councillor, a poetess the rank of a lady of honor or even empress. We read that the Shogun Sanetomo "was so extravagantly fond of poetry that any

---

[1] This little book has been translated by Flora Best Harris, and is published by Flood and Vincent, Meadville, Pa.

criminal could escape punishment by offering him a well-written stanza." To this day it is said that would-be suicides often leave behind a description of their woes and intentions in verse. One of the favorite amusements at social gatherings is the composing of impromptu verses on a given subject. But the most fanciful use of poems is the national habit of hanging them up among the plum and cherry blossoms. There is reason for thinking that this custom is particularly appreciated by maidens and youths in a country in which flirtation and courtship are not included among the legitimate arts of social life.

A few pages ought perhaps to be devoted in this chapter to certain branches of art in which Japan has gained unique distinction, such as the ornamenting of sword hilts, the fine porcelain and pottery, the exquisite cloisonné vases, and the incomparable lacquer-wares. But enough has been said to prove the thesis advanced — that Japan is the esthetic country *par excellence*. It has taught our greatest artists the charms of simplicity and irregularity; it has shown us that beautiful things can be made cheaply, and that the useful and the ornamental can be united in the humblest utensils in daily use. It has shown us that with the aid of training and hereditary transmission, the art sense can be made as keen and fervent as the religious sense; it might almost be said that David Friedrich Strauss's ideal of a nation whose civilization is based on esthetics instead of on theology, is realized in Japan.

Strange to say, there are radicals among the Japanese who resent our regarding their country as a dreamland of flowers, poetry, and art. Our electric machines, big factories, and Krupp guns have so dazed their senses that they harbor the delusion that capitalists, statesmen, and warriors make for civilization more than artists, poets, and the worship of nature. They will learn in course of time that esthetic culture is the crown and flower of civilization, and that a nation in which the love of art is universal stands on a higher level than the Occidentals, of whom not ten per cent enjoy the blessings of esthetic culture.

A SUPERIOR CIVILIZATION

CARE FOR PARENTS — A PARADISE OF BABIES — CHILDREN BORN CIVILIZED — SCHOOL AND HOLIDAYS — A THOUSAND YEARS OF POLITENESS — A LANGUAGE WITHOUT PROFANITY — SMILING IN GRIEF — ALTRUISM VERSUS EGOTISM — AMERICAN RUDENESS — TRANSITION PERIOD — NO FLAUNTING OF WEALTH — AMERICAN PLUTOCRACY — INSIDE AND OUTSIDE — KINDNESS TO ANIMALS — THREE KINDS OF PATRIOTISM — SHINTOISM — CRIMINALS AND CROWDS — SAILORS — HOW TO ENJOY LIFE

To be superior to all other countries in cleanliness and in the sincere appreciation of art and nature, would surely be sufficient honor for a nation which Occidentals, in their Pharisaic vanity, have been wont to treat as semi-civilized. But the Japanese may claim much more than that. In morals at least our equals, they are in general refinement of manners and in social culture far superior to Americans and Europeans. To prove this, we will briefly consider the following seven points: the attitude of parents and children, politeness, contempt for the display of wealth, kindness to animals, patriotism, the behavior of crowds and criminals, the rational enjoyment of life.

Parents and Children. — Mr. Herbert Spencer justly holds that of all the feelings which hold the family together, filial love, or the care of parents by their children, was the last to be developed. From this point of view, Japan represents a much higher stage of evolution than we do. There, filial affection has long been the strongest of all feelings, whereas we are still in that stage of semi-barbarism wherein children indulge in the "luxury of disrespect" toward parents. There is nothing that American and European parents dread more than the idea of falling a burden to their children in old age, although, since they took care of the children for twenty years, there is no reason why the children, in turn, should not provide for them. In Japan, says Miss Bacon, a man

"looks with scorn on foreign customs which seem to betoken a fear lest, in old age, ungrateful children may neglect their parents and cast them aside. An aged parent is never a burden, is treated by all with the greatest love and tenderness; and if times are hard, and food and other comforts are scarce, the children, as a matter of course, deprive themselves and their children to give ungrudgingly to their old father and mother. . . . Young America may learn a salutary lesson by the study of the place that old people occupy in the home."

Conversely, the treatment of children by parents makes Japan "a very paradise of babies," as Sir Rutherford Alcock called it. Here is the testimony of Miss Bird: —

"I never saw people take so much delight in their offspring, carrying them about, or holding their hands in walking, watching and entering into their games, supplying them constantly with new toys, taking them to picnics and festivals, never being content to be without them, and treating other people's children, also, with a suitable measure of affection and attention."

Possibly, Japanese parents do not love their children more deeply than American parents, but they certainly love them more wisely. They dress them more sensibly, keep them healthy by constant out-door life, bring them up on the food intended for them by nature. And what is the result? I was in Japan three weeks before I heard a baby cry, and I never saw any of them quarrel or fight, among all the thousands I saw in the streets and the open houses. Once more I beg permission to quote Miss Bacon, who had very unusual opportunities for studying Japanese family life. The following citation is so important and suggestive, that, contrary to the usual custom, I must ask the printer to put it into larger type than the author's text:—

"A JAPANESE CHILD SEEMS TO BE THE PRODUCT OF A MORE PERFECT CIVILIZATION THAN OUR OWN, FOR IT COMES INTO THE WORLD WITH LITTLE OF THE SAVAGERY AND BARBARIAN BAD MANNERS THAT DISTINGUISH CHILDREN IN THIS COUNTRY, AND THE FIRST TEN OR FIFTEEN YEARS OF ITS LIFE DO NOT SEEM TO BE PASSED IN ONE LONG STRUGGLE TO ACQUIRE A COATING OF GOOD MANNERS THAT WILL HELP TO RENDER IT LESS OBNOXIOUS IN POLITE SOCIETY."

The implication of this sentence is that the Japanese nation has been civilized so many generations that its children are born civilized, while ours too often pass through the evolutionary stages of monkey and savage, before they reach that of man; and some never reach it. There is no need of scolding or punishing Japanese children, no need of urging them to go to school. Japan is probably the only country in the world where children prefer school to holidays, dearly as they love the latter. As to their behavior in school, let me quote the testimony of Mr. Hearn after two years' experience in various places: "I have never had personal knowledge of any serious quarrel between students, and have never even heard of a fight among my pupils, and I have taught some eight hundred boys and young men." On another page he says: "Well, I have been fourteen months in Izumo, and I have not yet heard voices raised in anger, or witnessed a quarrel; never have I seen one man strike another, or a woman bullied, or a child slapped."

Japan has no society for the Prevention of Cruelty to Children. It does not need one. New York has one, and needs it badly. During the first twenty years of its existence it received and investigated 86,969 complaints, involving 260,907 cases. Yet we have sent six hundred missionaries to civilize the Japanese!

Politeness. — It is obvious that the esthetic taste of the Japanese could not be so genuine and universal were it not an inheritance — the cumulative result of generations of art culture and worship of nature. It has become an instinct, like a bird's untaught knowledge how to build a nest or bower.[1]

So, again, it is obvious that Japanese children would not be born free from the "savagery and barbarian bad manners that distinguish American children," were it not that civilization is so much older in their country than in ours that gentle manners have had a chance to become instinctive, through hereditary transmission. "Fine manners have always been a fine art in Japan,"

[1] The aptness of this comparison is proved by the fact that Japanese taste ceases to be infallible as soon as it has to do with new conditions — foreign costume or art methods, for example. A lark cannot build a swallow's nest. An interesting essay might be written on this theme.

says the Rev. W. E. Griffis. "Indeed, it is said that as early as the seventh century there were manuals or treatises on politeness." And in course of these twelve centuries the polish of the Japanese has gradually become so smooth and enduring that there is nothing to which it can be compared except their own lustrous lacquer.

What say you of a people whose language "affords absolutely no means of cursing and swearing," as we know on the unimpeachable authority of Basil Hall Chamberlain, emeritus professor of Japanese philology at the University of Tōkyō? Does it not sound almost incredible in this "Christian" country of ours, where street boys measure their relative "smartness" by their proficiency in profanity, and men are not far behind them? Mr. W. S. Liscomb, in a letter to the *Providence Journal*, gives an amusing illustration of the utter inability of the untutored Japanese mind even to comprehend the nature of profanity. His "boy" and cook one day had a slight misunderstanding, and the boy complained afterwards that the cook had said to him "G—d d—n your soul." But upon investigating the matter, he found that what the cook had really said was almost exactly equivalent to our slang phrase "What are you giving us?" The absence of profane words argues the absence of profane and ugly feelings. Dr. D. B. Simmons, after residing thirty years in Japan, says on the question of scolding by women: "I can hardly remember having heard this kind of language from their lips." Similar testimony is given by Maclay and other residents.

It is almost impossible to think of Japanese girls except as smiling, and this smile is taught them from childhood as an essential part of etiquette, which requires them to keep all painful emotions hidden from others. So far does this rule extend, that they must even wear a smiling face in telling you of a great loss or the death of a relative. Ignorance of this matter has been the cause of grave and absurd errors in judging Japanese character.[1]

In many details Japanese manners show a refinement and courtesy almost incomprehensible to coarse Western minds. To give only one illustration from Conger. Visitors are often invited to make extempore arrangements of flowers placed before them.

> "Should the master of the house produce a very rare and valuable vessel for holding the floral arrangement, it is polite for the guest to make objections, pleading want of sufficient skill to do justice to so precious a receptacle. If pressed, however, he must attempt a simple and unassuming arrangement of flowers *so as not to detract from the merit of the vessel itself.*"

The desire to please is the dominant feeling in the Japanese mind. Altruism takes the place of egotism, wherefore, "in Japanese society, sarcasm, irony, cruel wit, are not indulged." "No one endeavors to expand his own individuality by belittling his fellows; no one tries to make himself appear a superior being"(Hearn). Does not half the misery in Christian America spring from cruel gossip, from everybody's anxiety to appear socially superior to others, and to make them feel their inferiority?

If we could induce six hundred Japanese missionaries

---

[1] Many writers have discoursed on this matter, but Mr. Lafcadio Hearn has surpassed them all in a chapter headed "The Japanese Smile," which I commend to every reader as a masterpiece of comparative ethnic psychology.

to come to America, they might begin operations by contrasting the kindness of Japanese coolies, who would not run over or disturb even a dog in the streets, with the brutality of our drivers, which makes it necessary in our cities to place a policeman at every street crossing to enable persons on foot to get across without risk to life and limb. They might tell our lower classes that habitual rudeness toward their superiors is not a good way to show their "equality." They might explain that if a Japanese railway company hung up in its cars the notice, posted in every car of the New York elevated railroad: "Employees of this road are required to be courteous in their treatment of passengers," it would cause a ripple of laughter from Nagasaki to Sapporo. They might say to American women that their almost incredible rudeness in keeping on, year after year, their big hats in theatres, in spite of all entreaties and remonstrances from those who are thus deprived of pleasures much needed for recreation and dearly paid for, would be absolutely inconceivable in Japan, the only *nation* of ladies and gentlemen in the world. They might tell our women how un-Japanese, *i.e.* unladylike, it is to treat shopgirls and servants as superciliously as many of them do.

It is in such points as these — the consideration for the feelings even of servants, the avoidance of profanity and cruel gossip, the altruistic smile even in grief, the universal desire to please — that the Japanese show their true heart-politeness, rather than by their bobbing and bowing and kneeling, which, to tell the truth, are as exaggerated and absurd as their "honorifics"; that is, their habit of speaking of their "stupid" selves and wives, and of the "honorable" other persons. It is therefore just as well that this old-fashioned etiquette is no longer taught in boys' schools, and that even the girls are beginning to make fun of it. There is, of course, some danger of their going too far during the transition period and copying Miss Bird's guide Ito, who explained his occasional rudeness as "just missionary manners"; but we may feel sure that the inherited heart-politeness of the Japanese will survive the wreck of excessive bowing formalities and linguistic honorifics.

Contempt for Display of Wealth. — Once upon a time, in a certain American city, I met a girl who told me about a ball she had attended on the previous evening: "I danced with a young man who was an expert in women's gowns. Just think! he could tell me the price per yard of every woman's dress in the room, including my own. *Fortunately*," she added, "*mine was very expensive.*" At the risk of seeming rude, I could not help smiling at this very naïve illustration of the tendency of this Great Republic to drift into a state of plutocracy in which things as well as persons are estimated entirely by their money value. Flowers, for instance, are valued in "Society" only when they are out of season, because they are then more costly. Bouquets are judged, not by their beauty and arrangement, but by their cost, often even by their size. Newspapers chronicle the doings, not of men of brains (with a few conspicuous exceptions), but of men of wealth, no matter how illiterate, boorish, and rascally they may be. Rich women have their gowns described at the Opera and the Horse Show, and every rich girl is a "beauty" in the newspapers, though in life she may be a veritable fright. If the average American sees a fine building, his first question is "How much did it cost?" James Russell Lowell wrote that Thoreau's "whole life was a rebuke of the waste and aimlessness of our American luxury, which is an abject enslavement to tawdry upholstery."

From this point of view, again, Japan is infinitely more civilized than America. Why? Let Professor Chamberlain answer: —

"The bluster which mistakes bigness for greatness, the vulgarity which smothers beauty under ostentation and extravagance, have no place in the Japanese way of thinking. The alcove of a Tōkyō or Kyōto drawing-room holds one picture and one flower vase, which are changed from time to time. To be sure, picture and vase are alike exquisite. The possessions of the master of the house are not sown broadcast, as much as to say, 'Look what a lot of expensive articles I've got, and just think how jolly rich I must be!' He does not stick up plates on walls — plates are meant to hold food. He would not, whatever might be his means, waste £1000, or £100, or even £20, on the flowers for a single party: flowers are natural things, simple things; it is incongruous to treat them like precious stones."

Instead of valuing flowers out of season because of their expensiveness, the Japanese have a strict rule that they must be in season to be in fashion. They go so far as to taboo certain flowers at certain times because they properly belong to another season; for example, late peach blossoms.

Snobbishness, the insolent conceit of birth or wealth, or the aping and worshipping of it, is not a Japanese vice. "Daimyōs," says the *Tōkyō Times*, "have been members of college classes in Tōkyō for months before accident made their rank known to their foreign teachers." In Japanese towns you can rarely tell from the street side of a house whether its owner is rich or poor. He does not wish to flaunt his wealth any more than his rank in the face of others. Such wealth as he may have to spare, he spends on works of art and on his garden, which is behind the house. Only the foreign buildings in Tōkyō have their gardens in front.

Speaking of Japanese attire, Mr. Wores says that "the lining of their gowns is often of a more expensive and finer material than the outer stuff." Everybody knows, too, that it is a characteristic of Japanese embroidered silks that there is no seamy side to them, the lower side being as beautiful as the upper. I have before me a little Japanese metal tray, which cost fifty cents in New York and probably fifteen in Japan. The upper side represents a maiden standing on a fantastic dragon. On the lower side the artist has ingeniously shaped this haut-relief into an intaglio of a lotos plant. Only an inborn love of art for art's sake could thus induce a workman to emulate nature in making the unseen as beautiful as the seen. In such sincerity of soul there is infinitely more of the true spirit of Christianity than in the building of six denominational chapels for every sixteen missionaries.

The ostentatious display of wealth is in truth nothing but a phase of our Occidental lack of true politeness; it is an attempt to make others feel their "inferiority" and to arouse their envy. Here lies the true inwardness of our frequent changes of fashion in women's gowns, which cause so much needless expense and jealous heartburnings. The rich introduce these changes, knowing that the less favored cannot at once follow their example, whereby the desired plutocratic distinction is established.

Kindness to Animals. — From a moral point of view Christianity is unquestionably the greatest of all religions, but in one respect it is sadly inferior to Buddhism and even to ancient Paganism, or some of its representatives. The Old Testament forbade the muzzling of an ox that treadeth out the corn, the seething of a kid in its mother's milk, the taking of a parent bird sitting on its young or on its eggs; but the New Testament view is summed up in St. Paul's contemptuous question, "Doth God take care for oxen?"[1] It makes one melancholy to think what an incalculable amount of suffering might have been spared the animals of Christendom if the New Testament had emphatically enjoined the virtue and duty of kindness to animals; melancholy to read the annual reports of the New York Society for the Prevention of Cruelty to Animals with its sickening record of outrages on helpless animals, man's best friends; melancholy to think that Christian women encourage the slaughter of thousands of beautiful birds at nesting time for their feathers, leaving the young to die in the agonies of starvation. Buddhism may not have proved an unmixed blessing to Japan, but it has taught, among other virtues, that of kindness to animals. We may laugh at Buddhist priests sweeping the path before them lest they step on insects, or refusing to drink unfiltered water for fear of killing minute animals. We may smile on reading in Kaempfer that dogs are "treated like regular citizens of the town"; or on finding that to this day animals have their regular graveyards, and that in some temples prayers are even offered up to them: but we must admit, with Mr. Hearn, that "surely nothing save goodness can be expected from a people gentle-hearted

[1] See the fourth chapter of Lecky's *History of European Morals*, where this question is admirably discussed.

enough to pray for the souls of their horses and cows." And we must admit that the national kindness toward animals must have been enormously efficacious in making men kind to each other, since we know that nothing makes our own children so considerate as teaching them to treat their pets gently.

With the exception of the slicing of raw fish, the brutality of drunken soldiers (now suppressed), and the occasional maltreatment of a car-horse in Tōkyō, there are hardly any instances on record of Japanese cruelty toward animals, although there has never been a law against it. "The taking of life being displeasing to Buddha," says Mitford, "outside many of the temples old women and children earn a livelihood by selling sparrows, small eels, carp, and tortoises, which the worshipper sets free in honor of the deity." "In Tokio," says Mr. Griffis, "I used to notice old women sitting on the bridges and selling young eels. These were bought by passers by, and immediately dropped into the canal below, in pious memory of deceased relatives, and to shorten their pains in the Buddhist purgatory." All cruel sports, such as hunting and cock-fighting, come under the ban of Buddhism.

Patriotism. — There are three varieties of patriotism, one of which, however, hardly deserves so honorable a name. They are based respectively on vanity, defensive pugnacity, and real love of country. The first variety is that which leads a Hottentot to think he is better than a Kaffir; an Englishman, that all foreigners are stupid unless they conform to his insular prejudices; a German, that all other nations are ignoramuses; a Frenchman, that nothing important ever happens outside of Paris; and so on. It is a harmless but rather offensive form of vanity, a national egotism, the proper name for which is chauvinism.

The second form of patriotism wears a military cloak and has given rise to many noble acts of heroism and self-sacrifice in the past. Yet it must not be forgotten that many soldiers remain at their post only because desertion means death; nor must it be overlooked that in most wars men fight for their home and families, and therefore have a strong *selfish* reason for their courage.

The highest form of patriotism is the *altruistic* variety, which is manifested in love of one's country for its own sake, and in the willingness and desire to obey its laws, and preserve its honor at home and abroad. This phase of patriotism is still in its infancy in our Commonwealth. What ideas of devotion are evoked in the mind of an American by the words, "politician," "senator," "alderman"? Is public office generally regarded as a public trust, or as a public cow which every one who can get at the udders milks for his private benefit? What a noble exhibition of American patriotism is our pension system, the most gigantic swindle on record in all history—the annual expenditure of nearly $150,000,000, at least one-half of which goes to dishonest pretenders who, aside from their private immorality, are bringing the very idea of patriotic service in the army into disrepute, as a thing done for money!

In place of this what do our six hundred missionaries find in Japan? They find there Shintoism. And what are the virtues especially insisted upon and realized by Shintoism? They are cleanliness, courage, courtesy, personal honor, and above all, patriotism, or loyalty to the country and its ruler. A Japanese, be he a noble or a coolie, never hesitates to sacrifice his life for his personal honor. Shintoism has taught him that. "The spirit of Shintoism," says Mr. Hearn, "is the spirit of filial piety, the zest of duty, the readiness to surrender life for a principle without a thought of wherefore. . . . Ask a class of Japanese students — young students of fourteen to sixteen — to tell their dearest wishes; and if they have confidence in the questioner, perhaps nine out of ten will answer: 'To die for his Majesty, our Emperor.' And the wish soars from the heart pure as any wish for martyrdom ever born."

One Oriental genre picture must suffice to picture this phase of Japanese patriotism. Nine days after the murderous attack on the Czarewitch by a fanatic policeman at Otsu, in May, 1891, a young woman of respectable appearance cut her throat in front of the local government buildings in Kyōto. The wound did not prove fatal, and the girl afterwards confessed that she had come to apologize to the Czarewitch for the shameful crime of her countryman, but finding him gone she had resorted to this method to prove the sincerity of her motives. In Japanese annals suicide to vindicate national honor is an event of frequent occurrence. It may seem foolish to us, but it indicates the profound depth of patriotic sentiment.

Criminals and Crowds. — Nothing proves the innate, inherited culture of the Japanese more cogently than the fact that even their criminals are less degraded and brutal than ours. The reader may remember the surprise I expressed in the Yezo forest, among the "dangerous" convicts, at finding that "criminals could be so urbane and gentlemanly, so cheerful and musical." I got the impression that most of them must have committed their crime not from natural viciousness, but under the influence of drink; an impression confirmed by the fact that these men did not have the characteristic brutish expression which enabled Mr. Galton to make a composite portrait typical of the British criminal.

With these experiences I beg the reader to compare the account of a Tōkyō prison in Mr. Norman's *The Real Japan*, from which I will cite only two sentences: "I could not help wondering whether there was another prison in the world with no method of punishment for 2000 criminals except one dark cell, and that not used for a month." In one department of this prison he found "sixty men, common thieves and burglars and peace breakers, utterly ignorant previously of cloisonné making, now making beautiful and delicate ware. Fancy the attempt to teach such a thing at Pentonville or Dartmoor or Sing-Sing!"

Crowds in America or Europe are very apt to degenerate into mobs, and wherever they congregate squads of police are immediately despatched. Of Japanese crowds, Major-General Palmer says that "police in such a throng, it seems to us, can have no more to do than the lilies of the valley." The following clipping from the *Japan Mail* shows the efficacy of the police system where it is needed:—

"KANDA is a district of Tōkyō where all sorts of queer things are constantly happening. It is the great student quarter, the Quartier Latin, of the metropolis, and statistics show that it boasts the largest number of wineshops, tobacconists, bookstores, and sly brothels. The first and last of these categories generally run in couples. Fires are most frequent there; brawls and 'rows' of almost daily occurrence. Yet there is no part of the district through which one may not walk with perfect safety at night. And of what great Continental city may as much be said?"

Take one more illustration of our general theme that the Japanese are naturally more civilized than the corresponding class with us. Our sailors have not exactly an enviable reputation for refinement of manners. How is it in Japan? Mr. Hearn (238) has the floor: —

"These Japanese seamen are very gentle compared with our Jack Tars, and not without a certain refinement and politeness of their own. . . . It is quite pleasant to watch their feasting across the street. Perhaps their laughter is somewhat more boisterous and their gesticulation a little more vehement than those of the common citizens; but there is nothing resembling real roughness — much less real rudeness. . . . And as the wine flows, the more urbane becomes the merriment, — until there falls upon all that pleasant sleepiness which saké brings, and the guests, one by one, smilingly depart. Nothing could be happier or gentler than their evening's joviality; — yet sailors are considered in Japan an especially rough class. What would be thought of our roughs in such a country?"

Enjoyment of Life. — The Puritans, says Macaulay, "hated bear-baiting, not because it gave pain to the bear, but because it gave pleasure to the spectators." To-day the "infamous charge of Puritanism" (to quote a phrase of Swinburne) could hardly be brought against the English or Americans. A trace of it lingers, but the legitimacy, desirability, and hygienic value of pleasure are pretty generally conceded. Nevertheless, there has perhaps never been a people so unskilled in the art of enjoying life as Americans, although no other nation has ever been so plentifully supplied with the material comforts of life. Our men chase the dollar, not only while they need it, but long after it has become a superfluity and a burden, and finally die without having ever made any rational use of their wealth. Our millionaires are the unhappiest of mortals. And when

American men meet, as a rule, they do not rest or play, but weary their brains still more by "talking shop." Our women have learned the art of loafing gracefully, at least in summer; but at home they too often wear themselves out with social jealousies, household worries, gowns and other luxuries that are a good deal more of a bother and torment than a pleasure. On all these points we can learn a great deal by studying the higher civilization across the Pacific.

The Japanese are too wise to continue the chase of the dollar after they have earned enough to end their days in comfort. They altruistically give others a chance by voluntarily dropping out of the race and competition, and spending the latter part of their life in elegant leisure, enjoying nature, travel, art, literature, and the society of relatives and friends. Is not this infinitely more rational and civilized than our way of dying in harness, without having ever been turned loose in the green fields and pastures — a privilege we grant even to our old horses?

Our Japanese neighbors have learned that *happiness consists not in having all you want but in wanting no more than you have.* Their average earnings are estimated at twenty cents a day, yet they are the happiest people in the world. Many of the peasants are too poor to eat the rice they cultivate in the sweat of their brow. Yet after toiling all day they go home, take a bath, eat a frugal meal of millet, pickles, and tea, smoke a thimble pipe, play with their children, and look contented and happy. Of the coolie in general, Mr. Anderson says he is "childlike in his joys and sorrows, polite and kindly in disposition, . . . and careless as to who the masters, and what the state of religion, so long as his sufficient allowance of rice, his inexpensive luxuries, and periodic holidays come without undue effort to win them." And so on with the other classes, the shopkeepers, for instance, of whom Miss Bacon says that they "have still time to enjoy their holidays and their little gardens, and have more pleasure and less hard work than those under similar circumstances in our own country." So that in every sphere we find more pleasure and less grinding work than with us. Is not that the goal of our civilization; the object of all our labor unions and industrial wars? Yet we fancy it is our mission to civilize the Japanese!

Busy Americans have gradually reached a point where they consider it almost a crime, and certainly a waste of time, to read books, or attend plays; and when they take a vacation, they think it necessary to apologize for it, on the ground that they need it for their health and to gain fresh energy for work. We laugh at the Japanese for going to the theatre in the morning, and Richard Wagner aroused no end of sarcastic comment when he wanted people to look on his art seriously and come to it in the daytime with fresh and vigorous brains. But I think the Japanese could easily turn the laugh on us, and that too by quoting one of our own brightest social philosophers, Mr. Charles Dudley Warner, in a passage wherein he refers to

"the practice, if not the theory, of our society — to postpone the delights of social intercourse until after dark, or rather late at night, when body and mind are both weary with the exertions of business, and when we can give to what is the most delightful and profitable thing in life, social and intellectual society, only the weariness of dull brains and over-tired muscles. No wonder we take our amusements sadly, and that so many people find dinners heavy and parties stupid. Our economy leaves no place for amusements; we merely add them to the burden of a life already full. The world is still a little off the track as to what is really useful."

These are golden words of censure that could never have been written of the Japanese. But the climax is still to come. It is not in the enjoyment of Recreation, after all, but of Work that Japan will prove our most beneficial teacher, if we will but try to learn from her. The late Robert Louis Stevenson used to declare that machinery and the division of labor had utterly banished all a man's joy in his work; and that it was by insisting on the necessity for that joy that Ruskin had best served the world. The greatest objection to the multiplication of modern machinery is not that it takes away work from many (for they can still seek other employment), but that it makes all such work joyless, reducing laborers to the level of machines, caring no more than the machines how the goods comes out and what becomes of them. In Europe and America it is only the author, the scientific inventor, and the artist that enjoy the esthetic thrill of creative work. In Japan the humblest artisan, making the humblest kitchen utensil, enjoys his work because he uses his brain and his taste as well as his hands in shaping and adorning it. How much the greatest happiness of the greatest number is raised by this, is obvious.

The idea that Japanese civilization began with the appearance of Commodore Perry's gunboats, forty years ago, is still amazingly prevalent in our midst. I have before me a leading Boston paper of February 16, 1895, with an article entitled "Back to Barbarism," the author of which notes, among other oddities, the curious fact that such highly civilized persons as Sir Edwin Arnold and Pierre Loti should have been contented to live for a time in Japan! He admits, it is true, that "in the teeth of current cablegrams," about the war with China, "it may be presumptuous to class Japan among barbarous nations. But it is at least not the country of the steamboat and the railway, though it has adopted the ironclad with success." In this man's mind — and he represents a large class of persons — civilization obviously consists in railways, ironclads, and success in waging war. If judged by his own standard, he would have to acknowledge that our own "civilization" is very recent indeed, since we have had railways and ironclads less than a century. In truth, railways, telegraphs, telephones, and the like are simply comforts of life, having absolutely nothing to do with real civilization, which, in so far as it affects the refinement and happiness of mankind, is purely a mental product.

There is great danger ahead for Japan — danger that she will introduce our factory chimneys, and whistles, and soot, and machinery, and division of labor, and thus destroy the artistic joy in work, which is the highest product of her civilization. But if she will heed the warning voices from the West, and avoid that danger, it will be for us to be on our guard lest Japan entirely outstrip us in the race for supremacy. She is systematically adopting all that is really sound in our Western institutions, and unless we follow her example and graft the best features of her moral and social institutions on our own habits, we shall be left in the lurch, and the sociologists of the Far East will in a future century look at us across the Pacific as we

do at our untutored mediæval ancestors in Europe.
The reader may smile at this contingency, but it would
be simply a restoration of what has been before. A
few years ago Captain Brinkley heard an Englishman
say to his Japanese guide : "Japan has become quite
civilized, I suppose, in the last twenty years ; " upon
which he commented as follows in the *Japan Mail:*
" This very courteous representative of advanced civilization was evidently ignorant that when his own ancestors dressed in untanned skins and fed upon acorns,
the Japanese wore silks and had reached a high pitch
of refinement in their general mode of life."

INDEX

Ainos, 120, 174-177, 187, 197-202.
Alcock, 37, 94, 287.
America in Japan, 153-165.
Animals, kindness to, 205, 322-324.
Archery gallery, 64.
Architecture, 209, 229, 301.
Arnold, Sir E., 74, 79.
Art, at Exhibition, 104, 105; in inns, 137, 138; Nikko temples, 229; kakemonos, 265.
Asakusa, 63.

Bacon, Miss A., 77, 289, 314, 315, 330.
Barbers, 11, 138.
Bathing, 19, 140, 145, 149, 152, 162, 167, 170, 206, 241, 243, 286-297.
Bears, 159, 177, 208.
Beauty (see Women).
Beds, 126.
Beer, 27, 219.
Beggars, 16.
Bird, L, 44, 86, 290, 314.
Biwa, Lake, 248, 268.
Black, 109, 190, 288.
Blum, R., 26, 68, 78, 83.
Brinkley, 333.
Buddhist temples, 63, 136; and priests, 257-260.

Canadian Pacific, 1, 2.
Carriages, 12, 62.
Chamberlain, B. H., 7, 37, 82, 93, 112, 292, 304, 317, 321.
Chastity, 284.
Children, 50, 66, 67, 220, 313-316.
Cholera, 121, 207, 209, 215, 218, 244, 255.
Chopsticks, 85.

Christians in Japan, 280.
Chûsenji, 237.
Civilization, Japanese, 72, 313-333.
Climate, 54, 57, 117, 118, 178, 213.
Clogs, 25.
Clubs, 14, 15.
Coal mine, 168.
Conder, 305, 318.
Costume, 7, 42, 47, 112, 139, 144, 251, 286.
Criminals, 169, 184, 326.
Crowds, 66, 291, 327.
Curiosity, 16, 214.

Daimyos, 39.
Dancing, 87, 88, 230.
Dittrich, 120.
Dogs, 172, 205.

Earthquakes, 13.
East, A., 301.
Eating (see Gastronomy).
Enjoyment of life, 328-331.
Enoshima, 21.
Esthetics, at a banquet, 78-84.
Evening dress, 112, 115.
Exhibition, 103-116.
Expenses, 1, 127, 147, 188, 206, 211, 219, 234, 256.

Factories, 160.
Fenollosa, 303.
Filial love, 313.
Fire boxes, 80, 196.
Fires, 52.
Fireworks, 68-72.
Fish, 55, 136, 138, 237.
Flowers, 67, 304-308.

Food (*see* Gastronomy).
Forest, in Yezo, 171-188.
Fruit, 192.
Fuji, 3, 4, 244-249.

Gastronomy, 11, 27, 70, 77-86, 115, 130, 132, 143, 192, 209, 216, 220, 221, 246, 253.
Geishas, on river, 71; at banquets, 76; accomplishments and character, 76; music and chaff, 80-84.
Governor-General of Yezo, 154, 156, 167.
Griffis, W. E., 24, 33, 39, 43, 74, 273, 282, 285, 305, 317, 324.
Guides, 122, 171, 238.

Hakodate, 134-147, 206.
Hashiguchi, 158-168.
Hawaii, 1-3.
Hearn, L., 299, 318, 323, 328.
Henson, H. V., 206.
Horses, 173, 178.
Hotels, 9-12, 26-28, 256.

Ice, 59.
Ieyasu, 227.
Indians, 6.
Inns, 125, 138, 150, 161, 195, 221, 225.
Inundations, 210-219.

Jinrikishas (*see* Kurumas).
Journalism, 108, 123, 164, 189-191.
Journalists, 111.

Kaempfer, 74.
Kamakura, 21.
Kamikawa, 185.
Kissing, 75.
Kitabatake, 124.
Kneeling, 94, 95.
Kuro Siwo, 6.
Kurumas, 9, 10, 12, 22, 24, 32-35, 38, 42, 57, 215.
Kyōto, 255-266.

La Farge, J., 103.
Lamps, 163.
Language, Japanese, 273.
Lemons, 28.
Lotos, Preface, 193, 232, 269-272.

Merchants, 283.
Mikado, 106-115.
Milne, Professor, 122.
Miniatures, 161.
Missionaries, 63, 281-285.
Mitford, 324.
Moats, 40.
Money, 14.
Monkeys, 117.
Morality, 281-291.
Mororan, 203.
Morse, 289, 302.
Music, in cheap theatres, 18; native band, 19; Tōkyō city band, 71; geishas and samisens, 81, 82; drums, 87; in the theatre, 98; Professor Dittrich, 121; among convicts, 185; vocal quartet, 187; blind koto player, 264; Japanese versus foreign, 298-299.

Nature, love of, 227, 231, 304.
Nikko, 224-244.
Norman, H., 26, 74, 327.
Nudity, 49, 55, 57, 152, 204, 214, 222, 241, 286-297.

Okuma, Count, 100-102.
Oliphant, 38, 287.
Otaru, 148-150.
Otsu, 267.

Pacific Mail, 1-3.
Painting, 105, 302-304.
Parsons, A., 270.
Passports, 124.
Patriotism, 324-326.
Perry, 6, 287.
Piggott, 81.
Pilgrims, 226, 227, 238, 245.
Pine Islands, 128-130.
Poetry, 309-312.
Policemen, 41.
Politeness, 50, 149, 316-320.
Postal system, 122.
Poverty, 51.
Puns, 267.

Railways, 22-25, 167, 169, 248-251.
Rain, 219, 224, 245.
Rice, 85, 86.

Safety, 43, 44.
Saké, 86.
Samisen (see Music).
Sampans, 7.
Samurai, 39, 41.
Sapporo, 151-165.
School, of law, 100.
Sculpture, 301.
Sendai, 124-127.
Shintoism, 325.
Shopping, 139.
Shop signs, comic, 47; artistic, 53.
Shugio, H., Preface, 78, 83, 95, 100, 111, 122, 124.
Silk, 213, 260.
Smoking, 249-251.
Snakes, 244.
Stage ride, 204.
Steamers, 131.
Stores, 45.

Taste, 112.
Tea godowns, 20.
Tea house, 60 (see Inns).
Tea, stewed, 60; with milk, 106.
Theatres, 17, 91-99.
Tōkyō, railway station, 25; hotel, 26; in summer, 28, 119; at night, 29; clean air, 29; bird's-eye view and area, 30; parks, 31; distances, 30; street scenes, 37-48; yashikis, 39; moats, 40; policemen, 41; safety, 43, 44; stores, 45-47; comic signs, 47; costumes, 47; exposure, 49; bowing, 50; poverty, 51; fires, 52; shop signs, 47, 53; early morning, 54; chickens, 55; fish market, 55; wells, 56; summer heat, 57; freight coolies, 58; watering carts, 58; planed ice, 59; tea house, 60; carriage drive, 62; Tsukiji, 62; Buddhist temple, 63; archery gallery, 64; night crowds, 65; children, women, and foreigners, 67; flower show, 67; river festival and fireworks, 68-73; women, 74; a tea-house banquet, 77-86; Yoshiwara, 88-90; criminals, 90; theatre, 91-99; a high school, 100; Exhibition, 103-116.
Topsy-turvyness, 14, 71, 79-81, 83, 168, 273-279.
Tsukiji, 62.
Typhoons, 13.

Warner, C. D., 330.
Water, dangers of, 27.
Waterfalls, 234-243.
Wealth, display of, 329.
Wells, 56.
Wigmore, Professor, 282.
Wine, 11 (see Saké).
Women (see also Geishas), scarcity of foreign, 15; musicians, 18; in tea godowns, 20; costume, 48; brunettes in blue, 49; freedom of, 49; morning toilet, 55; archery girls, 65; and foreigners, 67; a baron's daughter, 73; beauty of, 74, 75; brunettes, 75; geishas and waiting girls, 76-89; grace and gait, 79; degraded class, 88; calls, 121; standards of beauty, 121; waiting maids, 125, 130, 140, 141, 161, 242; relations to men, 142; morals, 143; peasant, 148; at work, 154; Aino, 188, 198, 202; rural types, 217; smoking, 249; beauty after marriage, 251; costume, 251; Malayan and Tartar types, 261; Spanish resemblances, 262; in Kyōto, 261-263; chastity, 284; in public baths, 294-296; politeness, 317.
Wores, 301, 322.
Wrestlers, 252.
Writing, 164.

Yabi, Preface, 123 et passim.
Yashikis, 39.
Yezo, climate, 118, 178; features of, 120; and Russia, 152; forest, 171-188; clearings, 179; criminals, 169, 184.
Yokohama, 5-21.
Yoshiwara, 88-90.
Yumoto, 240-242.

www.ingramcontent.com/pod-product-compliance
Lightning Source LLC
Chambersburg PA
CBHW032032220426
43664CB00006B/452